Walking

Manchester University Press

Written as a sociological field guide, each contribution takes the reader on a walk, opening up attentiveness to embodied, situated spaces and connections between the local and global, pasts, presents and futures. This wonderful book will be invaluable to those researching, teaching and thinking with space, movement and everyday lives.

Rebecca Coleman, University of Bristol, UK

Engaging and illuminating at once, *Walking* holds the social, historical, political, and emancipatory possibilities of a stroll close. These are walks beyond the trope of the Romantic figure – in the city, down back alleys, through questions of access and activism. A much-needed contribution to our literatures of place.

Jessica J. Lee, author and environmental historian

A consistently unusual, thoughtful and original set of essays, full of gimlet-eyed observations and rich sociological insights. Taken together, they offer a compellingly diverse yet surprisingly unified account of walking – not walking as mere traversal of space but as a form of knowing, encountering, testing, clarifying, probing and above all listening to the complexity of places. Deeply informed, sociologically grounded, and politically astute, the essays also offer a glimpse of what walking, at its best, might be – a deeply intimate yet non-possessive mode of engaging with the world.

Michael Malay, University of Bristol, UK

This innovative 'field guide' offers a wonderful invitation to pay attention to and analyse our social worlds by engaging the peripatetic senses, the sensory affordances and creative understandings of the messy intersections of bodies, space, place, landscape, rhythms, sound, time and the more than human through a critical sociological lens by walking with contemporary sociologists! A book to read, share and savour! The power of sociological storytelling at its very best!

Maggie O'Neill, University College Cork, Ireland

This collection of walks tackles big social issues in a lyrical and reflective manner showcasing the creativity of movement as methodology. Read this timely book and be inspired to get walking and understand spaces and places differently.

Ruth Penfold-Mounce, University of York, UK

Richly textured, insightful and fascinating. Contributors share walks crossing both time and space, illuminating issues that resonate far beyond each writer's path. We travel along supply chains, rivers and disused railway lines, accompanied by dogs, songbirds, comedians and key social theorists. Subjects explored include complex histories and potential futures, regeneration, inequality, technology, racism, environmental injustices and more, alongside networks of care, community solidarity and everyday resistance. Power is revealed, disrupted and questioned with each footstep. Expertly crafted, each essay balances expertise with accessibility and is deeply engaging. Thoughtful prompts encourage the reader to embark on their own mobile research project. An essential guide for curious scholars across many fields – and for anyone who wants to understand the value of walking as, with, and in social research.

Morag Rose, University of Liverpool, UK

Walking

A sociological field guide

Edited by

Charlotte Bates and Emma Jackson

Manchester University Press

Published by Manchester University Press
Oxford Road, Manchester, M13 9PL

www.manchesteruniversitypress.co.uk

British Library Cataloguing-in-Publication Data
A catalogue record for this book is available from the British Library

ISBN 978 1 5261 8490 0 hardback

ISBN 978 1 5261 8491 7 paperback

First published 2026

EU authorised representative for GPSR:
Easy Access System Europe, Mustamäe tee 50, 10621 Tallinn, Estonia
gpsr.requests@easproject.com

Typeset
by New Best-set Typesetters Ltd

To James, Max, Lyra and Acorn, and all our walks together. CB

To Adey and Joanie – and in loving memory of my mum, Janet (1945–2025), walking with me always. EJ

Contents

List of illustrations ix
Contributors x
Acknowledgements xvii

Introduction: A sociological field guide – Emma Jackson and Charlotte Bates 1

Circulate 15

1 Pound shop: walking the intersections between Yiwu and Dalston – Laura Henneke and Caroline Knowles 17
2 Hiding in plain sight: walking through race and space on Brixton Station Road – Karis Campion 27
3 Walking routes, talking toilets: exploring pit stops of public toilet access in everyday life – Lauren White 41
4 Distribution landscapes: a walk through the trading estates of south London – Louise Rondel 53
5 Walking with nurdles: reflections on a plastic beach clean – Alice Mah 67

Trace 75

6 Breaking down the walls of Partick: tracing cycles of urban neoliberalism and resistance – Kirsteen Paton 77
7 Walls and bridges: or, what's so funny 'bout peace, love and understanding? – Daryl Martin 91
8 Traces of industrial York – Nicholas Gane 103

9 A walk along Chester's canal: peeling back the past to rediscover colonial era Cheshire – Julia Bennett 115
10 Walking the line: search practices, environment and the practice of care in mountain rescue work – Robin James Smith 131
11 Walking through waves: technology, the Thames and urban development – Alex Rhys-Taylor 143
12 In the Big Yin's footsteps: class, belonging and the long walk home – Les Back 161
13 Under a hawthorn tree or thoughts about Nightingales and war – Vron Ware 173

Recompose 187

14 The rhythms of walking and doing sociology on The Street – Dawn Lyon 189
15 Territory and temporality on the university campus – Katherine Quinn 199
16 Your feet may change size: murder mystery, motherhood and the anti-carceral imagination – Phil Crockett Thomas 213
17 Black dog, Brown disabled man, White world – Viji Kuppan 225
18 Listening to urban change on the River Ravensbourne – Emma Jackson 237
19 Walking into the current – Charlotte Bates 251
20 Walking away and returning: letting go of ashes in Blackpool and Stratford-upon-Avon – Nirmal Puwar 261

Hidden track 273

Index 275

Illustrations

Lily Mae Kroese is an animator and community artist based in Newcastle. The illustrations for this collection are hand-drawn in ink and were inspired by the Wainwright Guides – Alfred Wainwright's definitive walking guidebooks to the Lake District fells.

Map of walk locations
Pound shop, London, England
Firth of Forth shoreline, Grangemouth, Scotland
Glasgow Harbour housing development, Glasgow, Scotland
Mountain rescue team, Bannau Brycheiniog (Brecon Beacons), Wales
The Street, Whitstable, England
Laxman, the black English Springer–Labrador cross dog
Solva harbour, Pembrokeshire, Wales

Contributors

Les Back teaches sociology at the University of Glasgow. He is the former Director of the Centre for Urban and Community Research at Goldsmiths, University of London. In south-east London he combined his love of city walking with doing lectures on the move on issues including anti-racism and Black history. He is a researcher and author of books on migration, racism, music and urban cultures. In his contribution to this book, he brings this ambulant approach to sociology to his new intellectual home in Glasgow through his lifelong fascination with the urban storytelling of comedian Billy Connolly.

Charlotte Bates is a sociologist at Cardiff University, where she teaches courses on qualitative, sensory and mobile methods, walking, writing and cities. Her work explores the connections between the body, everyday life and place through different practices. Her co-edited collections include *Walking through social research* with Alex Rhys-Taylor (Routledge, 2017) and *Living with water: Everyday encounters and liquid connections* with Kate Moles (Manchester University Press, 2023). Her essay in this collection combines her interests in walking and swimming, and is part of a collaborative project with Kate Moles that explored the practice of swimming outdoors around the UK.

Julia Bennett is a Visiting Research Fellow at the University of Chester. She has written widely on belonging and place for both academic and literary journals. Research has included walking in parades, through parks, along the English coast and across the countryside in Cheshire and beyond. Her interest in the origins of the Chester Canal began as part of a walk to 'decolonise' the University of Chester, whose main campus sits alongside a branch of the canal.

Karis Campion is a Lecturer in Race, Ethnicity and Social Justice at City St George's, University of London. Her research interests include the relationship between race, place, identity and the city (particularly Black place-making practices and belonging), urban ethnography as method, Black mixed-race identities/families, and race inequities in higher and secondary education. Her recent ethnographic research incorporates art and photography to explore how barbershops function as counter-hegemonic spaces and community assets for Black communities in south London. The simple act of walking in the city is not so straightforward to Karis, precisely because it provides a rich subjective vantage point from which to analyse the everyday ways that race and racism are experienced, and communities are formed in the city. Who gives way? Who takes up space? What language are they speaking? Did they just do the Black nod? Walking opens questions and inspires sociological answers.

Phil Crockett Thomas writes fiction and poetry, and teaches sociology and criminology at the University of Stirling. Her research focuses on social harm, justice and creative and collaborative methods. Her fiction has appeared in *Granta* and on BBC Radio 4. She is the editor of *Abolition science fiction* (2022), a collection of creative writing by activists and scholars involved in the movement for prison abolition in the UK, and of *The moon spins the dead prison* (2022) with Thomas Abercromby and Rosie Roberts. Like many people she spent much of the COVID-19 pandemic walking around her neighbourhood (with a newborn) and is hugely grateful to have had the opportunity to reflect back on this experience for this book.

Nicholas Gane is Professor of Sociology at the University of Warwick. From the 2008 financial crisis onwards, his research has centred on neoliberalism and the increased powers of corporations, markets and finance over politics and all things social. His relation to the walk depicted in his essay is twofold. First, it is an encounter with neoliberalism from the ground upwards: from a repurposed factory at one end of the path towards a university and new housing development at the other, through sites that reveal the lived experiences of austerity politics: a food bank, social housing and public spaces such as the library. Second, following serious illness, the walk provided an opportunity to embrace life at a slower pace by being more attentive to urban surroundings that had previously gone unnoticed.

Laura Henneke is a researcher at the Habitat Unit of the Technische Universität Berlin. She contributes to projects focusing on sustainable urban development in China, Nigeria and South Africa. In London, Laura co-initiated the walkshop series 'Infrastructural Explorations' together with Louise Rondel, inviting participants to move through the city and critically engage with the infrastructures that sustain urban life. Individually, Laura applies walking as an investigative practice to large-scale logistics infrastructures along the China–Europe transportation corridor, also known as the New Silk Road. Her routes take her through wholesale markets, multi-modal transportation hubs and vast warehouse complexes. Walking in and around these infrastructures allows for an embodied understanding of global supply chains, their spatial footprints and their sociopolitical implications.

Emma Jackson is an urban sociologist and research consultant working on practices of place, belonging and the city. She is a Visiting Senior Research Fellow in Sociology at the LSE, and an Associate at Art of Regeneration. She is author of *Young homeless people and urban space: Fixed in mobility* (Routledge, 2015) and co-author of *The middle classes and the city: A study of Paris and London* (Palgrave Macmillan, 2015) and *Go home?: The politics of immigration controversies* (Manchester University Press, 2017). Walking has long been part of Emma's research, teaching and writing. She has organised multiple events on walking and sociology. She can be found wandering in south-east London, often chasing after her daughter, Joanie. Walking by and in Lewisham's rivers was central to the project Place-making and the Rivers of Lewisham, which her essay draws from.

Caroline Knowles is Global Professorial Fellow at Queen Mary University of London. She has been walking for many years across diverse landscapes and at varying scales. Sometimes she is trying to get a close look at how a small section of a city works, as in *Serious money: Walking plutocratic London* (Penguin, 2022). Walking slows everything down and allows her to see the city's textures and the infrastructures (in this case the infrastructures of wealth and luxury) at close quarters. The walks generating the material for this book were repeated over and over again looking for further clues and inconvenient facts. In other walks she is looking for a city's connective vectors, for the ways in which they are linked with other cities. *Flip-flop: A journey through globalisation's backroads* (Pluto Press, 2014) is an example of this kind of walking. Here, the aim was to trace the mechanisms of supply chains across neighbourhoods from Kuwait, Korea, China, to Ethiopia—an exercise that narrated the mobile biography of a pair of flip-flops. Her next book, *Uneasy Streets: How Chinese Money is Remaking Urban Britain* (Hurst, 2026) explores China's erratic economic and social footprint in British cities.

Viji Kuppan is an ethnographer and sociologist. He currently works as a researcher at Loughborough University on a project that connects cricket to caring for nature and the environment. Before this he worked as a researcher on the Rural Racism Project: Towards an Inclusive Countryside based at the University of Leicester. His writing, teaching and activism are most frequently animated by the intersectional inequalities of race, disability and gender. Viji enjoys walking both city streets and countryside locales with his partner, friends, and most frequently his dog, Laxman—the focus of his essay in this collection.

Dawn Lyon is a sociologist of work, time and everyday life with a keen interest in creative, audio-visual, sensory, temporal and mobile methods. As an Emeritus Professor of Sociology in the School of Social Sciences at the University of Kent, she lives (some of the time) in Whitstable, where she regularly walks on 'The Street'. In late 2024, Dawn was a Visiting Fellow at the Australian National University in Canberra where she had the opportunity to reflect on The Street from the shores of the Burley Griffin Lake.

Alice Mah is Professor of Urban and Environmental Studies at the University of Glasgow, with research interests in toxic pollution, environmental justice and just transformations. She was awarded the 2013 British Sociological Association Philip Abrams Memorial Prize, and her recent books include: *Red pockets: An offering* (Allen Lane, 2025), *Petrochemical planet: Multiscalar battles of industrial transformation* (Duke University Press, 2023) and *Plastic unlimited: How corporations are fuelling the ecological crisis and what we can do about it* (Polity Press, 2022). In this walk, Alice revisits a petrochemical complex in Grangemouth, Scotland, where she has done research before. This time, she approaches it from a different perspective: across the river, taking part in a beach clean and nurdle hunt.

Daryl Martin is a Lecturer in Sociology at Maynooth University. His research focuses on the intersections of architecture, embodiment and care. These complement his long-standing interests in northern landscapes, literary approaches to documenting the social, and processes of ruination within contemporary landscapes. Originally from Derry, the essay offers Daryl an opportunity to return to his home place, in order to think through the emotional charge of reconnecting with landscapes of his past, as well as acknowledging his blind spots about the city then, and listen to it with refreshed attention.

Kirsteen Paton is a sociologist of class and urban inequalities at the University of Glasgow. Hailing from the Clydeside area, Kirsteen has a deep-rooted interest in the relationship between class and the restructuring of the urban landscape. Her research explores class and the impact of urban restructuring, gentrification, evictions, and large-scale sporting events on working-class communities. This includes analyses of the changing urban political economy and class and everyday life in neighbourhoods and cities. This interest has inspired (and has been inspired by) walking in the city and along the River Clyde. Her book *Gentrification: A working-class perspective* (Routledge, 2014), focused on Partick, Glasgow, where the walk in this essay takes place. Her latest book, *Class and everyday life* (Routledge, 2023), traverses different geographies, including Liverpool, London and Glasgow, exploring local forms of class resistance. This interest in class resistance is expressed through her involvement in the radical archive project: Glasgow Housing Struggles Archive.

Nirmal Puwar is a Professor in the Department of Media, Communications and Cultural Studies at Goldsmiths, University of London. Walking has been a central feature of creative methods practised by Nirmal across sites and platforms. Building on her classic book *Space invaders: Race, gender and bodies out of place* (2004) she has designed feminist and post-colonial tours of consecrated institutions, such as parliaments and a cathedral. She has also developed a method of walking along with different kinds of knowledge makers: artists, botanists, activists, soil scientists and ghosts. This is realised in her book *One mile walk* (Punctum Press, 2026). Becoming writer-as-resident and comrade-for-the-city as she returned to her 'home' city, walking and writing are central to her way of making and being in space together, with human and more-than-human elements. Site-specific provocations and alternative mapping practices sit at the heart of her scholarship, including *Hear here: A modernist cathedral* (Mattering Press, 2025).

Katherine Quinn is an ethnographer interested in the interplay between classifications – epistemic, cultural, conceptual – in spaces and places of education, and a Lecturer at Cardiff University. Through her creative ethnographic research in sites like libraries, university campuses and academic workplaces, she is keen to understand how and to what consequence groups and individuals negotiate, maintain and transform boundaries. She is interested in what these practices reveal about the state and status of public goods, education and space. Additionally, Katherine's work engages in practices of creative non-fiction and drawing. In this walk, she combines both substantive and methodological interests. Walking from her office to a research site on the other side of the university she traces the shifting timescapes, while navigating writers' block by practicing a constrained writing method called *100s*.

Alex Rhys-Taylor is Associate Head of the School of Global Change at Goldsmiths, University of London. He is an ethnographer with a special interest in processes of change and how they are experienced. He lives in London, walks wherever he can, and has often used walking as method of data collection. He has been giving a shorter version of the walk featured in this collection to students for many years, but extended the walk further eastward after COVID-19 lockdowns, during which time he commuted to work by boat along the Thames.

Louise Rondel is an urban sociologist and Visiting Research and Knowledge Exchange Fellow at the Centre for Urban and Community Research, Goldsmiths, University of London. Her research interests include the relationship between bodies and cities, infrastructures, materials and geographies of toxicity. As well as walking around trading estates for work, she has walked along rivers, up and down high streets, across the Peak District and around different infrastructures of distribution, transport and waste. But most often Louise walks with Bo Thunder, a Staffordshire Bull Terrier cross, in their local parks in south-east London.

Robin James Smith is Professor of Sociology at Cardiff University and Visiting Professor at the University of Witwatersrand. His research is primarily concerned with social interaction, categorisation practices, mobility, and perception. He has completed various projects situated at the points where these interests intersect. He spends a good deal of time in the mountains: walking, running, and as a member of the Central Beacons Mountain Rescue Team. He joined the team in 2017 and is qualified as a party leader and casualty carer. He is also a navigation instructor and assessor. Happily, these two occupations come together in his academic work where he writes about the organisational practices of the team, such as in this current collection.

Vron Ware is a writer and photographer, having previously taught sociology, gender studies and cultural geography. Her published work has focused on the politics of gender and race, the social construction of whiteness, anti-racist feminism, colonial history, national identity, militarisation, the cultural heritage of war and ecological thought. Her most recent books are *England's military heartland: Preparing for war on Salisbury Plain* (co-authored by Antonia Dawes, Mitra Pariyar and Alice Cree, Manchester University Press, 2025) and *Return of a native: Learning from the land* (Repeater, 2022). This walk took place in June 2024 at a time when British weapons components were being supplied to the Israel Defence Force during the genocide in Gaza.

Lauren White is a Lecturer in Social Research Methods based in the Sheffield Methods Institute at the University of Sheffield. Her research focuses on the everyday experiences of health, illness and disability, utilising creative and participatory methods to explore these with communities. She is interested in creative, affirmative and co-produced research, doing meaningful public engagement and knowledge exchange. Part of this commitment is demonstrated through active participation and engagement with the social world with others, whether that be with objects as elicitation, artwork to co-create meaning or walking together to learn about everyday life. Lauren's interest in walking comes from a methodological curiosity in being alongside one another to learn and understand together, and through her substantive research areas where she thinks critically about access to space and place through the lens of health, illness, disability and social justice. Her essay in this book seeks to reflect this.

Acknowledgements

We would like to thank Shannon Kneis and the team at Manchester University Press for supporting this project, Lily Mae Kroese for illustrating the collection so magically, and the contributors for their wonderful essays and for staying with the project through a gruelling period in higher education.

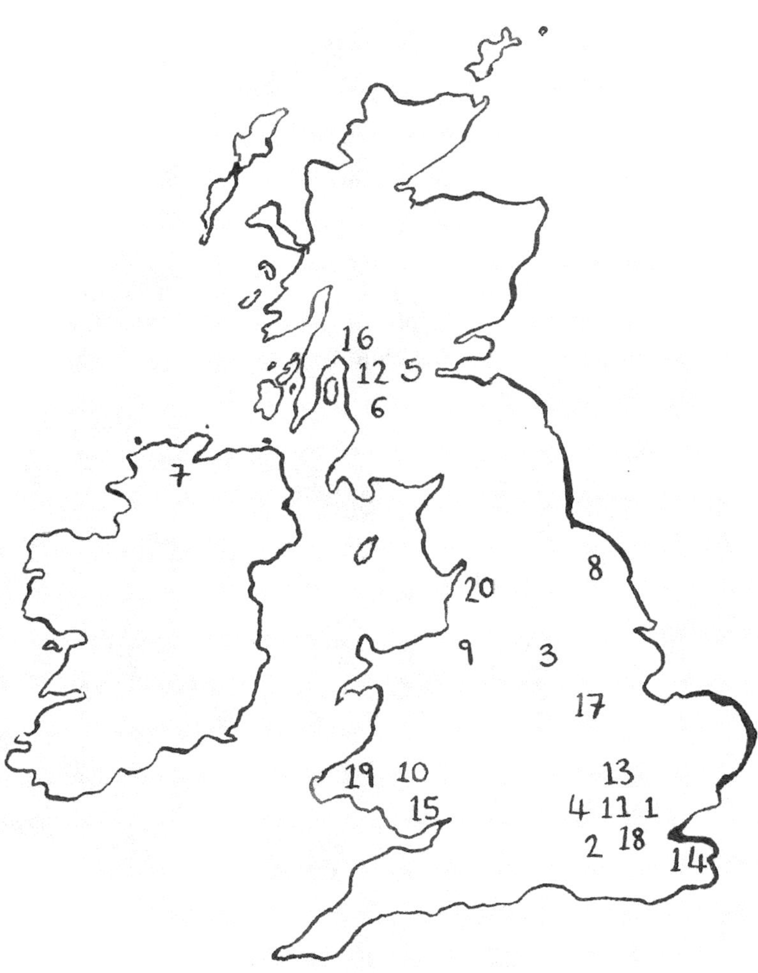
16
12 5
6
7
8
20
9 3
17
19 10
13
15
4 11 1
2 18
14

Introduction: A sociological field guide

Emma Jackson and Charlotte Bates

The walk from my house to Catford Bridge Station takes sixteen minutes.[1] I can push it to fourteen or fifteen if I'm prepared to run a bit. Like many London journeys, I know the time to the minute, as missing one train might mess up my day. This is a walk I usually undertake unthinkingly, periodically checking my phone for an update on my time. If I reach the shop on the corner with ten minutes to spare, I'll make it. But what if I tuned in?

If I listen carefully, from my front door I might hear the quacks of ducks or the honks of geese from the path by the River Pool some hundred metres away. I might look at the rows of 1930s terrace houses and wonder who built them? And who were they built for? I might say hi to my cat, Wilma, rolling around in the grass of next door's garden and look at the plants that have blown into this unmanicured space – asters, buttercups, nettles, brambles. Walking up to the main road, I pass the house where there is always reggae playing from the open window, past the Chinese takeaway which has a basket of toys in the window and the barbershop that reminds me of Karis Campion's rich ethnography of Black barbershops in Brixton. I turn right to head down to Catford Hill, a busy road with the red double-deckers rolling by to the heights of Crystal Palace and Blackheath. But who is waiting at the bus stop? What language are they speaking?

I cross the road and continue, past the junction where a homeless hostel faces the elite private Hogwartsesque school building. I might think about the marked disparities of wealth in this city, the facilities and large plot of land dedicated to a minority of children, while Lewisham local schools do so much with so little. Meanwhile, the homelessness crisis is intensifying. The multiple effects of a long period of austerity and cuts to mental health services can be felt in the middle of Catford. I might recall discussions by local policymakers on how to stop antisocial behaviour, the street drinking and the 'local characters' such as the unconventional man who tries to help people cross the road whether they want help or not. I might see children negotiating a hostile environment for pedestrians with the busy roads intersecting and dominating the street life. There are plans to move the South Circular Road; I might imagine this future.

As I turn towards the station, I might see workers in hi-vis grabbing a coffee and a cigarette in the sun outside Cafe Bonane. While inside, a group of tired new mums clutch their babies and reassure each other that they are doing ok. As I approach the station, I cross my old friend the River Pool. The proprietor at Beats and Grind is serving up coffees and playing techno from his van. The train I wait for is the commuter line from Kent that runs to London Charing Cross. I might think about the blurry character of London's edges.

You might find yourself walking or wheeling through the world on any given day. Moving around your home, walking the dog, commuting to and from university or work, running to catch a train, doing the school run. These journeys can be mundane and uneventful. But if you pause to pay attention, they can reveal the richness of the worlds we live in and move through. Of course, there are many ways of walking and a plethora of reasons why we walk, but the idea that walking is a way of observing and unfolding life is the impetus of this book. Not all walks are pleasant, we might not find what we are looking for, and it is important to notice both what is present and what is absent. But the invitation to pay attention to the world as we walk can remind us of the things we take for granted, things that too often fall out of our accounts. Walking attentively can be a way of reconnecting to our neighbourhoods, communities and the unfolding social life around us. It can help with what sociologist and contributor to this collection, Les Back, sets out as 'The difficult task of finding ways *to make the mundane remarkable*' (Back, 2020: xviii). Walking helps us to notice more and to ask different questions, and reminds us how to develop a felt relationship with the world and why that matters. It allows us to observe, feel and hear the impact of social issues in the places we move through.

It sounds deceptively simple, but walking is not always easy and opening to the world can be overwhelming. This book playfully engages with the idea of a field guide to provide some direction and to point towards some of the things you might pay attention to along the way. A field guide is a book packed full of information to help the reader locate and identify the life around them. The notes and illustrations within include detailed descriptions of various fauna and flora, including shapes and sizes, colours, calls and life cycles. Field guides are designed to be brought into the field and used outdoors; they are books to be carried with you and used repeatedly as a way of developing observational skills and building up knowledge. While this book is not a scientific identification tool, it is inspired by the idea that a field guide can help you to notice and be curious, to look around and learn about the life surrounding you in different ways. As Anna Lowenhaupt Tsing and colleagues (2024: 4) write, 'To head out into the world with a field guide in hand is to commit to opening and attuning in new ways'. This book is an invitation to explore some of the taken-for-granted and overlooked places we live in, to return to them, and to attend to them in a different way. It is an invitation to go for a walk and discover something new.

But this book is a *sociologist's* field guide. There is fauna and flora – in it you can find gatekeeper butterflies, fallow deer, green parakeets and curlews, as well as Himalayan balsam, buddleia and gorse. But you will also find other things in front of you – people, buildings, and all kinds of litter. In an essay on field guides, writer and naturalist Helen Macdonald (2021: 19) notes that 'even the simplest of field guides are far from transparent windows on to nature. You need to learn how to read them against the messiness of reality.' In this book we show how going for a walk is a way of expanding our sociological attention, generating different questions, and understanding the messiness of reality. Many sociologists are oriented towards making the links between forms of everyday social life and larger societal problems and questions, as C. Wright Mills (1959) puts it, being able to understand the interrelation of 'private troubles and public issues'. Walking sociologically might not instantly give us all of the answers about these relationships, but it may help us to develop a grounded way of thinking about sometimes abstract sociological theories and issues and open up new avenues for thinking about how inequalities and forms of injustice shape the places we traverse and occupy.

As Emma Jackson and Agata Lisiak (2025: 6) argue elsewhere, 'This discovery happens only if walkers are willing to engage the street beyond a surface level.' Even when we walk by ourselves, we are engaged with other people whose work helps us to understand what is unfolding, as well as the people we encounter in person. For example, in the opening walk, a connection was made to Karis Campion's (2023) work which might help us to better understand the social world of the Black barbershop, an urban interior that we merely pass by here. Links could also have been made to work on urban schooling (Kulz, 2017) or homelessness (Jackson, 2015), among many other sociological issues. As such, walking offers a set of dispositions and orientations that can both turn the everyday into something magical and illuminate untold stories and inequalities through a sociological lens.

For us, a key tenant of sociological walking is that it is approached as embodied and situated, challenging the idea of the universal walker. There is a close link between the critique of the 'lone enraptured male' hero of place writing (Jamie, 2008), the hero sociologist researcher (Jackson, 2024) and the durable and influential figure of the flâneur in traditions of urban walking and psychogeography. All of these masculine figures share an air of being able to intrepidly access even the most inhospitable places, and a lack of consideration within their writing about how they are situated in terms of race, dis/ability, class and gender and how this shapes their experience. While these kinds of approaches have generated some work and ideas that we have found useful and beautiful, this is not the approach to sociological walking that underpins this book. We cannot take walking for granted and must grapple with the exclusions that walking can be associated with and try to overturn the assumption of a certain kind of walking body.

The scholars influencing the approach taken here include those who recognise the situated and political nature of walking, bringing in the walker's position within the places they traverse (Brown and Shortell, 2016; O'Neill and Roberts, 2020; Rose, 2025), those who have grappled with complex histories of place through walking (Back, 2017), those who walk collectively and repeatedly in order to ask questions of a place and reimagine it (Lisiak et al., 2018;

Puwar, 2026), those who foreground the embodied and multisensory aspects of walking (Bates and Rhys-Taylor, 2017), and those who are attentive to the ethics and politics of walking in a more-than-human world (Springgay and Truman, 2018).

This book brings together place writing on the move in two ways. One, the places we walk through will not stop changing – we take from the geographer Doreen Massey the approach that places are dynamic, always changing, and always multiple. Catford, in the walk sketched above, or any other place in any other type of location, is always changing – albeit at different speeds and with different rhythms. If this walk was repeated at night, or in a different season or time of day, it would be different. The path that an author describes today might no longer exist tomorrow. The cafe may be closed due to the pressure of rising rents, by the time you get there. The tide may have come in, obscuring the shoreline. These scenes of life are never still. And two, as we write places, we are moving through them, rather than observing from the cafe (Perec, 2010) or the balcony (Lefebvre, 2004). This allows us to move with the world, and to link scenes and sites and think between them.

The walks in this collection take us to and through a wide range of locations. In urban writing, the masculine figure of the walker/explorer has tended towards the urban edgelands. This is at its most extreme in writing on urbex, the exploration of ruins and high up places – see Mott and Roberts (2013) for the pithily titled critique 'Not everyone has (the) balls'. But even in the more mainstream walking writing of Iain Sinclair and Will Self, we find a fascination with the out of the way and the liminal. These places are present here, in Louise Rondel's industrial estate and Alice Mah's exploration of the landscape of the petrochemical industry, although approached from a different angle. But we also visit places that are less difficult to access and, for many people, more mundane. This is a work of everyday sociology (Back, 2020) that asks the reader to re-engage with places that may seem very familiar, from the park to the pound shop. And while much of the literature on walking focuses on the urban, this book is not solely focused on cities or their edges. There is plenty of tarmac beneath our feet, but there is also mud, sand and water, blurring the boundaries between urban–rural distinctions.

But the scope of the walks goes beyond their immediate geographies. As we follow out objects, sounds, biographies to link the places we move through to elsewheres, again, we are influenced by Doreen Massey, who argues that places are always '*meeting* places' (1994: 154). This means that while these walks are all based in the UK, they are not contained there. The walk around the pound shop takes us to Yiwu, the Himalayan balsam on the London riverbank, and the canal path in Chester lead us not only to other places, but back through the extractive histories of colonialism. This process of following outwards, from the local and particular to the structural, infuses these walks with the sociological imagination.

While this book is framed as walking sociologically, walking is an important way of learning about and connecting with the worlds we live in that traverses rather than patrols disciplinary borders and boundaries. All the walks in this collection are made and written by sociologists, but through this book we hope to establish a common ground that connects the wide range of interest in walking as a methodology and a topic that currently exists across the creative arts, humanities and social sciences. As a critical, creative and interdisciplinary subject, walking emerges as a research method (Bates and Rhys-Taylor, 2017; Springgay and Truman, 2018; O'Neill and Roberts, 2020; Rose, 2020; Ernsten and Shepherd, 2024), a critical pedagogy (O'Neill et al., 2025), an arts practice (Jeffreys, 2024), and a technique that can tell us much about different social and cultural contexts (Ingold and Vergunst, 2008), contemporary urban life (Brown and Shortell, 2016; Shortell and Brown, 2016; Middleton, 2022) and leisure practices (Snellgrove, 2026).

Drawing on and contributing to this rich body of work, the sociologists and writers in this collection put on their boots and take to the streets to craft their work in lively, mobile and sensuous ways. Together, their work explores the significance of studying social life on foot, and shows what can be gained from thinking on the move. Interweaving key sociological ideas with walking concepts and methods, the collection opens new possibilities for both learning about and representing social life. By going for a walk, each essay develops an openness to the world around us and cultivates new ways of writing about people and places. At the same time, the book offers a distinctively sociological perspective. Each unique walk is an encounter with key sociological ideas, showing that sociology is for everyone and can be found everywhere, even in the most unexpected places.

There are many different routes through this collection. The structure is not prescriptive, and we invite you to explore and make your own paths. You might make a collection of city walks, follow the water through the collection, or look for your own sociological interests. But to guide you, the collection has been organised into three parts: *Circulate*, *Trace* and *Recompose*. The walks in *Circulate* contain circulations of people and all sorts of material things, and show how places are inextricably linked through social and material processes. Many of the walks in *Trace* connect the past and present, showing how places are forged through long and violent histories of extraction, exploitation and conflict. Others find traces of missing people on the hillside, traces of biographies on the city streets, or traces of neoliberalism in the urban landscape. In *Recompose*, a section that is inspired by and borrows from the title of Nirmal Puwar's latest book *One mile walk: decompositions and recompositions*, walks, people, relationships and places are constantly being remade and reworked. Hidden between these sections you will find practical exercises that are intended to encourage and support you to go out and conduct your own walks. We have used these exercises in the classroom and outside, as teaching techniques and as research practice. The exercises are playful, and can be tried in any order, at different times of day, and in different places.

Circulate

We begin in a high street pound shop in Dalston, east London. It is one of many pound shops on the street, all small and crammed full of everyday objects, from cooking pans and umbrellas to plastic flowers. Inside it is a bit of a squeeze, but as they negotiate their way around the shop Laura Henneke and Caroline Knowles move between different places and scales, connecting the commodities inside the shop to a giant wholesale mall in Yiwu, China. At the other end of the supply chain the sprawling mall holds bulk loads of this stuff waiting to be moved across the world, inviting different kinds of movement. Walking both spaces together reveals otherwise unseen places and connections, the cost-of-living crisis and the globalisation of everyday life. Moving from one busy cosmopolitan high street to another, in south London Karis Campion takes a walk down Brixton Station Road, where reggae music booms out from a large portable speaker and the aromas of Caribbean food drift through the busy street market. The walk weaves together tensions and conflicts, embedded histories and possibilities from the Brixton uprising in the 1980s, a watershed moment in the history of British race relations, to recent regeneration plans and the effects of urban renewal and gentrification on local Black communities. Next, Lauren White highlights the absence of toilet access for the people who make a living by moving around the city, from postal workers to parcel and food delivery couriers. Walking with participants from a research project conducted in and around Sheffield, England, we navigate the pit stops that punctuate and disrupt the day. Each journey and each stop reveal the everyday exclusions that are built into the fabric of the city, highlighting the urgent need for an urban infrastructure of care. The final two walks of this section resonate closely with Caroline and Laura's first essay, tracing the circulation of things. Returning to the edgelands of London, Louise Rondel takes a walk through south London's trading estates. Skirting warehouses, crossing car parks and roads, the walk takes us through an environment built for traffic and fumes, not people. This outside space contrasts with the inside of the warehouse, where beauty supplies are stacked up waiting to be bought and circulated through the city to salons and bodies. Across these spaces, the walk explores how the infrastructures of beauty practices entangle with gendered bodies at different scales. Walking along the Firth of Forth estuary across from the oil and petrochemical complex in Grangemouth on the east coast of Scotland, Alice Mah takes part in the Great Nurdle Hunt, an organised beach clean that aims to track the enormous volumes of tiny plastic pellets washing up along shorelines around the world. Together, the volunteers collect and sort all kinds of plastic waste and find countless nurdles. As she walks along the shoreline with her son, curlews cry and Alice reflects on the polluter across the water and the injustices and contradictions within the industry.

Trace

Kirsteen Paton opens this section, taking us on a walk around the neighbourhood of Partick in Glasgow, Scotland, including the Glasgow Harbour development. It is a place that she has studied and written about extensively, and a walk that she takes students on to animate the stories from her research. This huge state-led gentrification project tells a story of a housing crisis and makes neoliberalism visible in the landscape. We are also pointed towards what cannot be seen, including the histories of organising and resistance in the city. Next, we hop across the Irish Sea to accompany Daryl Martin who is revisiting the city he grew up in, Derry, in Northern Ireland. Walking the streets of the city, Daryl blends his recollections of the city and its pasts with his hopes for its future. The walls and bridges that divide the material city also divide the Catholic and Protestant residents, highlighting the violent histories, difficult heritage and contested political questions that continue to exist in the present. The walk connects the Northern Irish Troubles with everyday life in Derry, and moves from a traumatic and haunting landscape towards a love for place and a landscape of peace and understanding. We leave the murals of Derry Girls and Derry Boys to join Nicholas Gane as he walks through the suburbs of York in England. The city is a popular tourist destination, but there is a history that visitors do not normally see. Connecting the city's industrial past and famous chocolate factory with austerity politics and the cost-of-living crisis, the walk finds traces of the past on the streets in the present. Meanwhile, across the Pennines in north-west England, Julia Bennett follows the Chester canal from the city centre out through the suburbs to the countryside, and into the colonial history that the canal holds. Revealing histories of trade and commerce, exploitation and the violent regimes of slavery, walking the canal shows how the infrastructure of the United Kingdom is dependent on its colonial connections. Then we move to quite a different landscape. Somewhere along a mountain ridge a family has lost their way. Robin Smith is a member of the Central Beacons Mountain Rescue Team and in this essay he goes on a search and rescue, navigating the Bannau Brycheiniog (Brecon Beacons) in Wales on a cold dark night. The team are trained and equipped, working systematically up to the ridge before spreading out to walk the line, a kind of purposive wandering that produces as much coverage as possible. They find the family, and begin the difficult work of getting them safely off the mountain, step by step. Through this encounter, the essay highlights the relationship between movement and landscape, and ways of seeing, knowing and walking. Back in London, Alex Rhys-Taylor walks along the banks of the River Thames, chasing the waves of technology and urban development that have shaped and transformed the capital city over the last two millennia. Through technological revolutions of wind, steam, electricity and diesel, the walk takes in bridges, docks and power stations, before arriving at the Thames Flood Barrier and the climate emergency. Inspired by Billy Connolly, Les Back takes a walk up Buchanan Street and Kelvin Way, two very different streets in Glasgow. Drawing on Connolly's biography, the walk reflects on the relationship between street life and a sense of home and belonging. Vron Ware's walk begins on the outskirts of north London. Her destination is the Lee Valley Country Park, just beyond the busy M25 motorway that encircles London. Vron is hoping to hear Nightingales, and as she walks she weaves birdsong and England's military history together.

Recompose

The final section opens with a shingle strip known locally as 'The Street'. On the Kent coastline in southern England, Dawn Lyon walks along this vanishing stretch, then reflects on it from the shore, from Australia, and by walking it once more, piecing it together from shifting vantage points. We then head to Wales again, where Katherine Quinn takes a short walk across campus in Cardiff. As she walks, she reflects on the relationship between the university and the city, the shifting higher education landscape, and the precarity of beginning an academic career. Moving between a murder mystery novel and the first months of motherhood, Phil Crockett Thomas slips between fiction and reality, Blackheath House in the pages of the book and Pollok Country Park in Glasgow, and the connections between detective fiction and the anticarceral imagination. Next, Viji Kuppan and Laxman the dog take a walk together through their local neighbourhood on the edge of Nottingham in the East

Midlands of England. Walking together shapes their movements and their encounters with other people on the street, and the walk creates a space to reflect on connection and community, tension and conflict, racism and disability. In south-east London Emma Jackson follows the River Ravensbourne. Listening to the sounds of the river and the city, the walk reflects on the communities that live along the river and the processes of urban change that are shaping the area, from new housing developments to community clean-up groups. On a windswept peninsula in Wales, Charlotte Bates walks and swims with a group of outdoor swimmers in midwinter. Through these movements and moments she explores the body, landscape and immersion and the politics of trespass, nature and belonging. To end the collection, Nirmal Puwar brings a diasporic approach to walking. Moving between the roar of Blackpool in north-west England, a boat on the River Avon and the Royal Shakespeare Theatre tower, her essay intimately connects death rites, histories of migration and landscapes.

Note

1 The opening walk was written by Emma Jackson from her home in Catford, south-east London.

References

Back, Les (2017) Marchers and steppers: Memory, city life and walking. In Charlotte Bates and Alex Rhys-Taylor (eds) *Walking Through Social Research*. London: Routledge.

Back, Les (2020) Foreword: Making the mundane remarkable. In Helen Holmes and Sarah Marie Hall (eds) *Mundane Methods: Innovative Ways to Research the Everyday*. Manchester: Manchester University Press.

Bates, Charlotte and Rhys-Taylor, Alex (eds) (2017) *Walking Through Social Research*. London: Routledge.

Brown, Evrick and Shortell, Timothy (eds) (2016) *Walking in Cities: Quotidian Mobility as Urban Theory, Method, and Practice*. Philadelphia, PA: Temple University Press.

Campion, Karis and Nabisubi, Habiba (2023) *Bringing the Black Barbershop into Focus* [exhibition]. Gil's Barbershop, London, 12–29 June.

Ernsten, Christian and Shepherd, Nick (eds) (2024) *Walking as Embodied Research: Drift, Pause, Indirection.* Abingdon: Routledge.

Ingold, Tim and Vergunst, Jo Lee (eds) (2008) *Ways of Walking: Ethnography and Practice on Foot.* London: Routledge.

Jackson, Emma (2015) *Young Homeless People and Urban Space: Fixed in Mobility.* London: Routledge.

Jackson, Emma (2024) How to do social research with … a bowling ball. In Rebecca Coleman, Kat Jungnickel and Nirmal Puwar (eds) *How to do Social Research With ….* London: Goldsmiths Press.

Jackson, Emma and Lisiak, Agata (2025) You'll never walk alone: Theorizing engaged walking with Doreen Massey. *Sociological Review* [online first]. https://doi.org/10.1177/00380261241309715

Jamie, Kathleen (2008) A lone enraptured male. *London Review of Books*, 30 (5).

Jeffreys, Tom (ed.) (2024) *Walking: Documents of Contemporary Art.* London: Whitechapel Gallery.

Kulz, Christy (2017) *Factories for Learning. Making Race, Class and Inequality in the Neoliberal Academy.* Manchester: Manchester University Press.

Lefebvre, Henri (2004) *Rhythmanalysis: Space, Time and Everyday Life.* London: Continuum International Publishing Group.

Lisiak, Agata, Cox, Reece, Tienes, Flavia M. and Zbinovsky Braddel, Sophia (2018) 'A city coming into being': Walking in Berlin with Franz Hessel and Marshall Berman. *City*, 22 (5–6), 877–93.

Macdonald, Helen (2021) *Vesper Flights.* London: Vintage.

Massey, Doreen (1994) *Space, Place and Gender.* Minneapolis, MN: University of Minnesota Press.

Middleton, Jennie (2022) *The Walkable City: Dimensions of Walking and Overlapping Walks of Life.* London: Routledge.

Mott, Carrie and Roberts, Susan M. (2013) Not everyone has (the) balls: Urban exploration and the persistence of masculinist geography. *Antipode*, 46 (1), 229–45.

O'Neill, Maggie, O'Donovan, Danielle, Barimo, John, Mullally, Gerard et al. (2025) *Walking as Critical Pedagogy.* London: Routledge.

O'Neill, Maggie and Roberts, Brian (2020) *Walking Methods: Research on the Move.* Abingdon: Routledge.

Perec, Georges (2010) *An Attempt at Exhausting a Place in Paris.* Cambridge: Wakefield Press.

Puwar, Nirmal (2026) *One Mile Walk.* Rome: Punctum Press.

Rose, Morag (2020) Pedestrian practices: Walking from the mundane to the marvellous. In Helen Holmes and Sarah Marie Hall (eds) *Mundane Methods: Innovative Ways to Research the Everyday.* Manchester: Manchester University Press.

Rose, Morag (2025) *The Feminist Art of Walking*. London: Pluto Press.
Shortell, Timothy and Brown, Evrick (eds) (2016) *Walking in the European City: Quotidian Mobility and Urban Ethnography*. London: Routledge.
Snellgrove, Miriam (2026) *Walking and Leisure: Mobilities, Encounters, Critical Engagements*. London: Routledge.
Springgay, Stephanie and Truman, Sarah E. (2018) *Walking Methodologies in a More-than-Human World: WalkingLab*. New York: Routledge.
Tsing, Anna Lowenhaupt, Deger, Jennifer, Keleman Saxena, Alder and Zhou, Feifei (2024) *Field Guide to the Patchy Anthropocene: The New Nature*. Stanford, CA: Stanford University Press.
Wright Mills, Charles (1959) *The Sociological Imagination*. Oxford: Oxford University Press.

Circulate

Exercise 1: Setting the scene for your walk

Describe the physical landscape
What does this place sound, smell and feel like?
Who is there and what are they doing?
Can you hear any verbal exchanges?
What is the rhythm of this place?
How do you fit into or disrupt this scene?
How could you connect this scene to a sociological idea?

FLOWER
£1-00-
EACH

1

Pound shop: walking the intersections between Yiwu and Dalston

Laura Henneke and Caroline Knowles

There are many reasons to walk. But for urban researchers, walking is about unfolding city landscapes for their secrets, their inner recesses and their unacknowledged connections. Caroline and Laura have walked in cities around the world, but this particular walk is focused on the two ends of a supply chain – a local pound shop in Dalston, east London, and a giant wholesale mall in Yiwu, in eastern China, to which the pound shop is connected in ways that are not immediately obvious. We offer this two-part walk, not as a template for local or translocal walking research, but as an experiment in ruminating on the local and the familiar while exposing and exploring unseen places beyond and trying to draw connections between them. We have done each part of this walk alone and together, and this perhaps allows us to reflect on the benefits of walking together and combining different kinds of interest and expertise. Laura's expertise is in commodity supply chains linking China to Europe (Henneke, 2020). Caroline's is in the social morphology of London (Knowles, 2022) and the ways in which London is shaped by its many connections with China (Henneke and Knowles, 2020).

We meet up on Kingsland High Street in Hackney because several pound shops line both sides of the street, immediately posing the problem of which to choose. But as we wander between them, all concentrated in a small section of the street near Dalston Junction, Hackney's main commercial artery, we notice the cluster of commercial surfaces of which the pound shops formed a part, and which indicate who lives in this socially polarised neighbourhood. We walk past the hair shop with a permanent 'sale' notice outside, its wigs and African-Caribbean creams, oils and other beauty products displayed in the window: the wigs eerily set on faceless polystyrene heads stare out into the street. We wander past several open-fronted grocery stores with sacks of rice, onions and plantains next to giant freezers of large plastic bags of meat and fish. We take in several micro-shops or kiosks where customers buy phones, phone accessories and vapes from the counter outside, the shops themselves too small and stuffed with merchandise for customers to enter them. The pawnbroker has its treasure on display, precious items exchanged for instant cash that might tide someone over until their next pay cheque. We peer with difficulty through the windows of two betting shops – Ladbrokes and Paddy Power – offering the dream of lucky wins that could lift someone's fortunes, at least for a while. We notice a couple of pubs, recently revamped to attract a young crowd with a bit of cash to spare, and a shiny new aspirational restaurant called Africana.

We are standing on a cracked and uneven, worn concrete surface at the southernmost entrance to Futian Market in Yiwu, a city in Zhejiang province. We have travelled by train from Shanghai via Hangzhou, through the flatlands of the Yangtze River Delta, which suddenly gives way to a landscape of steep green hills and densely populated valleys. Since China's economic reform in 1978, the region has pioneered China's market-driven economy, becoming a hub for successful private enterprises that has integrated itself into global markets (e.g. Ding, 2006). At the station, a glaring white LED sign directs arrivals to the exit gates: WELCOME TO YIWU. The letters are attached to a vertical garden made up of dozens of plastic tiles that resemble greenery. The closer you get, the more you can see its imperfections. This is a typical example of plastics produced in one of countless factories in the area and sold in bulk at Futian Market: a sign of things to come on our walk there. Futian is Yiwu's wholesale market for small commodities, where everything from plastic toys to small electronics to household goods is on display and can be ordered in container ship or suitcase loads. Dalston and UK pound shops are full of such items, as we discovered.

Dalston's pound shops repeat the cost-of-living struggle imbricated in the commercial surfaces of which they form a part. Austerity in the UK from 2010, and ever tightening social welfare budgets, have torn through this neighbourhood like a tsunami as the huddled bodies of the homeless and people walking around in a daze talking to themselves attest. And pound shops are where those with the tightest of budgets meet their household needs. At one time everything in them cost a pound. Now they charge more, but are still the cheapest shops on the high street for everyday household objects. Moving inside of one of them we find an emporium of plastics, metals, fabrics and fluids used to fix and clean the house. Laura photographs the fabric and plastic flowers at the entrance – an inviting brightness that soon fades as we walk inside. We immediately discover that we can't walk side by side because the isles are too narrow and piled high to the ceiling with all manner of stuff. Every spare inch of space pays its way. We edge sideways past shoppers browsing shelves. They are browsing because it takes time to take it all in and to find what they might need. Our walking then is of a certain kind. Slow, ponderous, edging this way and that around piles of goods waiting to go on shelves and navigating around customers. No other high street shop crams as much into such a small space. Other shops might make attempts at display, but not pound shops, where it's all about stacking in as much stuff as possible. We soon get into the choreographies of the shop and find time to pause not within the isles but at the end of them where there is a little more place to stand and take it all in.

In stark contrast, Futian Market is a massive building. Originally located on the outskirts of Yiwu, surrounded by rural villages and productive landscapes, the market was gradually swept up in China's rapid urban development (Henneke, 2020). Today, these villages are unrecognisable: they have become highly specialised commercial zones of uniform multistorey blocks in close proximity to the market, offering all kinds of products, sometimes produced in the same building. These bustling neighbourhoods also offer a wide range of hospitality options, including eateries, hotels, KTV (Karaoke Television) bars and camouflaged brothels. Futian Market itself is now somewhat dated and very dusty. The entrance doors are covered with thick PVC curtains cut into wide strips. They are heavy and dirty and need to be pulled aside to enter the space. Laura tries to get through without using her hands. Caroline follows in her slipstream.

Like the pound shop, the lobby does not attempt to be welcoming; instead, it is purposeful and instrumental. The air is filled with a mix of food smells from the small canteen on the left, the smell of plastic fumes which linger everywhere in the market, mixed with sewage and bathroom smells. Despite this unpleasant mix, Laura is grinning, endorphins kicking in; she is keen to start walking into the madness of the market. She says it is like approaching a fairground or a music festival. She is happy to be back in the place she started visiting in 2013, and which has amazed her ever since. On her first visit, Caroline is wide-eyed in wonder and just a bit overwhelmed by Futian Market's sheer size. Steadily expanded since 2002, the market now has an L-shaped structure made up of five massive buildings (Districts 1, 2, 3, 4 and 5) with a total of 114 entrance gates, all numbered for better wayfinding and efficient shopping. It has a distinctive soundtrack too. The rattling of handcart wheels on tiled floors; customers calling on their phones to pass information to business partners or summoning drivers for a pick-up at the nearest exit. Most transactions are in Chinese or Arabic with a smattering of other languages too. The world comes to this place to buy and resell.

Pausing in the tiny, cramped entrance to the Dalston pound shop, we rapidly exchange our impressions – it is a bit of a squeeze – and take a few notes and photographs for later, having asked permission from Abdul who is serving behind the small counter which holds the cash desk. Caroline is a regular shopper here, scouring the shelves for hidden treasures, making it hard for her to see it as something strange to be investigated. Laura doesn't have this problem, although as a former London resident she is familiar with the concept of the pound shop. We resolve on ethical grounds only to photograph in ways that avoid customers and staff who have no option but to be there. Abdul isn't bothered. Looking at the low prices we understand that the pound shop operates with tight margins and relies on quick turnovers. The merchandise is arranged in small sections making it only slightly easier for customers to find what they are looking for as the shelves are crammed. Between us we draw up a small inventory of what we see: cuddly toys, metal pans for cooking, mops and mopheads, umbrellas, plastic dishes and bowls, vacuum jugs, kettles and other small electrical appliances, brightly coloured plastic fly swatters, folded woven plastic bags that unfold to absorb a whole life of stuff, plastic mats, rolls of paper towel, brushes and dustpans, scrubbing brushes, stepladders, tools, waste bins, plastic containers in all sizes, sunflowers and roses made from plasticised fabrics, glassware, crockery, plastic baskets, coat hangers, paper plates, suitcases, gift bags and fluffy blankets that are stored in see-through plastic cases to keep them clean.

There are more troubling products too, products not found in other kinds of London shops. We stand in front of them, picking them up and putting them back on the shelves after reading the instructions: glue traps for mice and rats, packets of fly papers, containers of flea powder, mothballs, heavy-duty cleaning products, candles and butane gas containers for those who cannot afford to use the gas and electricity supplied to their homes. While the pound shops' merchandise and the commercial cluster of which it forms a part suggests a local population on low incomes, these particular products suggest the poor quality of local housing and heroic struggles to make it habitable. At least for some. There is another version of Kingsland High Street with clubs, bars, restaurants and million pound plus housing for those who actually chose to live in run-down urban chic. The pound shop sits on the urban social landscape of this bifurcated neighbourhood: it serves the left behind and the struggling and provides doorways in which encampments of the homeless grow ever bigger.

In Futian Market we discuss a route through particular sections as we examine the goods on display. The market is mesmerising, disorienting, exhausting. Like the pound shop it demands a particular kind of walking – in this case all inside over vast distances. Starting in District 1 (artificial flowers, flower accessories, plush toys, inflatable toys, electric toys and ordinary toys, headdresses, festival and wedding crafts, decorations, porcelain, crystals, photoframes and accessories, home decorations, ornaments, Christmas supplies and artificial flowers as well as big distributors of jewellery and jade) and ending in District 5 (imported goods, bedding, wigs, textiles, festival and wedding supplies, knitting material, hotel supplies, automotive parts and accessories, aquarium supplies, delivery and e-commerce service area) takes about an hour walking in a straight line without visiting any of the shops. This does not account for the many opportunities for getting lost in the maze of uniform alleys, non-functioning escalators and unexpected dead ends. Futian Market has more than 75,000 stalls (Henneke, 2020), which vary in size but are generally between fourteen and thirty square metres in area and three metres high. In total, the market covers a gross floor area of more than 6.4 million square metres, spread over four or five storeys per building (Zhejiang China Commodities City Group Co., 2020) stretching over 2.6 km on the long side and 1.7 km on the short side. The buildings are connected by skywalks that span several multilane avenues, allowing people to walk from one end to the other without ever leaving this huge indoor complex.

The market's sprawling layout, with its seemingly endless rows of stalls, creates a disorienting environment where even the most organised visitor can lose their sense of direction. Adding to this complexity is the sheer volume of goods on display stacked high in colourful, chaotic arrangements. This is easily recognised as the stuff that finds its way to the Dalston pound shops. Each stall, we discover, is staffed by one or two people representing a factory or a small selection of manufacturers. The goods on display belong to one of the twenty-six commodity categories into which Futian Market is divided: toys, electronic appliances, ornaments, hardware and so on. This layout was designed to force traders to specialise in a single category of products, saving customers' time and allowing better management of the market (Rui, 2018: 20). The stalls have all kinds of functions. They serve as showrooms, sales offices, production areas and personal living rooms all at once. It is very common to see people eating, sleeping or watching films at their stalls. The market becomes the centre of their lives and involves the whole family: children often join parents after school and do their homework at tiny tables in a corner; grandparents take the youngest for a walk along the endless aisles while the parents go about their business. Young children play with the toys in toyshops or highjack a scooter and skid around the hallways between shops.

While it is impossible to assess the interior condition of the pound shop in Dalston as every wall and surface is covered with goods, in Futian Market the building's structure has started to crumble. Perhaps it was never in good shape. The concrete poured into this building must be enough to build a small town. The other dominant material surfaces are shiny slippery floor tiles that mirror the fluorescent white ceiling lights. As customers navigate this immense hub of global trade, the experience can feel as it did to us both exhilarating and overwhelming, offering a window into the vast scale and intricacy of modern supply chains.

The business model in Yiwu involves a Chinese entrepreneur who occupies a booth, and an associated factory often located elsewhere in Zhejiang Province, or, sometimes as far away as the Pearl River Delta in China's south-east. Although a considerable amount of the trade in Yiwu is handled online (Hulme, 2015: 54 ff.), stall owners still display their goods for those who want to inspect their products in person and those who prefer to wrap up a deal with a handshake instead of an agreement over WeChat. This is understandable in a system where much of the business is based on personal trust rather than trust mediated by a transparent credit score system. An estimated 210,000 people visit Futian Market every day, from 8am to 5pm, except during the Spring Festival (Zhejiang China Commodities City Group Co., 2020). This includes stall owners, delivery men and women, food vendors, shoe shiners, security guards, janitors and, of course, the Chinese and international traders who come to place their orders. It is a vast node of global commerce: a vibrant link between factory and retail.

Futian Market's clientele are traders in different kinds and scales of operation. Many of them are Chinese and international merchants whose main business is forwarding products to other wholesale markets and distribution centres, like the one in Enfield that serves the Dalston pound shops. Browsing our way through Yiwu Market, the pace of walking slowing as we became more tired, we see the omnipresent links to the pound shop in Dalston. But how are they made? How do these links materialise? How do the goods get from east China to the UK? These are just some of our questions and they demand further detailed research.

Back at the pound shop the soundtrack is relentless traffic and conversations in Bengali between staff. Customers with African and Caribbean accents enquire after this or that product. In just a few minutes it is possible to hear Turkish/Kurdish, a whole variety of Indian languages and UK east London accents, all in this tiny shop. The world lives in this neighborhood and passes through this pound shop on the quests of everyday life. We talk with Abdul, a relative of the owner who stands at the cash desk fiddling with his phone in between customers. Where does his stuff come from then? Many of the labels and QR codes point to China. We ask him about that. He says they have different suppliers for different kinds of goods. He has no sense that this shop has any connection to places in China. Why would he? He doesn't import the goods he sells. Instead, supply chains like these are fragmented into sections over which its operators have only partial oversight (Knowles, 2014). We zoom in on household items where plastic predominates and ask again where they come from. He tells us the names of some of his suppliers. They are from warehouses on the outskirts of London in places like Enfield from where they supply only to the trade. He phones Enfield when stocks are low, and more goods are delivered. Caroline phones Enfield. They are too busy to talk, but the boss says that a lot of the houseware items, party decorations, fake flowers and other things come from China, he supposes through shipping and other logistic and distribution centres. He doesn't know where in China. He doesn't need to.

Once an order has been placed at the wholesale markets of Yiwu, the goods are brought to one of the numerous warehouses and loading docks that can be found all around the city. Located close to Futian Market is a dry port, where a large part of Yiwu's international freight is handled. Huge logistics hubs relieve the operational burden of capacity-constrained seaports and improve the efficiency of inland intermodal transport making it more competitive on price (Zeng et al., 2013: 241). The basic functions of dry ports like Yiwu are cargo receipt and dispatch, truck operations, customs clearance, gate inspection and security, cargo and container storage, billing and cash collection. In Yiwu, the local government opened a dry port facility in 2013 in cooperation with the Ningbo seaport authorities (ownership 65–35 per cent to facilitate Yiwu's foreign trade; Chang et al., 2019: 111). The building has six loading docks spread over three floors, making it one of the largest of its kind in China with a capacity of 600,000 twenty-foot equivalent units – TEUs – a year. Drivers in vans and pick-up trucks unload boxes and bags of goods straight from the factory; workers at the loading docks receive and store the cargo in warehouses behind large roller shutters; traders arrive by car or scooter to check the quality of their order before it is reloaded into a container; noisy and smelly trucks drive in empty and drive out with full containers. They then head to the port of Ningbo-Zhoushan, where the cargo is reloaded onto container ships operated by major international shipping companies such as Maersk and China Shipping, for shipment to other ports around the world.

Only a fraction of the containers leaving Yiwu travel by rail. Most of them end up deep in China's landlocked provinces; some continue on to destinations in Central Asia, such as Almaty in

Kazakhstan. Contrary to the public image and messaging of the Belt and Road Initiative (BRI), a relatively small number of containers are transported by train to places in Europe, for example to Duisburg, which is a main hub of the BRI in Europe. Only on two test runs did trains from Yiwu actually arrive in London. London is effectively a railway siding, disconnected from China and mainland Europe by an underused tunnel and the 2016 vote to leave the EU. The goods in the pound shops must be transported as cheaply as possible given their slender margins and their function in serving the most underserved and under rewarded people of Dalston. Of course, UK austerity and neglect then rebounds in the factories around Yiwu in low wages and poor working conditions. The goods in the Dalston pound shops most likely travel by sea, taking more than forty days to arrive in Tilbury and the warehouses of Enfield, providing a material and largely unacknowledged link between low-income populations in both countries. Walking the vastness of Yiwu and the tight confines of the pound shop in Dalston both reflect the same economic reality – one of relentless circulation and squeezed living standards.

References

Chang, Zheng, Yang, Dong, Wan, Yulai and Han Tingting (2019) Analysis on the features of Chinese dry ports: Ownership, customs service, rail service and regional competition. *Transport Policy*, 82, 107–16.

Ding, Ke (2006) *Distribution System of China's Industrial Clusters: Case Study of Yiwu China Commodity City*. IDE Discussion Paper (075). Chiba, Japan: Institute of Developing Economies.

Henneke, Laura (2020) Small commodities, big infrastructure, *Articulo: Journal of Urban Research* [online], 21, article 4707. https://doi.org/10.4000/articulo.4707

Henneke, Laura and Knowles, Caroline (2020) Conceptualising cities and migrant ethnicity: The lessons of Chinese London. In John Solomos (ed.) *Routledge International Handbook of Contemporary Racisms*. Abingdon: Routledge.

Hulme, Alison (2015) *On the Commodity Trail: The Journey of a Bargain Store Product from East to West*. London: Bloomsbury Academic.

Knowles, Caroline (2014) *Flip-Flop: A Journey Through Globalisation's Backroads*. London: Pluto Press.

Knowles, Caroline (2022) *Serious Money: Walking Plutocratic London*. London: Penguin.

Zeng, Qingcheng, Maloni, Michael, Paul, Jomon Aliyas and Yang, Zhongzhen (2013) Dry port development in China: Motivations, challenges, and opportunities. *Transportation Journal*, 52 (2), 234–63.

Zhejiang China Commodities City Group Co. (2020) *Introduction of Yiwu Markets*. Chinagoods.com – official Website of Yiwu Markets. Available at: https://en.chinagoods.com/introduce [accessed 6 February 2025].

2

Hiding in plain sight: walking through race and space on Brixton Station Road

Karis Campion

On the approach to Brixton Station Road

I first hear the rumblings of Brixton town centre in south London as I cross the junction where Wiltshire Road meets the bend on Gresham Road. Before that point, my walk through the residential areas into the town centre is tranquil and quiet, peaceful almost. I call this bend on Gresham Road *death corner* because you cannot see or hear the number 35 bus swing around it on its way into Brixton until it is uncomfortably close.

As I cross the junction to continue up Wiltshire Road and turn right onto Canterbury Crescent, Brixton Police Station is just a stone's throw away. Along these roads you can always expect to find Metropolitan Police cars and vans taking up space in the parking bays or sitting with impunity on double yellow lines. The vehicles serve as a physical reminder of permanency of the police in the neighbourhood. Their distinctive blue and yellow Battenburg pattern can feel quite intimidating, despite attempts at friendly recruitment slogans emblazoned on some of them which vow to increase 'trust' in the community.

Trust in the police is hard-earned in a place like Brixton, the 'unofficial capital of Black Britain' (Elliott-Cooper, 2021: 21). It is where many early migrants from the Caribbean, and Jamaica specifically, settled in the 1950s and 1960s (Howarth, 2002; Mavrommatis, 2011). As of 2022, Black ethnic groups comprise a substantive 22 per cent of Lambeth's population (Lambeth Council, 2022: 4). Alongside places like Handsworth in Birmingham and Toxteth in Liverpool, Brixton is an important signifier of Black Britain and key nodal point in the urban topography of Britain, as a major *frontline* in resistance to racism and a place where Black intellectual thought has flourished (Brown, 2005; Connell, 2019; Palmer, 2020). Brixton has been the literal and intellectual home to prominent Black activists, writers, and musicians including Darcus Howe, Linton Kwesi Johnson, Olive Morris and C. L. R. James (Field et al., 2019).

April 1981 is an important period in Brixton's rich cultural and political history. Tensions reached a tipping point following an attempted arrest and the notorious Operation Swamp 81 (Elliott-Cooper, 2021). This brutal heavy-handed policing operation involved mass stop and searches and arrests of Black people. The community revolt, or 'insurrection', that followed caused widespread damage and is bookmarked as a watershed moment in the history of British race relations. It prompted the now widely cited Scarman Report, the official response to the disorders, which referenced the role of 'anger' and 'resentment' towards the police by Black people at the time (Hall, 1999; Scarman, 1981).

Up ahead on Canterbury Crescent, the twelve-storey building International House, which used to house Lambeth Council's Children and Young People's Services, now serves as workspace. The building is also the address location for an arresting sixteen-foot mural of Marvin Gaye by artist Dreph. The mural, just a few strides away from the police station, serves as a stark reminder of the fraught relationship between Brixton's Black communities and the police. The image of Gaye looking up defiantly, and in contemplation, is adapted from his album cover *What's Going On*. Facing the mural head on, across Gaye's chest on the right are protest placards with slogans like 'love over hate.' On the left side is a hellscape image of fire, burning buildings, an overturned car and the silhouettes of police wielding batons chasing shadowy figures. The mural celebrates the fiftieth anniversary of the album – a musical plea for peace abroad and a critique of police violence at home – and commemorates the fortieth anniversary of the 1981 Brixton Uprising. The mural, and its proximity to the police station, is a physical reminder that the collective memory of resistance to racist policing in Brixton is alive and well.

Turning left onto Pope's Road, for years blue, chipped, graffitied wooden hoardings on the left conceal an empty plot of land ready for development. The signage promises '1, 2 & 3 bedroom apartments coming soon' on the land that the Canterbury Arms pub once stood. The Brixton Recreation Centre (hereon: Brixton Rec) looms large on the right overhead. This huge leisure complex is a red brick brutalist Grade II listed building. Construction began in the 1970s and it completed in 1985, just a few years after the Brixton Uprising. In the summer of 1996, the South African President Nelson Mandela stood on the steps to the Brixton Rec as part of his state visit, waving at thousands of excited onlookers. His choice to visit Brixton was directly related to the area's historic role in domestic and global struggles for Black civil rights at home and decolonial movements abroad, including in apartheid South Africa.

Wells (2007: 201) has questioned whether this commemorative event linking the 'multiracial spaces of Brixton to the struggle against apartheid' smoothed over the contradictions of public space in the area which, in 1996, remained fractured by race and class. Just the year before, 1995, Brixton was rocked by more rioting, this time on a much smaller scale, after 26-year-old Wayne Douglas died in police custody, in Brixton Police Station. The recently developed Dogstar pub was set on fire during the riots. It had replaced the former Atlantic pub, the 'unofficial Community Centre of West Indians in Brixton' since the 1960s',[1] helped via the 'Brixton City Challenge', a state-funded initiative to regenerate the neighbourhood with a view to attracting private investment (Mavrommatis, 2010). The gradual whitening of the Dogstar's clientele was just one signifier of Brixton's vulnerability to expanding racialised gentrification (Okada, 2014). Throughout the 1990s, Brixton was increasingly perceived as a desirable location 'for middle-class habitation' (Jackson and Butler, 2015: 2353).

If Brixton was desirable then, it is coveted now. Analysis of gentrification in London during the 2010s shows that out of all the 'Inner London' boroughs, Lambeth, where Brixton is located, had the fourth highest 'mean gentrification' score (Almeida, 2021: 10). Just behind, in fifth place, Southwark, the neighbouring borough, home to the rival south London neighbourhood Peckham, scored 'severely gentrified' (Almeida, 2021: 6). The question of which neighbourhood floundered to gentrification earlier is yet to be settled, at least in conversations with locals. Whichever area won the historic race to the gentrification top spot, the local racially minoritised poor and historic Black populations remain the overall losers.

Property prices in Brixton rose by an average of 76 per cent between 2006 and 2016 (Marsh, 2016). At the same time presentations of homelessness and placements into temporary accommodation (TA) have steadily increased in the borough – up from 2,521 in 2019/20 to 3,710 in 2023/24 (Lambeth Council, 2024: 20). The majority of TA residents (55.8 per cent) are (disproportionately) from Black ethnic groups (Lambeth Council, 2024: 22). The Coldharbour Ward (electoral ward covering central Brixton, including Brixton Station Road, until 2022) has the highest homelessness application rates per thousand households alongside St Leonard's (Lambeth Council, 2022: 77).

My everyday walks into and through Brixton promote a 'more-than-rational' reading of these statistics (Wylie, 2005: 236, in O'Neill and Hubbard, 2010: 47) that takes me beyond an academic engagement with the facts and figures by placing me in the 'affective wash of everyday life' that orders this contradictory urban space (O'Neill and Hubbard, 2010: 47). As I walk along Pope's Road, I see the curated *edginess* of gentrifying neighbourhood institutions (Jackson et al., 2021), juxtaposed with the lives being *edged out*. This includes the stacked rusting shipping containers covered in graffiti, also known as Pop Brixton, which sit on the site of the old Pope's Road car park which used to serve the local markets and leisure centre.

Pop Brixton has been a site of 'transformation and contestation' (Jackson et al., 2021: 510) since Lambeth Council opened a bid to develop the space in 2014. Initially planned as a community growing space (Cobb, 2016), in 2015 it opened as the events space it is today, which reportedly struggles to turn a profit but continues to be given leases by the council (Cobb, 2024). Pop Brixton then, can be understood as part of the new(ish) Brixton night-time economy that has replaced 'an economy of necessity and thrift with one of distinction and display' (Hubbard, 2016: 4). On its website it is described as 'a creative event space for local independent business and the community',[2] but there are symbolic and physical barriers to universal participation (Jackson et al., 2021). Despite hosting some culturally tailored free Black music events, 'block parties' and pop-up markets, these can sometimes be ticketed after a certain time by promoters who hire the space. And it is not uncommon to see crowds of (mostly) young white people being ushered through the entrance by (mostly) Black security guards during watch parties for major sporting events like the Six Nations rugby. The securitised entrance does not invite the 'community' to come on in. It is a reminder that this pseudo-public space is in fact private land, which is guarded accordingly.

Ironically, just opposite this guarded 'block party' venue, you can often find authentic small street parties taking place. These gatherings of mostly (if not exclusively) Black people, take place on the street proper. There is music, drinking, smoking and the small crowds ebb and flow as people pass through on foot, scooters, mopeds and cars. The production of 'black sound *and* visibility' on the street signifies Black Brixton's staying power 'in a landscape where Black people are disappearing' (Summers, 2021: 43).

On the approach to Brixton Station Road, on quiet weekday mornings, I sometimes see the aftermath of these gatherings – Wray & Nephew bottles, empty cigarette boxes, vapes, cider cans and plastic cups – in the planter box where Pope's Road meets the pedestrianised half of Brixton Station Road. It is here where my walk typically begins.

Staying power: Black Brixton in the belly of the beast

These gatherings have the appearance of being fleeting and spontaneous. But at different times of the day, all along the pedestrianised half of Brixton Station Road and in nearby areas, there is a notable culture of hanging out. These groups of mostly Black men (and sometimes women) are determined by their 'blackness', their 'maleness' and 'what these attributes have come to stand for … in the ghetto' (Anderson, 2014: 187). This is especially true for those who 'don the urban uniform … athletic suits, gold chains, "gangster caps", sunglasses … large portable radios' and who socialise in groups (Anderson, 2014: 188). To the hurried passerby, at best these people are loiterers, at worst, they embody the figure of 'the predator' (Anderson, 2014: 188). However, when read against the historical disappearance of notable Black institutions like the Atlantic pub, this street sociability speaks to the 'unhoming' effects of gentrification in the neighbourhood (Elliott-Cooper et al., 2020: 498). Located on the street proper, many of these men lack the 'cultural capital

… and money to participate in the consumption' that takes place inside some of the nearby bars and restaurants (Jackson et al., 2021: 513).

Slowing down my stroll also reveals the complexities of the racial and class inequalities that structure the spatial relations along Brixton Station Road. Some of the men who hang out participate in a visible underground economy and subculture of drugs sales and consumption. Both the sellers and consumers are mostly, though not exclusively, Black, and are drawn from a diverse diaspora. At all times of the day you can encounter people in dire straits, openly smoking and injecting drugs, in the underpass to Brixton railway station, along Atlantic Road (which runs parallel to this end of Brixton Station Road) and, until recently, on the covered accessibility entrance ramp to the Brixton Rec. Public concern about Brixton town centre and particular hot spots are well known. Reporting in local news media and blogs about the town centre speak to a feeling of abandonment, lawlessness and a 'visible loss of control' by authorities (Russell, 2024). 'It's like something shut and everybody came here' – a friend once said to me during an impromptu meet on Brixton Station Road.

This notable hustle exists alongside the formal economy of small independent businesses along the road, many of them still Black owned. These independent businesses appear resilient and resolute and have resisted being taken over by wealthier, whiter owners as in other parts of Brixton (Hubbard, 2018), despite the recent histories of regeneration attempts in the neighbourhood. A Black-owned stall sells Caribbean flags, miniature Jamaica boxing gloves, t-shirts of all descriptions, Jamaica-themed Arsenal shirts, Bob Marley tees, interspersed with food and drink including sugarcane sticks, fresh ginger, tonics and bottles of artificial turquoise coloured Bigga fizzy soft drinks. A Pan-African tricolour flag flaps outside the front of One Love Cafe, a mobile Caribbean food vendor. A Taste of Ethiopia, another mobile vendor, dons the historic Ethiopian flag. Adopted as a symbol of Rastafari, the iconicity of the flag has deep connections to Jamaica and signifies the transnational Black diasporic connections that underpin the everyday relations and rhythms of the road. While the Portuguese, Algerian and Middle Eastern businesses next door are legacies of the 'churn … settling [and] mixing in' rhythm of multiracial migration that has characterised Brixton over the years (Noxolo, 2018: 806–7).

Unlike the success stories of Black Brixton entrepreneurs, the Black hustlers engaged in 'road life', excluded from the formal economy and 'well-paid legitimate employment', are perceived as a social problem (Bakkali, 2019: 1326). While destitute drug users appear zombie-like, pacing up and down, picking up stubbed-out cigarettes off the floor. Their repeated pleas for 'any spare change please?' are overlaid by Black sound aesthetics booming out from street vendors portable speakers and interlaced with the smells of berbere spiced lentils being cooked up in large pots. These parallel Black Brixtons are juxtaposed but interlinked by their 'personal, ancestral or geographical histories of colonisation' which brings them to the metropole (Nadine El-Enany, 2020: 1). For better or worse, *they are here because we were there.*[3] Notwithstanding their distinct social statuses, the street hustlers and beggars, to the food vendors and sellers, are still to varying degrees at the sharp end of 'spatial violence' in the locality (McKittrick, 2011: 956). Small Black-owned independent businesses remain vulnerable to displacement, hustlers face dispersal and enforcement, and drug users are confronted with a 'premature death' that institutional racism, poverty and social exclusion bestows on them (Gilmore, 2007: 28).

To witness these everyday racial and spatial relations on my utilitarian walks down the road to 'fulfil domestic and family tasks' like nursery drop-offs or shopping (O'Neill and Roberts, 2019: 15) suggests to me that Brixton Station Road is a contradictory space. In just a one-minute stroll down the strip you can witness the permanency of Black communities and culture, the continuing conditions of coloniality which weigh heavy on them (El-Enany, 2020), the casualties of racialised gentrification and the *broken promise of infrastructure* and regeneration (Davies, 2023). This also speaks to how the messiness of 'lived space' contrasts starkly with the 'conceptualised space' imagined by the urban planner (Lefebvre, 1991; see also Kindynis, 2018: 519).

In the 2009 Future Brixton Masterplan, this area of Brixton Station Road was described as lacking the much-needed night-time economy Brixton could benefit from (Lambeth Council, 2009: 34–5). In the report, these specific spaces in Brixton town centre were described as the epicentre of a 'no man's land', reportedly closing down at night, 'generating an empty, unwelcoming environment' (Lambeth Council, 2009: 34). The report set out 'a ten-year plan for the growth and evolution of Brixton town centre' (Lambeth Council, 2009: 8). In the decade that followed, developments like Pop Brixton, and the regeneration of the railway arches by Network Rail, were attempts to breathe new life into the road. The community campaign to #SaveBrixtonArches fought tirelessly against the eviction of longstanding businesses and rent increases. Despite their notable victories, by 2018 tenants had been moved out from the arches. The vacant arch units were eventually covered in soulless metal hoardings which intruded on pavement space while the works were prepared and carried out. These boards stayed up for far too long, disfiguring the area, and ironically contributed towards the creation of a new 'no man's land' once more. This time, the man-made void in the heart of Brixton's shopping district was named the Brixton Dead Zone (Urban, 2016), a critique levelled by community campaigners, not the developers.

A surface reading suggests that Brixton Station Road has been able to recover itself from this dip. In recent years development plans for the Brixton Recreation Quarter have ushered in more changes. The Brixton Rec has been restored to its former glory. An architectural luminaire now highlights the building's brutalist design. This includes the metal signage along its facade backlit by LEDs, and new warm lighting shines up on its grid waffle concrete ceilings. The signage on the entrance steps emits a bright light which can make the road feel a little warmer, even on the coldest of nights. The Rec's newfound glow is fitting considering its place in Brixton's political and cultural memory, as a symbolic site which memorialised the struggle against apartheid, and its role as a key landmark in the social life of residents over the decades.

Cleaning up the spoils of empire

Today, the Brixton Rec is also part of an infrastructure of surveillance in the area. Its height and grandeur make it an ideal building from which to position CCTV cameras. On Lambeth Council's website, it states that CCTV is used to 'assist in preventing and detecting street crimes such as assaults, vehicle thefts, and drug-related offences'.[4]

One summer morning I was sat having a coffee when a man, who I will call 'Uncle', came over to talk to me. In his distinctive

Trini accent, he explained that he regularly hangs out on the road, socialising and selling weed. Gesturing up to the CCTV cameras on the Brixton Rec opposite, he explained that local police were aware of the drugs economy, they just prefer it is not done in plain view, and you should avoid catching your face on camera to stay off their radar. On occasion, he explained, the police do a 'clear up' of characters whose criminal activities disrupt the spatial order. There appears to be a 'strange dance of criminality and enforcement' that takes place on the road (Ferrell, 1996 in Kindynis, 2018: 516). Just the week before, he explained, men who hang outside a nearby William Hill betting shop on Electric Avenue were moved on by police. In Uncle's words, they were now 'hiding out' in different places in Brixton.

As we are talking an elderly Caribbean woman walks past. 'Yo Grandma!', Uncle hollers at her. She strolls over and hands him a £10 note in exchange for a bag of weed. The quick sale takes me by surprise. A man with a loud south London accent shouts over to us, 'I know you can't believe she smokes innit!' He joins us and appears to know Uncle from their regular meets on the road. I later learn he's called Daniel and in his twenties. He works for 'the trains' and is responsible for monitoring 'issues', and cleaning the underpasses that run between Brixton Station Road and Atlantic Road. He starts each day before dawn, finishing by lunchtime. He often finds people sleeping here and wakes them. But if they are not ready, in a small act of care for the people he finds, and disobedience to the employer, he lets them snooze a little longer because 'they're only human'.

Just opposite us two white women walk past and take out their DLSR cameras by the Brixton Rec. Uncle calls over to them and asks them in jest, 'Are you visiting from Peckham?' Along the road Bubbles, a small vehicle 'streetscape cleaner' operated by the Brixton Business Improvement District (BID), like Daniel, is also tasked with cleaning and clearing up the streets. Bubbles, according to the Brixton BID website, 'will deliver a cleaner streetscape for Brixton … respond to concerns and issues from businesses' by attending to 'street cleansing issues affecting business premises including public urination, graffiti and tagging as well as jet-washing of pavements, bins and shutters'.[5]

From the formal enforcement of police powers to the business levy that funds jet washes, and the private train companies that hire caretakers to double up as cleaners and low-level security guards, there are multiple agencies involved in the cleaning, clearing and cleansing that takes place along Brixton Station Road – but in service to who, and to what end? When reading the descriptions of 'issues' and 'concerns' they are each responding to, on their websites and in the local media, the clean ups appear to be rational and reasonable responses.

But through my routinised walks along the road, with every step, it is clear that the 'issues' and 'concerns' that manifest here are euphemisms for the 'racialised poor living in the heart of the imperial metropole', including people like Uncle (Nadine El-Enany, 2020: 2). These are the 'wasteful leftovers' in the developers' dream (Davies, 2023: 105), a footnote in the Brixton Masterplan, and unaccounted for in the architect's concept drawing.

Doing it for themselves

It is Friday, early evening, autumn 2024 on Brixton Station Road. I am on the nursery run and see Uncle up ahead. He holds out his hand for a firms (fist bump). Lambeth Council have recently announced an initiative to respond to the persistent 'social issues' in the town centre, including drug outreach and community support, supplemented by a 'boosted' Met Police presence. Uncle explains that the police have been coming around lately, troubling some of his friends, but he has managed to avoid them so far.

I wonder who the intervention will service? I hope it will change or challenge the social status of the racialised poor – from the hustlers to the beggars – or the future security of the aspirational Black entrepreneur who pays his levy to Brixton BID to have urine cleaned off his shutters. I remain suspect about the existing cycle of repair and despair, the oscillating between social control and street sociability, which characterises the formal responses to the entrenched inequality that produces the spatial relations along Brixton Station Road. At the same time, I carry a cautious optimism in the strength and formidable resilience of the disorderly, slightly strange, but connected community and culture that exists along Brixton Station Road.

Nearby, some boys in balaclavas sit on the seating area outside a cafe drinking Wray & Nephew overproof Jamaican rum mixed with Boost energy drink. Just opposite, East African men gossip and vape over their coffees. Two men with XL bully dogs wander up and down the road. 'You not gonna say hello?', Uncle yells over to them. They walk over, let the dogs off their leads, step back a few yards and order them to 'stay' in a display of bravado and to showcase the skill, time and care spent on their (now illegal) pets.

In the distance I see a man with locs coming down the road towards us with a shopping trolley and long-life bags hanging off it. As he comes into view, I see he has a huge silver pot inside it. 'What's all this?' I ask. The smell of fresh thyme and spices wafts out, and I see hearty boiled dumplings bob around in the mix. He is cooking fresh vegetable soup packed with Caribbean delights to feed the homeless. The smells of the hot soup rises and, for a moment, warms my heart.

Acknowledgements

Thanks to Reid Allen, whose literature review for a separate project on Black barbershops in Brixton inspired and guided some of the readings and topics that feature in the essay.

Notes

1 https://brixton-timeline.maydayrooms.org/#atlantic
2 www.popbrixton.org/
3 https://asivanandan.com/key_sayings/we-are-here-because-you-were-there/
4 www.lambeth.gov.uk/streets-roads-transport/public-space-surveillance-pss-cctv-lambeth
5 https://brixtonbid.co.uk/streetscape-cleaning/

References

Almeida, Adam (2021) *Pushed to the Margins: A Quantitative Analysis of Gentrification in London in the 2010s*. London: Runnymede Trust and Centre for Labour and Social Studies (CLASS). Available at: www.runnymedetrust.org/publications/pushed-to-the-margins [accessed 6 October 2025].

Anderson, Elijah (2014) The black male in public, from Streetwise. In Mitchell Duneier, Philip Kasinitz and Alexandra K. Murphy (eds) *The Urban Ethnography Reader*. New York: Oxford University Press.

Bakkali, Yusef (2019) Dying to live: Youth violence and the munpain. *Sociological Review*, 67 (6), 1317–32.

Brown, Jacqueline N. (2005) *Dropping Anchor, Setting Sail: Geographies of Race in Black Liverpool*. Princeton, NJ: Princeton University Press.

Cobb, Jason (2016) Exclusive: Grow Brixton to Pop Brixton – how a green oasis for the community turned into a 21st century business park. Brixton Buzz, 4 June. Available at: www.brixtonbuzz.com/2016/06/exclusive-grow-brixton-to-pop-brixton-how-a-green-oasis-for-the-community-turned-into-a-21st-century-business-park/ [accessed 16 October 2025].

Cobb, Jason (2024) The loss making Pop Brixton gifted yet another lease extension by Lambeth as Brixton Buzz FoI reveals that the car crash project has paid zero profit share to the Council. Brixton Buzz, 15 July. Available at: www.brixtonbuzz.com/2024/07/the-loss-making-pop-brixton-gifted-yet-another-lease-extension-by-lambeth-as-brixton-buzz-foi-reveals-that-the-car-crash-project-has-paid-zero-profit-share-to-the-council/ [accessed 16 October 2025].

Connell, Kieran (2019) *Black Handsworth: Race in 1980s Britain*. Oakland, CA: University of California Press.

Davies, Dominic (2023) *The Broken Promise of Infrastructure*. London: Lawrence Wishart.

El-Enany, Nadine (2020) *Bordering Britain: Law, Race and Empire*. Manchester: Manchester University Press.

Elliott-Cooper, Adam (2021) *Black Resistance to British Policing*. Manchester: Manchester University Press.

Elliott-Cooper, Adam, Hubbard, Phil and Lees, Loretta (2020) Moving beyond Marcuse: Gentrification, displacement and the violence of un-homing. *Progress in Human Geography*, 44 (3), 492–509.

Field, Paul, Bunce, Robin, Hassan, Leila and Peacock, Margaret (2019) *Here to Stay, Here to Fight: A 'Race Today' Anthology*. London: Pluto Press.

Gilmore, Ruth. W. (2007) *Golden Gulag: Prisons, Surplus, Crisis, and Opposition in Globalizing California*. Berkeley and Los Angeles, CA: University of California Press.

Hall, Stuart (1999) From Scarman to Stephen Lawrence. *History Workshop Journal*, 48 (1), 187–97.

Howarth, Caroline (2002) 'So, you're from Brixton?' *Ethnicities*, 2 (2), 237–60.

Hubbard, Phil (2016) Hipsters on our high streets: Consuming the gentrification frontier. *Sociological Research Online*, 21 (3), 106–11.

Hubbard, Phil (2018) Retail gentrification. In L. Lees and M. Phillips (eds) *Handbook of Gentrification Studies*. Cheltenham: Edward Elgar Publishing.

Jackson, Emma, Benson, Michaela and Calafate-Faria, Francisco (2021) Multi-sensory ethnography and vertical urban transformation: Ascending the Peckham Skyline. *Social and Cultural Geography*, 22 (4), 501–22.

Jackson, Emma and Butler, Tim (2015) Revisiting 'social tectonics': The middle classes and social mix in gentrifying neighbourhoods. *Urban Studies*, 52 (13), 2349–65.

Kindynis, Theo (2018) Bomb alert: Graffiti writing and urban space in London. *British Journal of Criminology*, 58 (3), 511–28.

Lambeth Council (2009) *Future Brixton Masterplan*. London: London Borough of Lambeth. Available at: www.lambeth.gov.uk/sites/default/files/EB09_09_Future%20Brixton%20Masterplan_0.pdf [accessed 2 October 2025].

Lambeth Council (2022) *State of the Borough 2022*. London: London Borough of Lambeth. Available at: www.lambeth.gov.uk/sites/default/files/2022-07/state-of-the-borough-2022-report.pdf [accessed 2 October 2025].

Lambeth Council (2024) *Homelessness Review 2024*. London: London Borough of Lambeth. Available at: https://haveyoursay.lambeth.gov.uk/uploads/f43a1bbd-d83a-47db-99cb-525df665d771/project_file/file/a7e4871d-2759-4869-9f94-6e986afce577/Lambeth_Homelessness_Review_2024pdf.pdf [accessed 2 October 2025].

Lefebvre, Henri (1991) *The Production of Space*, trans. D. Nicholson-Smith. Oxford: Basil Blackwell.

Marsh, Sarah (2016) How has Brixton really changed? The data behind the story, *Guardian*, 14 January. Available at: www.theguardian.com/cities/datablog/2016/jan/14/how-has-brixton-really-changed-the-data-behind-the-story [accessed 16 October 2025].

Mavrommatis, George (2010) A racial archaeology of space: A journey through the political imaginings of Brixton and Brick Lane, London. *Journal of Ethnic and Migration Studies*, 36 (4), 561–79.

Mavrommatis, George (2011) Stories from Brixton: Gentrification and different differences. *Sociological Research Online*, 16 (2), 29–38.

McKittrick, Katherine (2011) On plantations, prisons, and a black sense of place. *Social & Cultural Geography*, 12 (8), 947–63.

Noxolo, Patricia (2018) Flat out! Dancing the city at a time of austerity. *Environment and Planning D: Society and Space*, 36 (5), 797–811.

Okada, Shuhei (2014) Transformation of Spaces and Places in Inner Cities: The Case of Gentrification in Brixton since the Riot in 1981. PhD thesis, Royal Holloway, University of London.

O'Neill, Maggie and Hubbard, Phil (2010) Walking, sensing, belonging: Ethno-mimesis as performative praxis. *Visual Studies*, 25 (1), 46–58.

O'Neill, Maggie and Roberts, Brian (2019) *Walking Methods: Research on the Move*. Abingdon and New York: Routledge.

Palmer, Lisa A. (2020) 'Each one teach one' visualising black intellectual life in Handsworth beyond the epistemology of 'white sociology'. *Identities*, 27 (1), 91–113.

Russell, Herbie (2024) Brixton 'twenty times worse' than '24-hour crack supermarket' of the early 2000s, locals warn, *Southwark News*, 12 October. Available at: https://southwarknews.co.uk/news/crime/brixton-twenty-times-worse-than-24-hour-crack-supermarket-of-the-early-2000s-locals-warn/ [accessed 16 October 2025].

Scarman, Lord (1981) *The Brixton Disorders 10–12 April 1981: Report of an Inquiry by the Rt Hon. The Lord Scarman, OBE*. London: HMSO.

Summers, Brandi T. (2021) Reclaiming the chocolate city: Soundscapes of gentrification and resistance in Washington, DC. *Environment and Planning D: Society and Space*, 39 (1), 30–46.

Urban, Mike (2016) Brixton Dead Zone: Local activist highlights the damage caused by Network Rail's plans. Brixton Buzz, 23 December. Available at: www.brixtonbuzz.com/2016/12/brixton-dead-zone-local-activist-highlights-the-damage-caused-by-network-rails-plans/ [accessed 16 October 2025].

Wells, Karen (2007) Symbolic capital and material inequalities: Memorializing class and 'race' in the multicultural city. *Space and Culture*, 10 (2), 195–206.

3

Walking routes, talking toilets: exploring pit stops of public toilet access in everyday life

Lauren White

Each place a pit stop

The COVID-19 pandemic brought to the fore inequalities of all kinds: health, education and, significantly, work, with those 'on the frontline' faced with the increased risk of illness when attending to others. Alongside this, caring for one's own health and well-being became a focal point, with regular walking becoming more broadly viewed to harness rhythms, routines and reach out to connect with the social world (Bates and Rhys-Taylor, 2017). What also accompanied this was a cultural realisation of an absence of welfare infrastructure. Through spending increased time walking (or being) outdoors, coupled with the closures of (or limited access to) commercial settings including bars and restaurants, the notable absence of toilet facilities became increasingly obvious. Newspapers reported the littering and fouling of parks and places of recreation. This was not news for many who experienced, or continue to experience, barriers to access, supported by a wealth of sociological literature whereby access to toilets is socially shaped (Slater and Jones, 2018) and infrastructures of provision are necessary for everyday mobilities (White, 2021). These barriers to access were too made visible by the daily walks during COVID-19 and the project I undertook during this time.

In this essay, I will take you on a walk in my local area in Hillsborough, Sheffield. Sheffield is a large city in the north of England, and the suburb of Hillsborough in the north-west of the city is the place I most frequented on my daily walks during the pandemic (see White and Carter, 2021). Accompanying us on this walk are a selection of stories and accounts from postal, fast food, supermarket delivery and parcel workers navigating toilet access amid lockdowns during the COVID-19 pandemic. Despite their work in keeping society running throughout the restrictions and beyond, this group faced (and continues to face) intersecting precarities of work with the absence of infrastructure in the form of toilet provision and broader welfare facilities. On our walk together, we will pause for 'pit stops'. These pit stops are moments that highlight and sensitise you as the reader to both the personal challenges and political signifiers of accessing facilities. My local area and my individual walking route are not synonymous with that of participants and there is a fictionality in the accuracy of the places described, but not in the experiences or the accounts. Rather, the pit stops offer potential in illustrating what may be commonplace and relatable in urban and public life. This may be an appreciation of what facilities may be present in your local area, noticing your own embodiment in line with walking and welfare requirements, and of course, recognising that this is not an even playing field for all involved.

Our walk is structured with three main pit stops. First, we pause by recognising the communal places that punctuate many routes and become unlikely places for provision. Our second stop is perhaps more profound in terms of infrastructure, encouraging the reader to consider the contradictory circulations of consumption via the local supermarket. Third and finally, I want to walk through an absence of place, space and infrastructure where risk, fear and embodied realities become apparent on side streets and in plastic bottles. Together, they tell a story of the longstanding closure of public toilets, the increasing reliance on commercial spaces and broader social infrastructures coming into play in times of crisis and limited resources. As Star (1999: 379) notes, '[s]tudy a city and neglect its sewers and power supplies, and you miss essential aspects of distributional justice'. And on this walking route, toilets are no exception.

Cafe, care homes, community

We begin this route from my house as I close my front door and head out to the main street in the late morning. I live in a mid-terrace house, 'two up two down', with the road squeezed as the sheer volume of cars no longer meets the sizing of the street. Often at this time cars have left the street, their owners headed off to work, though the patterning of this has changed with many now working from home offices, kitchen tables and spare bedrooms. Those pottering up and down the street include retired people out with their dogs, tradespeople renovating a recently sold house for first-time buyers or to meet the strained rental market, the local window cleaner who appears every few weeks and charges £5 for all the windows, and workers hurrying between houses on delivery rounds. One person who is key to the fabric, rhythms and sociality of the street is the postal worker.

As we leave for the day and walk down the street, we meet Doug. Doug has worked as a postal worker, or 'postie' as colloquially known, for many years. Typically, posties travel in twos. Their walking rounds are relational and collaborative. When COVID-19 hit, posties were required to walk alone. Alongside the loss of the company of a colleague was the acute realisation of an absence of facilities amid the closure of many public spaces. Doug tells me about his postal routes, walking and talking through the people and places that make toilet access possible. We notice the sounds of the street during the postal round (Gallagher and Prior, 2017) with drills from local roadworks and beeps from the bin lorry and the calls between workers pacing up the road. Within the circular routes of his postal round, Doug tells us about the pit stops where access can be granted or negotiated. As we pace across pavements, up and down the side streets in the residential area, we reach the local residential care home for older people. Though implicated in health and safety protections, Doug described the reciprocal, interdependent care and community offered by those living there: 'One of the guys that lives there I know very well. I delivered his mail, he was kind to me and said, "Anytime postie, you want to use my toilet, my door is always open."'

I think about the ways in which postal workers become permanent figures in the rhythms of everyday life and what this means to others in their mundane routines, with the mundanity felt ever more profoundly during the peak of the pandemic. We continue to walk, red bag over his shoulder and lighter in load as the morning progresses. By late morning we reach the end of the postal circuit. We arrive at the high street of shops, cafes and charity shops. The high street of Hillsborough is now thriving with independent cafes, shops and spaces of creativity. Doug tells me of his experience with his local cafe: 'It's almost the end of my round and it's ten to one. There's a very small Polish cafe. I used to go there for a toilet break and sometimes have a cup of coffee, but they're closed as they're having some renovations done. Fortunately, I know the owner and he was in today, so I managed to slip in and use the toilet.'

Cafes are not merely places of consumption – they are places of care, community, conviviality and serve the circulations of everyday rhythms and routines. With Doug's daily walking route comes a familiarity and intimacy with the people, streets, businesses and places around him. Kindness is significant here, and as sociologists we must notice this as we walk within our landscapes and notice our 'affective localities' (Hall and Smith, 2015; Brownlie and Anderson, 2017). For Brownlie and Anderson (2017: 1226), 'the acts and emotions have a background or infrastructural quality, little noticed and yet also fundamental. Like the pavements we talk on and the electricity we use, these low-profile acts and relationships – lifts to work, bins put out, children cared for or asked after – enable other things to happen.' Many of us know our postie as part of the rhythms of our everyday lives and our walks up and down the street. They become known to spaces and places of community, from the local care home to the cafe. There are circulations and reciprocations of care. Yet with this intimacy, conviviality, familiarity and kindness comes a smoothening of access to toilets in public life that is not granted to everyone.

Supermarkets: 'A haven with jacket potatoes'

We continue our walk from the cafe and head up the road to reach the top car park of the local supermarket. When not being used for shoppers popping in for their daily or weekly bread and milk, this car park is a hub of young people hanging out in their cars eating McDonald's, groups rollerblading on the open space of tarmac and Yorkshire Water van drivers pausing to park in fleets to rest between jobs. Car parks, parking spaces and pavements often turn into obstacle courses of access (Imrie and Kumar, 1998), where walkers may sidestep around others, observing the contrast between those who pause or gather and those hurrying on. Travelling down the escalator from the top car park, we walk into the entrance of the Morrisons supermarket. When thinking back to the COVID-19 pandemic, nothing quite demonstrated the circulations of care, consumption and crises than joining the line of the supermarket queue at the entrance and often into long lines taking up space in the car parks. By the entrance we meet Andy. Andy is a courier delivering everything from parcels to food. There is a paradox in workers distributing resources of replenishment while lacking such provision for themselves. Essential workers, making essential journeys to deliver essential items, and yet denied essential facilities within public infrastructure. Stopping our walk at the entry point of the supermarket entrance, Andy tells me: 'The first lockdown, the first few weeks were really strange and there was nowhere you could go. The only thing that was open was supermarkets, but people were queueing for hours to get in. And when you're working, you don't have time to queue, so you've got no access, basically, to any toilet facilities.'

Thinking about infrastructural injustice, Tonkiss (2015: 384) notes 'infrastructures produce and reproduce distributional inequalities … in material, and deeply spatial, ways'. The supermarket queue for drivers demonstrated this spatial inequality and infrastructural injustice in the absence of facilities and the time required to access them. When walks to the supermarkets and queueing eased, and when track and trace (the government monitoring system that attempted to track, and seek to halt, infection transmission) was not a condition for entry in such spaces, access became a central focal point, and supermarkets were celebrated as a reliable source for rest and replenishment. Supermarkets provide parking, seating, often a convivial cafe space (Jones et al., 2015) with affordable food and drink, and of course, toilet facilities. Key to this is the absence of questioning or the requirement to purchase items often felt in smaller commercialised franchise and non-franchise cafe spaces (White, 2021).

As we enter the supermarket, the first points of reference are nearby accessible toilets and a cafe. I find comfort in these spaces, carrying with me memories of childhood – lunches in the supermarket cafe with my grandparents during school holidays, watching older people socialise over cups of tea in white porcelain, and eating plate after plate of fish and chips. I'm not alone in this. Andy describes supermarkets as 'havens' with 'no one watching if you aren't spending anything'. Supermarkets are places where 'you can park your truck, nip to the loo, get a quick drink, go to the café ... [it's] £1.50 for a jacket potato' or, during the winter months, a place of warmth as you pause en route. This was especially true during COVID-19 when park benches were taped up, taken away and people discouraged from lingering (White and Carter, 2021). And yet these are the workers providing sustenance and resources to others (Jones et al., 2024).

Beside the cafe, the toilets and the key-cutting shop in the supermarket entrance is the customer services. Here, you can often notice the pacing of 'click and collect' – circuits of passing back and forth with food delivery items, where the click of a supermarket app pings a driver to bring the order. This is a space where couriers often gather, and it is evident they are watching the clock. As we walk back into the car park, we see the sheltered section of supermarket vans loading up. We meet Emily who is busy preparing a supermarket home delivery. We get chatting and Emily tells us that despite the regularity of stops for delivering food items to customers, her breaks are few and far between. She stresses that she enjoys chatting to people on her rounds, but there's a challenge in doing this when schedules are tight, and delivery stops are frequent. Emily tells us how she often walks into their kitchen and 'puts stuff in the freezer for them': something unofficially done during COVID-19. In return, she often receives a cup of tea and an offer to use the toilet as the low-profile, relational exchange (Brownlie and Anderson, 2017). I think about how this work highlights the hidden sociality, care and kindness between houses, people and streets as workers walk into the homes of those who live alone and who often crave conversation. Of course, time is pressured, and journeys must continue. This means back on the roads and the streets. Questions must again be asked about the places where pauses can be made and access granted within the fabric, infrastructure and socialities of urban and suburban life.

Out in the open, old water bottles and back alleys

We walk out of the supermarket and head out on to the high street. Opposite us is a Wetherspoons pub, and by this is a back alley by the side of the pub. I think about how I would only walk through here in the daytime, and how short the alley is. Often there is litter, empty bottles or smashed glass, and the lingering scent of half-drunk pints of lager. This becomes our next pit stop. In many ways, we notice this as an absence of place, a lack of infrastructure. Andy again reminds us that this becomes the place where workers often have to relieve themselves 'out in the open', in 'old water bottles' or secluding oneself in a back alley. He elaborates on such harsh realities: 'I've always carried a two-litre bottle of water with me which I'll drink throughout the day. On occasions, if you do get caught short, I know it doesn't sound very nice, but I do have another empty plastic bottle. If there isn't any, especially at the moment or reduced toilet access, you do on occasion have to pull up and get in the back of the van.'

Resting by the side street is a bicycle and a takeaway backpack. We get chatting to Sajid who works as a platform food delivery driver. Sajid tells us that following contracting COVID-19, he stopped working for a platform delivery company due to the working conditions. His walks between restaurants, fast food outlets and homes were speedy, squeezed and sporadic as the clock ticks for customer ratings. He tells us about his anxiety over lateness and 'bad publicity' on the app, stressing how he 'doesn't want to be seen as a liability for using the toilet on shift'. Our pit stop of the side street marks a stark fearful account shared by Sajid: 'I'm a heavy coffee drinker so the toilet can become a big issue. On one occasion, it was six or seven o clock. I had to use a passageway, but I felt uncomfortable. Imagine if the police came, I'd be fined. If you're in a public space urinating and then doing food deliveries, it feels very disrespectful, but the platform delivery company gave very limited instructions.'

Stopping on side streets and similar spaces is always a last resort, causing major anxiety for many, with streets as sites of scrutiny with fears of repercussions (Hubbard and Lyon, 2018). An absence of places to rely upon within regular or irregular routes leads to an embodied urgency and a temporal pressure. An awareness of bodily need in conflict with the rush of schedules and the rush of not being caught or others being suspicious, or shaming actions in the event that they become visible. Badger and Armston-Sheret (2021) argued in the *Tribune* that, 'Every day, workers find themselves bursting to go to the toilet, risking the sack if they do so in the wrong place … When they do so, they run the gamut of responses from the public – from disdain to shame.' What these journeys – and the absence of infrastructure – reveal are circulations of harm, oppression and exclusion, patterned by the intersecting social dynamics of gender, race, class, wealth, age, disability, sexuality, migration status and place.

Walking between places and pit stops, and tuning into the body in the absence of infrastructure, also raises questions of when one last drank or ate, and of the need for hydration or hot drinks in keeping with the seasons, the weather and the exertion of walking at pace. The circulations of consumption and bodily rhythms and clocks become noticeable. As we walk these routes and note these pit stops, we may also be faced with a sign at the entrance of pubs or cafes which read 'toilets are for customers only', illustrating how access is conditional on consumption. And yet those we have paused with on our walk have pointed out that they are the very people providing the comforts of consumption for others. Circulations of care continue – fragmented and broken. Pacing and provision halted, altered, made conditional.

Conclusion: Forgotten buildings, changing places

At our final pit stop, I want to point out the parks and places in which empty old Victorian toilets may stand. Often, these fade into the derelict landscapes that surround them, or are gated, fenced or boarded to hide what was once operational. Often the only notable clue is the gendered signage etched into the stone above the old door entrance. And yet, despite the passage of time and the progression of society, such infrastructure has not been sustained, nor has it been replaced. Then arrived the commercial landmarks in the city that informally took the role of public toilet access for many. Department stores such as Debenhams and John Lewis: spaces that were once hailed as permitting access to the city. And yet, in my hometown on the high street of Sheffield, neither of these – nor the toilets that people relied on – exist, closed among the chaos of COVID-19. Buildings stand empty, with only promissory architectural projects proposed. Toilets, convivial cafes and spaces of rest and welfare have yet to be made a priority on the urban landscape map.

There are, however, pit stops and places of hope in my local park, which I routinely frequented and took daily walks in during lockdown (White and Carter, 2021). Of course, my walk may be a slow amble and comes with a bodily privilege in contrast to those described in this piece and beyond. The bench on which I rested, and continue to rest, is a bench shared and a point of connection with couriers in this essay who rest between delivering takeaways when the cold isn't too much (Risbeth and Rogaly, 2017). This park now has new toilet access and provision, following major investment in leisure infrastructure. A new cafe, a revived library, a community arts and crafts hub for older people, a bike track and tennis courts – to name but a few. In this park, by the library, there is now a Changing Places Toilet (larger accessible toilet provision for wheelchair users who may need hoists and other assistive equipment) and a toilet by the cafe to which the door remains on the outside of the building and access is not necessarily conditional on a coffee purchase. So, there are spaces, places and people that move forward access and provision, taking seriously the centrality of toilets to inclusion and participation in everyday life.

My local walk has sought to take the reader on a route whereby we can reveal broader insights into the intricacies of everyday mobilities for those who often pass us by on the roads, streets and pathways as they deliver, service and support broader circulation of consumption. Some of us may know our postal worker and wave as we begin our walk to work, but only smile and quickly exchange items with those rushed to deliver food items on our doorstep. We must pay attention to these circuits and care for those who are on them. Despite their work in keeping society running throughout the COVID-19 restrictions and beyond, couriers and food delivery workers faced (and continue to face) intersecting precarities of work with the absence of infrastructure in the form of public toilet provision. Such pit stops point to the longstanding closure of public toilet provision and to the circulations of harm, oppression and social exclusion. Harm such as the fear and worry of the street surveillance of Sajid, or harm such as having to hide away with a water bottle. There is a reliance on the 'kindness' of others or the informality of community spaces, whether it be care homes or supermarkets, with a recognition of the universal need of human bodies and dignity. But this is not something afforded to everyone, nor equally experienced by workers in how their actions are perceived, their bodies read, and consequently how they are treated. These are the workers and community circuits that form the fabric of our everyday urban landscapes, servicing leisure and enjoyment in some cases, and essential services in others. The pandemic revealed this starkly – those delivering parcels and food were supporting and servicing others, even as their working environments, access to facilities and, indeed, their health were put at risk. And my hope is that, through my local walk with its points, people and pit stops, the experiences and necessities of such workers are centred as part of a broader care – one that replenishes bodies and recognises the universal need for access to welfare facilities that bind us all together. These pit stops with people on everyday walks and routes are not only personal but political, reminding us of our structural commitments to rethink care and inclusive provision for bodies in public life – with access to toilets at the forefront.

Acknowledgements

Thank you to the nine couriers and delivery drivers who generously gave their time and shared their personal and working lives, shaping this piece. Thank you also to the Economic and Social Research Council for funding this research (ES/V009397/1).

References

Badger, Adam and Armston-Sheret, Edward (2021) Public toilets are a workers' right, *Tribune*, 17 May. Available at: www.tribunemag.co.uk/2021/05/public-toilets-are-a-workers-right [accessed 13 December 2024].

Bates, Charlotte and Rhys-Taylor, Alex (eds) (2017) *Walking Through Social Research*. New York: Routledge.

Brownlie, Julie and Anderson, Simon (2017) Thinking sociologically about kindness: Puncturing the blasé in the ordinary city. *Sociology*, 51 (6), 1222–38.

Gallagher, Michael and Prior, Jonathan (2017) Listening walks: A method of multiplicity. In Charlotte Bates and Alex Rhys-Taylor (eds) *Walking Through Social Research*. New York: Routledge.

Hall, Tom and Smith, Robin (2015) Care and repair and the politics of urban kindness. *Sociology*, 49 (1), 3–18.

Hubbard, Phil and Lyon, Dawn (2018) Introduction: Streetlife – the shifting sociologies of the street. *Sociological Review*, 66 (5), 937–51.

Imrie, Rob and Kumar, Marion (1998) Focusing on disability and access in the built environment. *Disability & Society*, 13 (3), 357–74.

Jones, Charlotte, White, Lauren, Slater, Tig and Pluquailec, Jill (2024) Hospitality work as social reproduction: Embodied and emotional labour during COVID-19. *Sociology*, 58 (2), 471–88.

Jones, Hannah, Neal, Sarah, Mohan, Giles, Cochrane, Allan and Bennett, Katy (2015) Urban multicultural and everyday encounters in semi-public, franchised cafe spaces. *Sociological Review*, 63 (3), 644–61.

Rishbeth, Clare and Rogaly, Ben (2017) Sitting outside: Conviviality, self-care and the design of benches in urban public space. *Transactions of the Institute of British Geographers*, 43 (2), 284–98.

Slater, Jen and Jones, Charlotte (2018) *Around the Toilet: A Research Project Report about What Makes a Safe and Accessible Toilet Space (April 2015–February 2018)*. Sheffield: Sheffield Hallam University. Available at: https://shura.shu.ac.uk/21258/1/Around%20the%20Toilet%20Report%20final%201.pdf [accessed 2 October 2025].

Star, Susan Leigh (1999) The ethnography of infrastructure. *American Behavioral Scientist*, 43 (3), 377–91.

Tonkiss, Fran (2015) Afterword: Economies of infrastructure. *City*, 19 (2–3), 284–391.

White, Lauren (2021) 'I have to know where I can go': Mundane mobilities and everyday public toilet access for people living with irritable bowel syndrome (IBS). *Social & Cultural Geography*, 24 (5), 851–69.

White, Lauren and Carter, Adam (2021) Solidarity through routine: Relations and rhythms of regular lockdown walks, *Sociological Review Magazine*, 7 September [online]. Available at: https://thesociologicalreview.org/magazine/september-2021/new-solidarities/solidarity-through-routine/ [accessed 2 October 2025].

4

Distribution landscapes: a walk through the trading estates of south London

Louise Rondel

I am spending the morning on a trading estate in south London where I am going to be shown around a beauty supplier's wholesale store. As part of my research project mapping the commodity chains of beauty products, I am following the goods (as much as is possible) to and through beauty salons, arriving at these sites of consumption where they are quickly used and quickly discarded, before the whole process starts again in a seemingly interminable cycle. As I move with the products, I am trying to understand the relationship between this intimate bodily work and the infrastructures upon which beauty practices are predicated, exploring how their circulation through the city is enabled by *and* simultaneously shapes the places through which they move, leaving potentially pernicious traces in spaces and in bodies. As I walk around the trading estates – a thoroughly embodied and emplaced act itself – I tune into my corporeal and emotional experiences, attending to what they indicate about the space, how it is made, and who or what is prioritised here (Rondel and Henneke, 2024).

This trading estate is where the hairdressers and beauty therapists, with whom I have been spending time in their salons, drive to buy shampoos, conditioners, nail polishes, dyes and tints, false lashes, nail products, spray tan, depilatory waxes, lotions, waxing strips, bed roll, cotton wool and all the other goods involved in beautifying bodies. And to buy them in bulk. Indeed, upon entering the store I am first taken aback by its scale, writing in my field notes that it is like 'walking into a Superdrug on steroids'. Familiar like the high street beauty chain, but in a slightly weird, distorted way where it makes me feel like I have been shrunk, such is the massive size and the amount of products.

The store's location on a light industrial estate – overwhelmingly grey, tarmac, breeze blocks and corrugated metal – is a far cry from its brightly lit, colourful and semi-familiar interior. And even further from the stylish and cosy salons where I have been spending much of my research time, with warm hues, soft towels, floral scents and chill-out music. The store is basically a giant windowless aluminium box on a trading estate lined with other warehouses, similarly box-like. It is neighboured by other trading estates with still more warehouses as well as retail parks with big-box stores and their shadeless car parks which seem to stretch to the horizon. These are the 'edges' of the city – 'the grey area that lies between the brown and the green of town and countryside' 'characterised by rubbish tips and warehouses, superstores and derelict industrial plant, office parks and gypsy encampments, golf courses, allotments and fragmented, frequently scruffy, farmland' (Shoard, 2017: 5). Far from a place only for brave, macho urban exploration, different forms of everyday life unfold at these edges and they are inextricably linked to the beautifying and feminising work that happens in the city's salons – for this is where beauty products are brought to, stored and sold in bulk (and where they return to, once used and disposed of, to waste plants, tips and incinerators). The landscape forms a 'grey' and 'scruffy' backstage to the carefully decorated salons in which I started my study. It is also a landscape shaped by the city's insatiable consumption habits, where space is continually formed by the processes of receiving, distributing, and receiving again an unending flow of goods and waste.

Cycling from my home in another part of the south London suburbs, and always concerned about getting lost and arriving late, I am characteristically early for my appointment at the store. I am pleased as this will give me some time to have a walk around the area. However, pulling into the trading estate the first challenge is to find somewhere to lock up my bike. It is clear that cycling is not the expected mode of arrival, but I eventually locate a token bike stand down the side of one of the units. The gap is slightly too narrow and there is a makeshift ashtray at the base of the stand, but I manage to squeeze in with my bike and lock up.

From here I set off on foot. With nearly an hour to kill, I walk in a loop. I begin in the trading estate itself. There is a wide entrance off the main road with a sign listing the different businesses. This is one of many light industrial estates in the area. In addition to bulk buying beauty supplies, here one can find builders' yards, electrical stores, car parts, food wholesalers, MOT and car-valeting services, self-storage units and industrial catering businesses.

Although each trading estate is differently configured, they all share particular characteristics: wide roads, narrow pavements, ample parking spaces, big wheelie bins and large bin storage areas. There is some plant life, although any greenery feels unplanned and looks uncared for. Mainly buddleia, this plant is indeed an opportunist and needs little encouragement to set down roots and grow (Gupta, 2014). Buddleia's purple flowers are much loved by butterflies, and it is sometimes known as the butterfly bush. Another moniker is the 'bombsite plant'. Introduced in Britain from China in the 1890s as a decorative plant, it grows wherever it can take root and thrives in quick-draining stony or (concrete-y) ground (The Wildlife Trusts, n.d.). Unchecked, buddleia quickly spreads: 'widespread and common across the capital, found in gardens and parks, but more typically the scruffier parts of town – wastelands, railway linesides, scrapyards and other unkempt curtilages of business parks, transport corridors and derelict land, where it is almost ubiquitous' (Frith, n.d.). It is truly a plant of the 'edgelands'. As I walk past, its flowers stand out starkly against the grey metal walls of the units. But somehow it's not cheery; its droopy and unkempt demeanour instead adds to the rather bleak, functional and neglected atmosphere of the trading estate.

Occasionally there are also green privet hedges – that classic greenery of suburbia – planted around the entrances to some of the units. These are not overgrown looking, so clearly someone is maintaining them, cutting them back into neat, uniform rectangles. But like the buddleia, they do not offer any cheer. A pretty uninteresting green mass, bits of rubbish have got caught up in the privet's thick leaves. Small bits of plastic are tangled there, possibly forever, and cigarette butts litter their base. In the suburban neighbourhoods closer to home, privet hedges contribute a brightening splash of green to the rows of off-white terraced housing with red-tiled roofs, orange stone masonry and neatly planted gardens. Here against the greyness of the rest of the industrial estate, like the buddleia, they appear dreary and forlorn.

The trading estate feels a very masculine space. It is reminiscent of when I worked at a builders' merchant on a similar estate in the summer after my A levels when it was just me, the other 'office girl' and the woman who worked in the burger van among the male builders, plumbers, car-valeting service, mechanics and delivery drivers. However, there are women here. I see a woman in a black uniform and hairnet having a smoke at the side of one of the units. I assume that she must work in one of the catering units, which are becoming more and more common on the city's edges with the increase in home food delivery and the attendant 'dark' or 'ghost' kitchens (Shapiro, 2023). And, of course, there are the beauty therapists who come here to buy supplies. I watch them as they arrive in their shiny cars. Well-presented, manicured, made-up, they disrupt the scruffy, dreary and masculine surroundings.

As I walk, the soundscape is dominated by the constant low-key buzz of traffic: cars, vans, the distinctive throaty rumble of a heavy goods vehicle's (HGV's) engine. The trading estate is surrounded by dual carriageways, eventually leading to the motorway which connects the city to the towns and ports of the south-east. The occasional reversing-beeps from lorries parking up to unload their goods cut through the traffic hum. In the trading estate itself, the pavement along which I am walking is narrower than average. As a single walker who is able-bodied and without a pushchair or any kind of mobility device, I can just about walk along comfortably. The pavements are punctuated every five metres or so to allow vehicles to pull into the parking bays in front of each unit, and I have to check both ways and step down off the kerb to cross the entranceways before stepping back up onto the opposite kerb. This is a landscape designed around vehicles, built with driving in mind. I feel out of kilter with the scale of the landscape; am out of place as a walker. Especially as a woman walker. I cross paths with a man in a hi-vis yellow jacket who is unloading boxes from a van. Does he look at me inquisitively? Wondering where I'm going? I decide that if somebody asks what I'm doing or if I'm lost, I will say that I'm just waiting as I have my car valeted. This seems like a semi-plausible reason why somebody – a lone woman, not in a uniform, without an obvious purpose – would be walking around a trading estate.

What is moving through this space are goods. This is what this space is for. Taking into consideration only cosmetic products already highlights global networks of circulating stuff passing through the trading estate: false lashes manufactured in Indonesia (Chamberlain, 2013; Diani, 2013); nail polishes produced in China, the UK, Spain and the USA; hair extensions made in China with hair from India or Myanmar (Tarlo, 2016); and spray tan from China, Australia or Scotland. Like nearly every other thing we consume – in fact, like '90% of everything' (George, 2013) – most of these will have arrived in the UK by sea. Packed into twenty-foot equivalent unit (TEU) metal shipping containers and piled high on massive ships up to the size of four football pitches, the goods land in Tilbury, Harwich, DPD London Gateway or one of the other seaports dotted around the coast and in the estuaries. Docking in these ports, containers full of goods are quickly unloaded onto waiting HGVs and driven onwards to distribution centres and then to the beauty wholesalers' central warehouses in the south-east or the Midlands, before a daily van is dispatched to each of the stores.

It is axiomatic to say that the now ubiquitous shipping container 'changed the world' (Donovan and Bonney, 2006) in how stuff is produced, transported and consumed. Shipping containers have changed the world in more literal ways too as they have transformed the physical make-up of cities. This has been most acute in the shift from city-centre docks to down-river ports as the increase in size of the ships which are necessary to carry containers and the ways in which the uniform, stackable TEUs enable goods to be unloaded and transported onwards needed deeper water and new technologies (El-Sahli and Upward, 2017). As old docks closed in the 1970s and 1980s, urban waterside geographies – both physical and social – were significantly reconfigured; in London, places such as Bermondsey, the Isle of Dogs and Deptford were 'ruined' by containerisation (Back, 2017: 21; Watson, 2019). More recently, dockside 'regeneration' or 'redevelopment' projects have made these areas into 'luxury' places for living and leisure (Massey, 2007; Mah, 2014).

As the container moves off the vessels, through the ports and further inland, it textures spaces in other ways. To facilitate the distribution of the stuff transported in the TEUs (or the FEUs – forty-foot equivalent units) and with the aim of getting the goods ever closer to the marketplace of the city centre, places have been sought which have easy access both from the ports and to the consumers; places where roads are wide and so navigable by large vehicles, and where land is (relatively) cheap and conducive to large constructions such as warehouses (Parker, 2013; Cowen, 2014; Chua et al., 2018). In this way, the city's edges have been made both as a physical landscape shaped by *and* for the circulation of goods (Danyluk, 2018). They are a key site in London's geographies of beauty, a place upon which the city's beauty work (and myriad other consumption practices) is contingent.

Exiting the trading estate and walking next to the four-lane A-road, I continue my loop. The flow of traffic is constant, only slowing and pausing at traffic lights where the vehicles idle for a minute or two while waiting for the green light. Heading north, I walk in the opposite direction to where the dual carriageway will meet the motorway. Along this main road, on one side, there are houses, a newsagents, a Chinese take-away, a secondary school, bus stops, everyday scenes of domesticity and city life; opposite, another trading estate, a car showroom, retail parks and big-box stores, the sort of places one only visits if you need to buy a fridge or a mattress. Passing these, I turn right into a local park. The noise of traffic subsides somewhat, never quite disappearing but turning into a low hum. I can even hear birdsong. This is accompanied by a less pleasing avian sound as I pick up on a cacophony of crows. I follow their caws and, over the top of a wall, half-hidden by the tree line, I can see what has grabbed the birds' interest: a fleet of refuse lorries and a mound of rubbish. Not only are these edges a place for the distribution of goods, but also for their disposal. Here one finds the municipal refuse truck depot, a rubbish tip, recycling facilities, scrapyards collecting metal, and, in the near distance, an incinerator chimney and its plume – all an equally integral part of consumption practices. This is where the spent beauty products and their discarded packaging will return as they circle from the edges to the centre and back again. As Wang Min'an (2011: 346) precisely describes, '[s]uper-stores and rubbish mountains are the two extreme ends of modern cities, calling out to one another across the borders of the city … To some extent, the rhythm of the city can be understood as the non-stop humming rhythm of commodities marching from one empire to the other.' The retail units on the trading estates work in neat synchronicity with these waste disposal sites as they fuel one another.

I leave the park via a different gate and head back towards the A-road which I cross. In total I need to traverse seven lanes of traffic using the pelican crossings. It takes ages. The crossings are staggered so I have to wait for three different sets of lights. Non-motorised movement is slow here. As a steady stream of cars, lorries and HGVs pass, I stand and (im)patiently wait. But there is no chancing it and trying to dash across the road. Pedestrian movement is not the priority.

The big-box stores are now on my right, the houses and parade of small shops are on the other side of the road. Rather than carrying on along the pavement on the A-road, I decide to take a short cut across a planted verge which marks the boundary between the public pavement and the private space of a retail park. This involves stepping over a low wooden barrier and walking across some woodchip where a few sorry-looking perennials are planted, strewn with plastic bottles and empty fast-food wrappers. Crossing into the retail park's car park, I can see that other people have also made this cut through as there is a distinctive path trodden into the verge. I have heard somewhere that it only takes fifteen passes for a path – or a desire line – to become visible, walked into the ground and there for others to follow. I walk diagonally across the giant car park of an extra-large supermarket, starting to feel the heat bouncing off the asphalt with no shade to temper its effects, heading back towards the trading estate where the beauty wholesalers store is.

Finally, it is time for my appointment, and I head inside the double glass doors. I am greeted by a part-time sales assistant and part-time beauty therapist, who will give me a guided tour. The inside of the store is brightly lit with fluorescent lights. And colourful. The products themselves and their packaging create a rainbow in neon plastic. It is a stark contrast to the greyness and dreariness of the outside. It feels familiar. Also contributing to the un/familiarity of the store, there are shelves where you can get appointment books and reminder cards, the type I have in my wallet from my own hair appointments. Upstairs, on a mezzanine level, you can purchase salon chairs, manicure stands, hair-washing basins and massage couches.

I am shown around the various products with my guide emphasising the discounts that the store offers for buying in bulk. A case of twenty-four pots of depilatory wax offers much better value than buying a single one; likewise, twelve packets of one hundred fabric waxing strips rather than one pack. A quick calculation – a case of wax weighs about eleven kilograms (plus packaging). No wonder everyone drives here! Bulk buying also requires a steady supply of deliveries and the store manager tells me that they receive a pallet-load of goods every day or every other day from their central warehouse, the vans travelling via the motorway and A-roads to replenish the fast-emptying shelves. The unit is shaped to accommodate these daily deliveries with a wide unloading bay, up-and-over loading doors and a large stockroom plus big wheelie bins to dispose of the folded-down cardboard boxes in which the goods arrive. The never-ending process of beauty work and the associated bulk buying of beauty products are both made possible by *and* make the landscape.

Cycling home after my visit I cannot stop thinking about the houses I saw along the A-road and wondering about who lives there. Incongruous with the rest of the outsized landscape, the houses themselves – 1930s terraces with bay windows, brick arches over the front doors and red tiled roofs – could have been in any suburb in south London. But unlike the street on which I live, their front doors are a mere five metres from a dual carriageway, their facades look grubby and worn-out from the emissions of the constant traffic almost literally on their doorsteps and the view from their windows is across a massive car park onto the big-box retailers. Inside, net curtains were hung to shield the life within from the drivers sat idling in the queue of traffic and, even on this warm day, all the windows were closed.

The goods and the vehicles which contain them are not the only things moving at these edges. The exhaust fumes from the incessant traffic also circulate here, invisibly, perniciously. The London Air Quality Network's (2018) map of annual mean pollution for 2016[1] shows this stretch of dual carriageway as experiencing levels between 46 and more than 58 micrograms per cubic metre ($\mu g/m^3$) of nitrous dioxide (NO_2) (significantly higher than the EU limit of $40\mu g/m^3$ of NO_2 and far exceeding the World Health Organization's guideline figure of $10\mu g/m^3$, a figure exceeded in every London borough [Mayor of London Assembly, 2023]). A short distance from these houses, the incinerator plant is also proved to be a significant source of greenhouse gas emissions and other forms of air pollution (Citizen Sense, 2017; Stallard et al., 2024), in addition to the other noise, dust and olfactory pollutants associated with waste disposal. The work of clean-air activists and research across the environmental health and social sciences has shown that pollution from vehicles disproportionately impacts on minority ethnic in the UK communities and people from lower socioeconomic groups (Barnes et al., 2019; Choked Up, 2021; Ella Roberta Family Foundation, n.d.).[2] Following a similar pattern, Greenpeace research found that 'people of colour are overrepresented in the neighbourhoods where existing incinerators are sited' and these waste-burning facilities are 'three times more likely to be built in the UK's most deprived neighbourhoods than in the least' (Roy, 2020). As well as the physical fabric of the landscape surrounding the trading estates, the air here is equally permeated by the circulation of these consumer goods, and is itself circulating in uneven and harmful ways.

A week later, I am back in the salon as the beauty therapist carries out a leg-waxing treatment. I now recognise nearly everything she is using from the wholesalers' store. I am starting to piece together the journey that the products have taken to get here: the places through which they have moved (and will later move as rubbish when the salon's bins are collected that evening), the infrastructures which enable this movement as well as the traces left by this movement and who is most impacted. The treatment lasts about forty-five minutes and, on her way out, the customer makes a repeat appointment for a month's time as the hairs will have regrown. The utility of the products is as fleeting as the outcome – smooth legs, manicured hands, tinted eyebrows, a new haircut only last for so long, and the inexorable 'march' of stuff (Min'an, 2011) continues apace, goods circling from the warehouse at the edges to the salon and back to the edges as waste. The interminable beauty practices are predicated upon the city's edges and how they are landscaped, not only enabling but prioritising the movement of stuff. The circulation of these goods also makes the edgelands. The waxing treatment, manicure, brow tint or haircut are inseparably and co-constitutively bound up with these spaces of distribution, as well as with the airborne emissions also circulating there.

Largely obscured by the giant aluminium boxes and inaudible among the constant rumble of traffic, people are circulating in these places of distribution too. As a visitor from a more residential part of the south London suburbs, walking here, the scale feels inhuman. But people live in the row of terraced houses. People are walking to the corner shop or the take-away; walking to wait at the bus stop; walking to school or work; creating desire lines as they cut across the verges and the car parks. Distribution dominates in this edge landscape; every facet seems to be shaped for and by the movement of stuff. But this is not all that is moving here, and the traces of distribution are both visible and perniciously invisible, especially for those who (have to) walk here.

Notes

1 The London Air Quality Network (LAQN) is based at Imperial College London. The LAQN (2018) explains that '[t]he annual map uses a detailed model to show a prediction of what air quality is like across the whole of Greater London' for 2016 where this 'is the latest year for which an accurate model is available'.

2 Based on air quality data from 2019, the Greater London Authority (2023: x) reports that while there might be some improvement in overall air quality, the uneven distribution of air pollution across neighbourhoods and social groups in London persists.

References

Back, Les (2017) Marchers and steppers: Memory, city life and walking. In Charlotte Bates and Alex Rhys-Taylor (eds) *Walking Through Social Research*. London: Routledge.

Barnes, Joanna H., Chatterton, Tim J. and Longhurst, James W. S. (2019) Emissions vs exposure: Increasing injustice from road traffic-related air pollution in the United Kingdom. *Transportation Research Part D*, 73, 56–66.

Chamberlain, Gethin (2013) Sore eyes, bad backs, low pay: The cost of false eyelash glamour, *Guardian*, 28 December. Available at: www.theguardian.com/world/2013/dec/28/false-eyelash-industry-indonesia-low-pay [accessed 8 June 2015].

Choked Up (2021) Post on pollution zones, Instagram, 11 March, www.instagram.com/p/CMScYSzsj6E/ [accessed 26 October 2023].

Chua, Charmaine, Danyluk, Martin, Cowen, Deborah and Khalili, Laleh (2018) Introduction: Turbulent circulation: Building a critical engagement with logistics. *Environment and Planning D: Society and Space*, 34 (6), 617–29.

Citizen Sense (2017) *Deptford Data Stories: Deptford Park*, Citizen Sense, 14 November. Available at: https://datastories-deptford.citizensense.net/deptford-park [accessed 14 January 2022].

Cowen, Deborah (2014) *The Deadly Life of Logistics: Mapping Violence in Global Trade*. Minneapolis, MN and London: University of Minnesota Press.

Danyluk, Martin (2018) Capital's logistical fix: Accumulation, globalisation, and the survival of capitalism. *Environment and Planning D: Society and Space*, 34 (6), 630–47.

Diani, Hera (2013) False lash industry changes women's lives in Java town, *Magdalene*, 13 December. Available at: https://magdalene.co/story/false-lash-industry-changes-womens-lives-in-java-town/ [accessed 25 February 2025].

Donovan, Arthur and Bonney, Joseph (2006) *The Box that Changed the World: Fifty Years of Container Shipping – An Illustrated History*. East Windsor: Commonwealth Business Media.

Ella Roberta Family Foundation (n.d.) *Clean Air for All*. Available at: http://ellaroberta.org/ [accessed 21 November 2024].

El-Sahli, Zouheir and Upward, Richard (2017) Off the waterfront: The long-run impact of technological change on dockworkers. *British Journal of Industrial Relations*, 55 (2), 225–73.

Frith, Mathew (n.d.) *Buddleia; Butterfly Buffet or Bush of Burden?* [blog post], London Wildlife Trust. Available at: www.wildlondon.org.uk/blog/frith/buddleia [accessed 21 November 2024].

George, Rose (2013) *Deep Sea and Foreign Going: Inside Shipping, The Invisible Industry that Brings You 90% of Everything*. London: Portobello Books.

Greater London Authority (2023) *Greater London Authority Air Quality Exposure and Inequalities Study: Part 1 – London Analysis*. Oxford: Aether. Available at: www.london.gov.uk/sites/default/files/2023-06/Air%20quality%20exposure%20and%20inequalities%20study%20-%20part%20one%20-%20London%20analysis.pdf [accessed 26 October 2023].

Gupta, Tanya (2014) Buddleia: The plant that dominates Britain's railways, BBC, 15 July. Available at: www.bbc.co.uk/news/magazine-28196221 [accessed 21 November 2024].

London Air Quality Network (2018) *Annual Pollution Maps*. Available at: www.londonair.org.uk/london/asp/annualmaps.asp [accessed 20 August 2020].

London Assembly (2023) *New Highly Localised Data Shows Every Borough in London Exceeds World Health Organization Limits for Toxic Pollution*, 25 April. Available at: www.london.gov.uk/New%20highly%20localised%20data%20shows%20every%20borough%20in%20London%20exceeds%20World%20Health%20Organization%20limits%20for%20toxic%20pollution [accessed 26 October 2023].

Mah, Alice (2014) *Port Cities and Global Legacies: Urban Identity, Waterfront Work, and Radicalism*. Basingstoke and New York: Palgrave Macmillan.

Massey, Doreen (2007) *World City*. Cambridge (UK) and Malden, MA: Polity Press.

Parker, Martin (2013) Containerisation: Moving things and boxing ideas. *Mobilities*, 8 (3), 368–87.

Rondel, Louise and Henneke, Laura (2024) Walking the (infrastructural) line: Mobile and embodied explorations of infrastructures and their impact on the urban landscape. *Sociological Research Online*, 30 (1), 325–38.

Roy, Inori (2020) *UK Waste Incinerators Three Times More Likely to be in Poorer Areas*, Unearthed, 31 July. Available at: https://unearthed.greenpeace.org/2020/07/31/waste-incinerators-deprivation-map-recycling/ [accessed 23 February 2021].

Shapiro, Aaron (2023) Platform urbanism in a pandemic: Dark stores, ghost kitchens, and the logistical–urban frontier. *Journal of Consumer Culture*, 23 (1), 168–87.

Shoard, Marion (2017) The peri-urban fringe: Edgelands. *Land Magazine*, 21, 5–8.

Stallard, Esme, McGrath, Matt, Clahane, Patrick and Lynch, Paul (2024) Burning rubbish now UK's dirtiest form of power, BBC, 15 October. Available at: www.bbc.co.uk/news/articles/cp3wxgje5pwo [accessed 21 November 2024].

Tarlo, Emma (2016) *Entanglement: The Secret Lives of Hair*. London: One World.

Wang, Min'an (2011) On rubbish. *Theory, Culture and Society*, 28 (7–8), 340–53.

Watson, Sophie (2019) *City Water Matters: Cultures, Practices and Entanglements of Urban Water*. Singapore: Palgrave Macmillan.

The Wildlife Trusts (n.d.) *Buddleia*. Available at: www.wildlifetrusts.org/wildlife-explorer/trees-and-shrubs/buddleia [accessed 21 November 2024].

5

Walking with nurdles: reflections on a plastic beach clean

Alice Mah

Today is a beautiful space of endeavour, a small group of friends coming together. My 10-year-old son and I pack raincoats and sandwiches and set out after breakfast. I admire the shifting grey clouds from the car window. The skies in Scotland never cease to amaze me, so alive. I know that we are close when we see the petrochemical chimneys through the trees. I have never approached them from this angle before. We follow signs to the nature reserve, turn left, and stop at a car park. At the entrance, a black chalkboard mounted on a metal gate invites us to join the 'Plastic Free Beach Clean & Nurdle Hunt Today, 11am–2pm.'

In our wellington boots, we stride along the path with a sense of purpose. The path leads us over a railway crossing overgrown with weeds to a junction, where we find a handwritten sign affixed to a post, with green arrows pointing the way to the beach. We follow a gravel trail into the willows, nettles and grass, their colours fading with the end of summer. Every few hundred steps, there is another marker: a red ribbon tied to a tree; a piece of driftwood covered in felt pen writing; and a scrap of cardboard perched in the grass, which says: 'Beach Clean: almost there'. At last, we come to an opening, where the greenery meets the estuary, marked by two bright flags. As we walk down to the rocks and sand, my son remembers his fear of touching the nurdles. There will be gloves, I assure him.

Nurdles are lentil-sized plastic pellets, produced by petrochemical companies, which get transported in giant bags and containers around the world to make plastic products. Every year, an estimated 230,000 tonnes of nurdles spill into the oceans, one of the largest sources of marine microplastic pollution. Nurdles are 'toxic sponges', and their surfaces can carry very high concentrations of chemical pollutants and bacteria (McVeigh, 2021).

After all the signs, I expected a large gathering of people on the beach, but I smile when we are greeted by three familiar faces: my climate activist friends. There is only one other person who has come to the beach clean so far, a woman who lives in a neighbouring town, already hard at work some distance along the shore, black bin bag in hand, combing for plastic litter. But it is still early, and they are hoping that more people will come, maybe after church.

The main organiser is a local environmental activist named Bryan. I first met Bryan in the spring of 2019, when he invited me to walk with him along a public road through the heart of the oil refinery and petrochemical complex in Grangemouth. The walk took just over an hour, and it felt like we were trespassing, getting so close to the flares, industrial infrastructure, and rusted pipes. We would get in trouble from security if we took photographs, Bryan warned me. Over the past decade, he had brought at least a hundred people on tours of the Dirty Oil Road, including politicians, journalists, activists and community groups, as a way of showing them the scale of heavy polluting industries. As we walked, Bryan told me about growing up in this former British Petroleum (BP) boom town, living with fears of nuclear attack and industrial accidents (see Mah, 2023). The air was heavy and sulphurous.

Bryan shows us our equipment for the beach clean: bin bags; litter pickers with claws; gloves, as promised; and tweezers and glass jars for the finer work of collecting nurdles. He explains our mission for the day: pick up plastic waste and count nurdles.

For the plastic waste, we should sort out what plastic can be recycled and what needs to go in the rubbish. We can also keep track of our most interesting and surprising finds. So far, they have found a doll's leg, several cotton bud sticks, and a 'prize': a pink product label from INEOS, the petrochemical company flaring across the river … a fingerprint. INEOS claims no responsibility for the nurdles accumulating on this shore; its corporate representatives say that the nurdles come from elsewhere. Like other petrochemical companies, INEOS makes corporate pledges to have 'Zero Pellet Loss' (INEOS, 2020) and blames transporters and other companies for the spills.

It was along the verge of the Dirty Oil Road, Bryan says, recalling our walk five years ago, that he saw his first nurdles. During one of his tours, an activist pointed the tiny pellets out to him and explained what they were. Since then, Bryan has participated in a number of nurdle hunts here along the Firth of Forth, on the opposite site of the petrochemical complex. These are part of the Great Nurdle Hunt which is organised by local environmental groups around the world every September.

There is an art to hunting nurdles. One nurdle is the industrial equivalent of a grain of sand, found in great heaps on beaches, and floating in vast quantities in the oceans. A nurdle count can only ever be an estimate. If we see a clump the size of a handful, that would be about one hundred nurdles. We should take photos of our findings to submit as evidence. Our estimate will almost certainly exceed the highest number that is possible to record in the Great Nurdle Hunt submission, above one thousand. We can collect nurdles, too, but mainly for campaigning purposes. Cleaning them up would be an impossible task.

I have never seen a nurdle in the wild before, only in jars and in photographs. Already, as we gather our bin bags and litter pickers, I can see hundreds of them, nestled in the ground, mixed with sand, weeds, sticks, and pebbles, blue, white, black and translucent.

More than the nurdles and the other plastic fragments, though, it is the petrochemical complex that I am drawn towards, seeing it so clearly across the water, the line of chimneys, storage tanks and cranes. For a long time, my attention has been trained upon this polluter, the most noxious of industries, producing petrochemicals, linked to cancer, neurological diseases, respiratory illnesses, and reproductive problems, together with chronic issues of headaches, sleep deprivation, anxiety and depression, for people living in fenceline communities in close proximity to the plants (Allen, 2003; Mah and Wang, 2019; Feltrin et al., 2022).

Despite the overwhelming evidence that petrochemicals are toxic (harmful to health and ecosystems across all stages of the petrochemical lifecycle); fossil-fuel dependent (99 per cent of petrochemicals are derived from fossil fuels; the largest industrial consumer of fossil fuels; and one of the largest industrial emitters); wasteful (major contributors to plastic pollution; 80 per cent of petrochemical products are plastics, 40 per cent of which are for plastic packaging); and unjust (causing the most harm to poor, ethnic minority and working-class fenceline communities), petrochemicals are tolerated by governments and societies as necessary to the functioning of everyday modern life. After all, they are in our communication devices, roads, buildings, transport, medical equipment, household products, wind turbine blades, and even in our food (see Azoulay et al., 2019; Hamilton et al., 2019; Mah, 2023).

It is a difficult industry to get close to, as an outsider: highly securitised, walled off by fences and gates. There is also good reason not to get too close; there are lots of dangerous, flammable, toxic and explosive chemicals; and workers need safety equipment and specialist training to navigate these spaces; they are not for wandering about. People living in houses adjacent to petrochemical plants are equipped with emergency phones and protocols in case of accidents, a regulatory legacy of the disastrous chemical explosion in the 1970s in Seveso, Italy (see Barca, 2012; Brown et al., 2021).

Yet here, I see the petrochemical industry from a different perspective. I am not so close that I am in its securitised walls, nor am I fully enveloped in its pollution. I am not so far away that I can map its sprawling global contours. Instead, I can see it with an unobstructed view, from across the water, and confront it with a less guarded gaze, taking stock of its nurdles, and its hubris. Framed against the tides of the Firth of Forth, it is not all-powerful.

We search along the shoreline of the muddy estuary, finding crumpled brown plastic bottles encrusted in barnacles, and plastic bags so thin that they resemble crepe paper. There is a disturbing number of cotton bud sticks, blue and white, given that these are now banned. We find lots of tampon applicators, crisp and sweet packages and bottles. My son recognises some of the brands. The claws of the litter picker are awkward, and the objects are by turns too heavy, light, slippery, or sticky to pick up easily.

Our first bag fills up in about twenty minutes. We falter at the task of sorting: how much is still recyclable, after it has been sullied and eroded by sea and sand? How can there really be so many cotton bud sticks? Do they travel from landfill overflow, or from sewage? It is disturbing, this constant circulation of plastics from land to sea and back.

We walk further along the shore, clearing all the visible plastic that we can find. With each step, we feel the crunch of pebbles and the squelch of wet sand. As we cast our gaze up, out, around and down, the world becomes at once larger and smaller. Time slows and expands. Even our sense of purpose fades in the rhythms of water and sky.

At noon, we lug our bin bags back to our friends, sanitise our hands, and find a rock to sit on for lunch. My son takes a few bites of his sandwich but cannot finish it, unnerved by the toxic plastic around us. Two other activists join us, gather equipment, and set off in different directions. One man sits on a rock with a jar and a pair of tweezers, mesmerised by the task of sifting through nurdles. We spot some curlews in the mudflats, at low tide, and look through binoculars.

Bryan points out the place where they are building the fuel import terminal across the river now that the oil refinery is scheduled to close. There is lots of talk about the need for a 'just transition' for Grangemouth (Shibe, 2024), and many people think that the petrochemical company will close, too. But INEOS plans to expand, continuing to make petrochemicals, using imported shale gas from the US, as it already does, instead of oil from the North Sea.

Our other friends are local medics who are worried about the impacts of climate and pollution on health. We eat rather soberly and talk sheepishly about the packaging we have brought with us, the guilty pleasure of fresh strawberries in clamshell containers.

After lunch, my son wants to try searching for nurdles. We find some bountiful places, revealing thousands at a time, under rocks, between logs, following the curve of the shoreline. But it is frustrating work. The tweezers take too long, allowing him to pick up just one at a time, and using a scoop catches too much sand. We could have tried a sieve, except that nobody has brought one.

This intricate task illuminates other treasures, crab legs, blanched pinecones and long spiral shells. Somehow it softens the darkness of what we face, on the horizon, that looming industrial skyline. The tides of the estuary move as ever before, and birds still play and rest.

In all my years of researching the plastics and petrochemical industries, this is the first time that I have participated in a beach clean-up. It always seemed like a superficial act, in a way, because it only deals with the froth, and it cannot begin to make a difference, materially speaking, to the endless volumes. Yet I realise that in this simple work, there is insight; a minor perturbance in the cognitive dissonance that underpins everyday life. It is a jarring reminder, seeing these objects we have consumed, and still consume, knowing that they never go away; that to cast off material as if it can disappear is an act of violence, as much as it is one of convenience.

When we are finished, we have filled several bin bags and glass jars between us, catalogued some of our most surprising findings, and determined what is recyclable. Not much of it is. As a memento, my son gets to keep a half-filled jar of nurdles. We take a group photo, and retrace our footsteps along the path, walking slowly, removing all the carefully placed signs along the way.

As we approach the railway crossing, an old-fashioned coal-powered steam train passes by, rattling and whistling, leaving a trail of black smoke. One of our friends, a retired doctor in his seventies, admits to a certain nostalgia for this creaky old fossil-fuel-based form of transport. We reflect on the contradictions it represents. Back in the car park, we divide out the spoils, the bin bags to take away in different car boots, the equipment for cleaning.

Plastic pollutes the shores; we cannot contain it. By tomorrow, or the day after, the plastic will have returned. But that is not really the point. Today, we experienced a form of communion: reclaiming some part of ourselves that we have lost. We created a small clearing in a continual churn, a collective sifting over a couple of hours. Curlews cried, and the mudflats gleamed at low tide. We walked with nurdles.

References

Allen, Barbara L. (2003) *Uneasy Alchemy: Citizens and Experts in Louisiana's Chemical Corridor Disputes*. Cambridge, MA: MIT Press.

Azoulay, David, Villa, Priscilla, Arellano, Yvette, Gordon, Miriam, Moon, Doun, Miller, Kathryn and Thompson, Kristen (2019) *Plastic and Health: The Hidden Cost of a Plastic Planet*. Washington, DC: Center for International Environmental Law.

Barca, Stefania (2012) On working-class environmentalism: A historical and transnational overview. *Interface: A Journal For and About Social Movements*, 4 (2), 61–80.

Brown, David, Mah, Alice and Walker, Gordon (2021) The tenacity of trust in petrochemical communities: Reckoning with risk on the Fawley Waterside (1997–2019). *Environment and Planning E: Nature and Space*, 5 (3), 1207–29.

Feltrin, Lorenzo, Mah, Alice and Brown, David (2022) Noxious deindustrialization: Experiences of precarity and pollution in Scotland's petrochemical capital. *Environment and Planning C: Politics and Space*, 40 (4), 950–69.

Hamilton, Lisa A., Feit, Steven, Muffett, Carroll, Kelso, Matt et al. (2019) *Plastic and Climate: The Hidden Costs of a Plastic Planet*. Washington, DC: Center for International Environmental Law.

INEOS (2020) *Zero Pellet Loss? This is How We're Doing It*. Project One. Available at: https://project-one.ineos.com/en/stories/zero-pelletverlieszo-doen-we-dat/ [accessed 2 October 2025].

Mah, Alice (2023) *Petrochemical Planet: Multiscalar Battles of Industrial Transformation*. Durham, NC: Duke University Press.

Mah, Alice and Wang, Xinhong (2019) Accumulated injuries of environmental injustice: Living and working with petrochemical pollution in Nanjing, China. *Annals of the American Association of Geographers*, 109 (6), 1961–77.

McVeigh, Karen (2021) Nurdles: The worst toxic waste you've probably never heard of, *Guardian*, 29 November.

Shibe, Riyoko (2024) Grangemouth: A story of unjust transition? [blog post], 9 February. *Centre for Energy Ethics Blog*. Available at: https://energyethics.st-andrews.ac.uk/blog/grangemouth-a-story-of-unjust-transition/ [accessed 2 October 2025].

Trace

Exercise 2: Beneath your feet

Look down at the ground where you are walking
Is there concrete, earth, or rubbish beneath your feet?
Are there any footprints?
What does the surface tell you about where you are?
What do you imagine lies beneath the surface?
Consider what is hidden or invisible in the physical landscape all around you

6

Breaking down the walls of Partick: tracing cycles of urban neoliberalism and resistance

Kirsteen Paton

For many years, I have played a word game with my friend Robbie where we work Scottish places into song titles: 'Fly me to Dunoon', 'He ain't Heavy, He's Anstruther' and George Michael's classic, 'Careless Whifflet'. In this vein, Robbie suggested that I title my PhD, 'Breaking Down the Walls of Partick' after the Dexy's Midnight Runners song, 'Breaking Down the Walls of Heartache', to describe the process of gentrification in the neighbourhood. I went for something far straighter and more academic in the end, that better captured the process which I saw around a wider neoliberalisation of housing that constituted a hegemonic shift in this industrial working-class neighbourhood. Gentrification in a traditional sense of a replacement of a working-class population by incoming capital and middle-class residents, didn't happen, at least not during that period of fieldwork from 2005–08. Partick Housing Association, the social housing provider, despite its own neoliberal activities and enterprises, did largely prevent displacement and full-scale gentrification in the neighbourhood. 'Breaking Down the Walls of Partick' stayed with me like an earworm. Seventeen years after my initial research, did neoliberalism and gentrification prevail? Did they break down the working-class walls of Partick? A lot has happened since.

The walk tells the story of my PhD study and subsequent book on Partick, *Gentrification: A working-class perspective* (Paton, 2014), which explored the experiences of gentrification processes in the neighbourhood initiated by the Glasgow Harbour housing development on the banks of the Clyde which had once been a site of industry. I take students on this walk to animate the stories from the research. So much has changed, yet not necessarily what was anticipated in terms of what the community feared would change and the change that was desired to be manufactured in the neighbourhood through state-led gentrification. This huge state-led gentrification Harbour project was delivered around the time of the 2007/08 financial crash; it didn't drive the gentrification desired by the local state and summon thousands of well-heeled young professionals to the riverside. But many hands have been greased and pockets generously lined since, through land deals, property development, buy-to-let and build-to-let deals. The changes in the urban economy have left its mark in the landscape. I left Glasgow just before 2014, which was the year of the Glasgow Commonwealth Games, another large-scale gentrification project in the east end of the city and a few years after that Living Rent, Scotland's first tenant union, was formed in the city. Glasgow is a paradigmatic post-industrial neoliberal city. State-led gentrification and boosterism have been the key local state governance strategies for over thirty years. The urban form that neoliberalism takes, how it is expressed in different ways through the landscape along the route of this walk, can be read in what haunts the landscape as well as new additions to the space, but also in what's missing and in what is not visible.

The walk begins and ends back in Partick by way of Glasgow Harbour. It is a full circular walk. It loops westbound along Dumbarton Road, the main bustling high street in Partick, which runs parallel to the River Clyde, down to the Glasgow Harbour development which runs directly riverside, walking eastbound along its deserted, privately owned promenade, meeting the sites recent mass purpose-built student accommodation, and ending back at Dumbarton Road, crossing with Byres Road, where Partick begins. In following this loop, we can see read the cycles of neoliberalism, market failures and undeterred new attempts: same song, different dance.

'From the Ground Up'

The walk starts where the research project began. At the WestGAP office, 65–7 Hyndland Street – except WestGAP are no longer there or operate at all. In its place sits a hair salon and a homeware and furniture shop selling modern and vintage pieces. There are no traces at all left of this group at this spot, who were the heart of resistance and organising in Partick and in Glasgow at that time. My PhD study was a collaborative project with WestGAP, an anti-poverty community group run by and for people in Glasgow who have first-hand experience of living in poverty who provided welfare advice and advocacy in the neighbourhood. Their slogan, 'From the Ground Up', expressed their commitment to the local community and grassroots organising. WestGAP were deeply concerned with the Glasgow Harbour development, the fallacy of trickle-down economics it was premised upon, and which was used to placate Partick residents – that they too would benefit from the 'uplift' in the area. They saw the Glasgow Harbour development plainly for what it was – gentrification. And in 2004 in Glasgow, that was not a process much known or experienced, despite the dedicated boosterist efforts of Glasgow City Council for decades which attempted to rebrand the gritty city into something more cosmopolitan and profitable. I was the PhD researcher taking on the task of investigating the impacts of gentrification in the neighbourhood. One day a week I would work in the WestGAP office. The front of the office had sofas and plants; it was where local residents seeking support would be met. The back of the office housed some desks; it was dark, often lamplit, cold yet cosy and cluttered with pamphlets, flyers, reports, books and files. Tea was in constant supply.

At that time in Glasgow there was not a strong tenant or housing movement. There had been a significant campaign against the Housing Stock Transfer in 2002,[1] but by and large the housing movement had waned. WestGAP had a broad anti-poverty remit and provided welfare advocacy rather than being primarily concerned with housing inequality; however, the changes in the area due to increased housing privatisation and gentrification and compounding welfare benefits cuts, stagnated wages and rent price increases, meant housing inequality was an emerging issue in their work. Many people interested in activism and working-class organising in the city at that time found their way to WestGAP, including Ruth Gilbert, who would go on to be part of Living Rent as well as people who have become academics, involved in critical and radical research around class, race and housing financialisation, such as Ashli Mullen and Damien Dempsey. One of the founding members of the WestGAP collective, Kait Laughlin, later worked at the University of Glasgow as a Knowledge Exchange Lead in Social and Political Sciences, and led a programme called Community Matters that trained researchers on how to work with communities. Community Matters was central in promoting the work of Castlemilk Souper Heroes project, run by local women helping their community in the face of food poverty.[2] While WestGAP is no longer there, its legacy is rich, powerful and rhizomatic, shaping me and many others in the work that we do with communities in the city today.

If you cannae get it in Partick you cannae get it anywhere

This was apparently a local Glasgow saying, which expressed the vibrancy of its main shopping street Dumbarton Road in the 1960s and 1970s. It was said to me in an interview as a lament, as it was believed by that resident to be no longer the case, and that Dumbarton Road was 'dead'. On my walk, it's 2pm on a Monday afternoon, and Dumbarton Road is busy. There are people everywhere, dashing to the transport interchange to catch a train, subway or bus, going to the bank and post office, heading to cafes and bakeries for lunch, or heading to the nail shop, vape shop, mobile phone shop, for bubble tea, vegan Chinese food. There are the Rangers supporters' pubs, Celtic supporters' pubs, cheap hot or cold rolls, advertised on a sandwich board alongside a restaurant specialising in expensive small plates. It is multicultural. It serves the working-class residents, middle-class young professionals and students, both international and home. I pass the nail shop which I wanted to feature on the front cover of my book; with its colourful, carnivalesque neon lights shining, it has stood the test of time. All the same pubs remain, stalwarts too. Long gone are those cafes and restaurants which were seen as the signifiers of gentrification in the neighbourhood, but they have been replaced by more modern versions. The row of bars which at the time encapsulated gentrification in the neighbourhood, are gone, but new ones stand in their place – one painted a chic moss green, which has been vaunted in the media and Michelin guide featured. This is a stop point in the walking tour that I give. It's here I tell the story of Sylvie from my book. This was once the place where we met for an interview, where she sat in the sunshine in her sunglasses, drinking white wine, aged 19, on the waiting list for a social rented flat in Partick, but longing for the sleek contemporary lifestyle branded by the Glasgow Harbour promotional material. I have often thought about Sylvie. Did she get a socially rented flat in Partick? Did she rent a Harbour development flat? Many units went straight on the private rental market. Or was she forced out, outpriced from Partick?

Here, I turn left and head to the river. Partick and Glasgow Harbour are separated by an expressway. It is connected by an underpass tunnel, or by a series of crossings that allow pedestrian access. Today I take a different, longer route down to the Harbour development, taking in a housing development which sits across the expressway which separates Partick and Glasgow Harbour. The expressway cuts directly through Dumbarton Road, and on the other side there is an island of housing, at Inchholm Street, cut off on both sides by the expressway. On the street there is a mix of housing: on the right-hand side of the street, housing built around the 1990s; and across the street, more contemporary housing built around 2010s. Most of these are socially rented. Partick Housing Association is the main social housing provider in Partick, managing a stock of 1,802 homes in the area (as of their 2023 annual report). This provision of socially rented housing in the area has been a key stabiliser in protecting tenants from displacement due to rent rises induced by gentrification. However, Glasgow is in the grips of a housing crisis. The local council declared the city to be in a state of housing emergency in 2023, and the root cause of the city's housing emergency is a chronic lack of social housing. Rents have gone up twice as fast as earnings in the last three years in Glasgow, which has seen the largest rent increases in the UK between 2020 and 2023, at 38.9 per cent (Peachy, 2024).

Partick Housing Association is increasingly marketised in their housing provision, setting inflated rents in newer housing developments. In 2017, residents at 7 Inchholm Street noticed that their rents were much higher compared to other properties across the street and across the city. The average rent for a three-bedroom flat with Partick Housing was only around £315 per month, and the Scottish average even less at £295pm, while they were paying around £614pm. Social housing providers can include a 'new build levy' in their pricing matrix. Residents in the block joined their tenant union Living Rent and successfully campaigned to lower not only their own rent, but win a reduction for everyone in their block, as well as extensive repairs for the full block. To the passerby, it's just a housing block, but it's the site of vital tenant organising in Partick. Living Rent formed as a campaign group in 2014, the year after I left the city, before becoming a tenant union in 2016. Their work has been pivotal in protecting tenants from the worst aspects of the housing crisis and organising for decent and affordable housing. The housing crisis and chronic lack of social housing in the city means that Partick Housing Association can't stave off gentrification in the neighbourhood as they once did. In 2015, Partick Housing Association had 1,719 socially rented homes; nearly a decade later, they have 1,802 – only 81 more. This does nothing to offset the housing crisis in the city. Now, it is tenant unions who are doing the vital work in protecting tenants from displacement.

Designed for life

I walk towards the river. There is no blend between the neighbourhoods. As Gray (2021) points out, it was called *Glasgow Harbour* not *Partick Harbour*. The intention was to detach, protectionism designed in: '*[t]his is indicative of a strategy that is not so much aimed at integrating the harbourside with Partick but of generating an intrusive form of 'new build gentrification' from the riverside into Partick*.' (Gray, 2021: n.p.)

The neighbourhoods still sit like oil and water.

A key marketing slogan for the Harbour Development was 'Designed for Life'. However, it seems anything but. Developers promised the site would have shops and amenities for Harbour and Partick residents. There's a Starbucks and Burger King drive-through awkwardly placed, sitting just off the expressway and parallel to the Glasgow Harbour flats. It's ill-fitting and unnecessary. Part of that blend could have been achieved in this area by closing this gap between the neighbourhoods and connecting them through creating shared community spaces and amenities. Instead, it's bland commercialism.

There were plans to deliver a £100 million 'retail destination' on the banks of the river. In 2020, Glasgow City Council gave planning approval to Peel L&P, part of the Peel Holding group, who bought and developed the Glasgow Harbour site. They planned to extend the project with the Glasgow Harbour Lifestyle Outlet emulating their other retail parks in Manchester, Lowry Outlets and at Gloucester Quays. Peel claimed that the Glasgow Harbour Lifestyle Outlet '*will provide VIP and concierge shopping services and will work with agencies, airports and airlines to promote Glasgow to the national and international market*' (Sandelands, 2020). Typical boosterist hyperbole. Peel later withdrew their plans, but offered up the site to another company who have signed terms to develop a spa resort.

You do see signs of life in the Harbour flats. Pushchairs, bikes and washing fill the balconies. It's busy and disordered. There's a row of blue plant pots of different shapes, shades and varieties, running along the ledge of a balcony. The colour is vibrant against the decaying grey cladding. And while the signs of life are clear in the flats, this is not matched by a support system for that community. Scaffolding on the flats, but no social scaffolding. There are no parks, community centres, shops, cafes or amenities which the hundreds of residents living there can access. This has not materialised and as a neighbourhood it feels barren, tired, forlorn and deprived. Currently only the Starbucks and Burger King service the community. That these amenities are drive-throughs expresses what has been clear about the development from the beginning – it is not a place meant for gathering or socialising. It speaks to the secessionary network spaces as described by Graham and Marvin in *Splintering urbanism* (2001) – you can leave your flat, via underground parking, to the drive-through to get your coffee on your way to work, without being in the space, but protected by the bubble of your car.

Maybe that protection isn't from the people of Partick but from industrial remnants which still encroach on the space. The Glasgow Harbour development smells like industry and sounds like industry. The region is one of the most industrialised and urbanised areas in Scotland. There is a constant, low but unmistakable thrum from BAE Systems across the river in Govan. Brewerton-Harper (2024) uses the geological term 'superposition' to describe Glasgow's urban landscape and the ways that it reflects layers of history and architecture that coexist and overlap: 'The past within the present. This "lingering" feeling, an affect, a sense, a shared sociocultural experience, made Glasgow in my eyes a place that could be better understood through a hauntological lens.'

Brewerton-Harper draws from Mark Fisher's notion of hauntology and applies it to examine post-industrial Glasgow, with particular attention on the East End and Glasgow Commonwealth Games. At Glasgow Harbour, it's hard to know who is haunting who. Who is the ghost? It doesn't seem like industry is haunting – BAE business is booming. BAE recently opened a new £12 million state-of-the-art training facility at BAE Systems' Scotstoun shipyard, and a new ship build hall at the Govan shipyard is underway creating a facility large enough to construct two Type 26 frigates simultaneously. The Type 26 is one of the world's most advanced warships, fitted with armour developed by Israel. The plant in Govan produces the Type 26 for the Royal Navy. BAE is the UK's leading military manufacturer and makes 15 per cent of the components for F-35 stealth bombers. At the time of writing, Israel has taken delivery of thirty-nine of the jets and ordered seventy-five, with the aircraft deployed in the ongoing offensive on the Gaza strip (McKay, 2024). Not designed for life, but designed for death. What is haunting here, is killing there.

The River Clyde smells. The river has been subject to historical and contemporary deposits from hazardous substances from industrial and domestic waste and is one of Scotland's most contaminated bodies of water (McIntyre et al., 2012). More recently, a report (REHIS, 2019) warned that contaminated land under Clydeside, caused by poisons dumped by a former chemical factory, poses an immediate risk to human health because of toxic waste leaking into the river. Another study (Wilkinson et al., 2022) found the Clyde to contain the highest levels of toxic pharmaceuticals in the UK. While these flats were designed as part of sanitised living, the interplay of nature and industry fill the sound and scent of the space. But this isn't the only man-made hazard at the Harbour flats.

From Glasgow to Grenfell

These flats, which were said to revolutionise the Clydeside, are covered in scaffolding, undergoing reconstruction. These so-called luxury buildings were in fact made of cheap and dangerous material. The combustible cladding, ACM (aluminium composite material), was the same type used on Grenfell Tower and was responsible for the fire spreading so quickly. It is currently being removed and replaced with non-combustible solid aluminium cladding. In 2018, the UK banned the use of combustible cladding on high-rise buildings (more than eighteen stories). The government first received data demonstrating the danger of polyethylene-cored cladding in 2002, with deadly fires[3] caused by cladding dating back to the 1970s, and campaigners since then have been demanding stronger building regulations (Hodkinson and Murphy, 2020). But ACM cladding is cheaper, and over time health and safety regulations have been steadily diminished by successive governments. Hodkinson and Murphy (2020) attribute what happened at Grenfell to a series of political and ideological decisions over decades which prioritised profitability over social and state protections.

Resident leaseholders at the Glasgow Harbour were facing a £10m bill to remove and replace the cladding. But Taylor Wimpey, which completed the development, eventually took on the costs, and work to replace the cladding is ongoing. There is an irregular, tinny percussion from the hammers and steel wielded by workers on the scaffolding enveloping one of the tower blocks. The sound echoes across the river sky. It isn't the professionalised, sleek, gentrified space of the architectural plans. You see the consequences of profiteering and deregulation. You also see signs of disrepair. Discoloration and tarnished building parts, films of moss, water stains, made brown with iron. It was presented as a desirable location for investors, developers and residents alike. Instead, it looks like cruel optimism (Berlant, 2011).

The global corporate landlord revolution: Purpose-Built Residential Accommodation (PBRA)

The promenade I walk along which skirts the river is a private promenade owned by Glasgow Harbour Ltd (which is part of Peel L&P). The Peel Group also own half an acre of land around the iconic Finnieston Crane, further along the river. The ownership of this land has changed hands over the last few decades, changing the use and purpose of that land. When Glasgow City Council sold the 130-acre Glasgow Harbour site land to Peel Holdings, it announced it as heralding a change not seen on the site 'since the industrial revolution'. While grandiose, the shift in land use from industry, the grain mills and associated shipbuilding industries, to 'luxury' flats and now student housing does speak to a revolution of sorts – of corporate ownership and landlords.

Peel Holdings might not announce their ownership of the streets and promenade, yet they brand the landscape with their standardised developments. You might not have even heard of Peel Holdings, but they own land you have likely walked on, swam in, or shopped in. Peel owns the Manchester Ship Canal, and until recently the Trafford Centre shopping complex which was sold in the largest single property acquisition in Britain's history. It owns Liverpool Docks and Liverpool John Lennon airport and MediaCityUK in Salford. And when I first walked this landscape there was much land still empty, with what Neil Smith (1987) would call a ripe rent gap. Now new developments crowd the landscape. It's not only Peel. The other stealthy, fast-growing developers and landlords in the UK are student housing providers, which feels increasingly precarious in relation to the UK higher education sector and international student market governed by the Home Office. Student housing is big business, with investment in such developments hitting a new high in 2022 of £7.2 billion – a 69 per cent increase (Knight Frank, 2023: 2). The high-yield return has seen student housing becoming highly appealing to international investors. As Kallin (2024) notes in his research into the Edinburgh student housing market, Blackstone's – who hold one of the largest property portfolios in the world – acquisition of UK student housing company iQ for £4.66 billion in 2020 (Christophers, 2022) 'was the UK's largest ever private property transaction in any sector' (Sanderson and Özogul, 2022: 170). This goes far beyond notions of previously discussed studentification.

And we see that materialised on the walk. Just beyond the Harbour development flats is more brownfield land with a sizable rent gap. The vacant site formerly comprised the Partick Central Railway Station, which was demolished without warning at 6am one morning in 2005 when I was conducting my fieldwork, to the dismay of residents. Massive student housing blocks replaced it in the mid-2010s and more plans are in place for 424 private homes 'built to rent'. Gray (2021) notes that, in late 2020, there were 5,465 designated units of student accommodation in South Partick/Yorkhill, and 3,359 in South Partick alone. And while it is worrying regarding the concentration of private units in the area, it points to something far more nefarious emerging – a new kind of corporate development.

Reflections

Walking this route again makes me think about what this landscape tells us and what it doesn't. Neoliberalism is distinctly evident in the landscape: from speculatively built, expensive private housing that is not only decaying but dangerous; to the broken boosterist promise of new professional living, home to diverse, privately rented tenants; to the surge in monolithic, purpose-built student accommodation and corporate landlord-driven residential blocks. We can trace the failures of neoliberalism; it reinvents itself cyclically and spatially, reproducing dysfunctional social consequences (Brenner and Theodore, 2005).

But there is so much unseen, unreadable, imperceptible from the space. So much that is either erased or implicit. I carry with me on that walk the knowledge of the past and that which lies beyond the surface. Where people see a hair salon, I see an important site of organising in Glasgow. You might see rows of red sandstone tenement housing, and not a growing tenant movement. Living Rent passed a motion at their 2022 AGM to commit to a programme of housing decommodification, based on lobbying for social housebuilding. The branch that brought that motion was the Partick branch. That commitment to resisting housing neoliberalism is deeply embedded in the neighbourhood. While the walls of Partick might have been broken down, residents are fighting hard to build them back up. The social consequences of the cycles of neoliberalism are not always dysfunctional; they can be galvanising and coherent, producing powerful counter-hegemonies. Disentangling where that power and knowledge comes from and where it goes has been something that I have been thinking about a lot. The walk teaches us that we have to look up and out, and down and in to understand the forces of urban restructuring, its past and its futures. It is not simply a seamless cycle, it is challenged by interruptions. 'From the Ground Up', WestGAP's commitment, seems more important than ever. That resistance is on ground we walk on.

Notes

1 Glasgow Anti-Stock Transfer campaign was established by local tenants and campaigners to challenge the transfer of Glasgow's council housing stock of 81,000 homes out of public ownership and into the hands of specially created 'social' landlord, Glasgow Housing Association. They lost the vote: 58% Yes, 42% No.

2 Listen to the podcast episode with Les Back and the Castlemilk Soup'erheroes here: www.gla.ac.uk/schools/socialpolitical/recoveringcommunitypodcast/season2episode2/

3 www.bbc.co.uk/news/uk-england-45982810

References

Berlant, Lauren (2011) *Cruel Optimism*. Durham, NC: Duke University Press.

Brenner, Neil and Theodore, Nik (2005) Neoliberalism and the urban condition. *City*, 9 (910), 101–7.

Brewerton-Harper, Dylan (2024) The ghosts of the 2014 games, *Scottish Left Review*, 142. Available at: https://scottishleftreview.scot/the-ghosts-of-the-2014-games/ [accessed 10 December 2024].

Christophers, Brett (2022) Mind the rent gap: Blackstone, housing investment and the reordering of urban rent surfaces. *Urban Studies*, 59 (4), 698–716.

Graham, Steve and Marvin, Simon (2001) *Splintering Urbanism: Networked Infrastructures, Technological Mobilities and the Urban Condition*. New York: Routledge.

Gray, Neil (2021) If Beith Street could talk: 'Build to Rent', studentification and 'Purpose built residential accommodation', *Bella Caledonia*, 9 February. Available at: https://bellacaledonia.org.uk/2021/02/09/if-beith-street-could-talk-build-to-rent-studentification-and-purpose-built-residential-accommodation/ [accessed 10 December 2024].

Hodkinson, Stuart and Murphy, Phil (2020) Grenfell, three years on: A preventable disaster that could still happen again [blog post], 17 June. *Greater Manchester Housing Action Blog*. Available at: www.gmhousingaction.com/grenfell-preventable-disaster/ [accessed 30 December 2024].

Kallin, Hamish (2024) Victims of studentification? Variegated student experiences of housing precarity and homelessness in Edinburgh. *Scottish Geographical Journal*, 1–19. https://doi.org/10.1080/14702541.2024.2372623

Knight Frank (2023) *2023 Student Property Report*. London: Knight Frank. Available at: https://content.knightfrank.com/research/169/documents/en/uk-student-housing-2023-9846.pdf [accessed 10 December 2024].

McIntyre, F., Fernandes, P. G. and Turrell, W. R. (2012) *Scottish Marine and Freshwater Science*, 3 (3), *Clyde Ecosystem Review*. Available at: www.gov.scot/publications/scottish-marine-freshwater-science-volume-3-number-3-clyde-ecosystem/pages/5/ [accessed 10 December 2024].

McKay, Gabriel (2024) BAE Systems in Glasgow shut down in Israel arms protest. *Herald*, 1 May. Available at: www.heraldscotland.com/news/24287555.bae-systems-glasgow-shut-israel-arms-protest/ [accessed 10 December 2024].

Paton, Kirsteen (2014) *Gentrification: A Working-Class Perspective*. London: Routledge.

REHIS (The Royal Environmental Health Institute of Scotland) (2019) SEPA seal off Glasgow burn over dangerous levels of chromium. Available at: https://rehis.com/news/sepa-seal-off-glasgow-burn-over-dangerous-levels-of-chromium/ [accessed 11 December 2025].

Sandelands, Drew (2021) Glasgow riverside shopping outlet plans withdrawn but leisure resort could be built instead, *Glasgow Times*, 12 October. Available at: www.glasgowtimes.co.uk/news/18186700.major-retail-development-banks-clyde-move-forward/ [accessed 10 December 2024].

Sanderson, Danielle and Özogul, Sara (2022) Key investors and their strategies in the expansion of European student housing investment. *Journal of Property Research*, 39 (2), 170–96.

Smith, Neil (1987) Gentrification and the rent gap. *Annals of the Association of American Geographers*, 77 (3), 462–5.

Wilkinson, John L., Boxall, Alistair B. A, Kolpin, Dana W., Teta, Charles et al. (2022) Pharmaceutical pollution of the world's rivers. *Proceedings of the National Academy of Sciences*, 119 (8): article e2113947119.

7

Walls and bridges: or, what's so funny 'bout peace, love and understanding?

Daryl Martin

It is a bright Saturday morning in February as I trace my way around the city centre of Derry in Northern Ireland. I don't live in Derry now, and I have spent longer in other cities, but it is where I was born and still the place I would call home. This sunny morning I cannot shake the song '(What's so funny 'bout) Peace, Love, and Understanding', specifically the cover by Elvis Costello and the Attractions. It might be the urgency of the rhythm, or it might be the intensity of the vocals … but I find that I'm thinking about its animating themes as I walk. And so, I will take each of its keywords in turn to guide my reflections on Derry in the present, my recollections of the city as it was, and my hopes for its future. I will be reflecting on the intersections between history and biography, between politics and place, and – to subvert C. Wright Mills' (1959) formulation ever so slightly – between the very public troubles this city is known for and the private issues that still reverberate for me into the present, as I walk the streets as a kind of urban pedagogy (Back, 2017). Derry feels like a threshold space, or a 'thin place' (Ní Dochartaigh, 2021) which holds the ghosts of its past close to the surface of its present form: the very stones of the city seem to articulate the memory of those who have passed through its streets (Edensor, 2013).

Peace

I'm following the edge of the River Foyle, at the Peace Bridge, whose two pylons stretch into the crisp blue sky, and whose reflections shimmer beautifully in the water underneath. Technically, the Peace Bridge comprises two separate suspension bridges, curved in shape, identical in structure, opposite in orientation, and designed to overlap gracefully at a middle point on the river without merging into one. You get the best impression of it by walking towards it from either side of the river's cycle path; either approach offers the optical trick of its two arms seeming to edge towards each other, appearing to momentarily touch and intersect as one. Its architects designed the two halves of the bridge to meet in a kind of 'structural handshake', relishing the symbolism of connecting the west of Derry, the Cityside, to its east bank, the Waterside – and by extension its Catholic to its Protestant residents, its Nationalist to its Loyalist communities, and those with Irish cultural identities to those who identify as British (Abdelmonem and Selim, 2019: 163).

The Peace Bridge provides a visible path between the city's two major public squares – the gathering point outside the Cityside's Guildhall building and the refurbished plaza set among the buildings of Ebrington Barracks on the Waterside. Both spaces speak to Derry's colonial past, and Ireland's relationship with Britain more widely. Ebrington Barracks was home for almost two centuries to British army troops, and the Guildhall is a grand nineteenth-century building 'gifted' to the city by The Irish Society, a consortium of companies within the City of London Corporation established to fund the Plantation of Ulster (where Irish land was confiscated and given to British settlers). The bridge was funded by EU money, prior to the Brexit referendum that resulted in a sea border for trade between Northern Ireland and the rest of the UK. So, the bridge spans sites that are drenched in violent histories, difficult heritage and contested political questions in the present.

Addressing the legacy of communal violence in places such as Northern Ireland requires an acknowledgement of the deep social fissures that fed the conflict from different directions. Recognising the current difficulties faced by its residents is also important to any political process: the River Foyle is notorious as a popular place for people who want to end their lives (Capener, 2018). What is clear from Northern Ireland's recent history of power-sharing between Loyalist and Nationalist political parties is that peace processes are fragile and provisional in character, never settled entirely. The Peace Bridge certainly captures the essentially liminal state of Northern

Irish politics, as a country uneasily positioned within a wider state, and where the tensions of the past remain lodged within visions of the future (Coulter and Shirlow, 2023). Spanning the Foyle as an expression of the complexities of peacebuilding, a pair of bridges that never quite merge in the middle of a deep estuarial river seems an entirely appropriate metaphor.

Love

I cross the busy road that passes by the Guildhall and walk through Guildhall Square. I climb the steep Magazine Gate stairs to the City Walls. These walls were constructed in the early 1600s and funded by The Irish Society to protect the Planters' business interests (it is from this time that the city was legally named Londonderry). Whenever I walk along Derry's Walls, my instinct is to gaze upwards and out, following the long views to the city's rural hinterlands – County Londonderry to the east and County Donegal on the west and south. Donegal, although across the border in the South of Ireland, is less than five miles from where I am standing, and its hills frame Derry's west bank. When I was growing up, the proximity to the Republic meant that we had enough reception to get Irish radio and television channels from its broadcaster RTE in addition to the UK broadcasters. Each weekday evening, I could listen to John Peel on BBC Radio 1, as well as his equivalent Dave Fanning who promoted independent music in Ireland on RTE 2FM. Because of this, I knew Irish bands as well as the British and North American scenes championed by Peel. Geography can feel imprisoning in contested places, but Derry's closeness to the Irish border exposed me to more music than would have been the case on the UK's mainland (or elsewhere in Northern Ireland). I felt less a prisoner of geography than a prisoner of history when growing up in Derry, given the cultural drag of old conflicts.

I feel lucky to have grown up around the time of the first albums of The Undertones, whose faces beam down at me in the first of the murals I encounter on my walk around the walls. This mural recreates an image taken for the cover of the first Undertones album in Derry's Bull Park. Growing up in Derry in the 1980s, there was enormous pride in The Undertones, not just because the band members were all *from* the city, but also because of they were *of* the city:

they looked like they were from Derry, and Feargal Sharkey sang in a Derry accent. Most of their lyrics stressed the everyday concerns of teenagers, such as chocolate, girls and irritating family members. Did this mean that The Undertones, and the type of life they wrote about, were any less important than more politically pronounced artists, such as their contemporaries Stiff Little Fingers? I don't think so; as Martin McLoone has suggested, the levity of The Undertones meant that the ordinary subject matter of a song like 'Teenage Kicks' made for 'an extremely political statement in the highly charged, extraordinary atmosphere of Northern Ireland at the time' (McLoone, 2004: 37).

I continue walking, past the Apprentice Boys of Derry Memorial Hall. I am at the nearby plinth that is all that remains of the Walker's Pillar monument which was blown up by an IRA bomb in 1973 and was only known to me through archival photographs. I lift my eyes and try to trace in my mind's eye the sculptural form of George Walker, the governor of the city during its siege in 1689 by Jacobite and Irish armies. I drop my gaze to survey an incredible urban landscape, with the west bank of the city built into a hill which is framed by the high ground of Donegal's surrounding hills. Just outside the walls is Derry's Bogside, scene of the Bloody Sunday massacre in January 1972, where thirteen residents attending a peaceful protest were shot dead by British paratroopers, and eighteen more were wounded (one of whom died later that year from his injuries). The army commanders claimed that they were fired on by paramilitaries first, but later enquiries confirmed that half of the victims were teenagers, all were unarmed, and many were shot in their backs while fleeing for shelter (Campbell, 2022). The consequences of that day have been profound – most obviously for the families of the victims, but more widely for those living in the city. As Brian Conway (2003: 313; emphasis added) notes, collective traumas such as Bloody Sunday become 'the lens through which people think about themselves – their past, goals, and ideals – and *orient their behavior toward the other*'. That is how it was for me growing up in a city still raw from that day's pain – Bloody Sunday cast a permanent shadow on my relationship with the city, and still does. The memory of the day is palpable from this vantage point – I wasn't even born then, but the television cameras were there, I grew up with the accounts of those who were present, and I know the streets where those lives were lost. I move along and stop at the Roaring Meg cannon that was originally placed by Planters on the walls during the 1689 siege, observing how its line of sight remains trained on the working-class communities of the Bogside. Bewildered, I am struck by the (in)sensitivities of how we deal with heritage in Northern Ireland.

I lift my eye to the horizon again, tracing a path to the place where the journalist Lyra McKee lost her life when she was struck by a stray bullet at a riot in the Creggan estate in April 2019. I remember being in Derry that night and feeling that the public anger at her death could be a turning point in resetting Northern Ireland's political deadlock (the power-sharing government was paused at that time). McKee had been a key voice in putting the issue of high suicide rates in Northern Ireland since the Peace Process of the late 1990s on the agenda. She concentrated her reporting on the deaths of those born just before the decommissioning of paramilitary weapons – 'ceasefire babies' – by highlighting the underlying factors of high unemployment, poverty and poor mental health among young people in the North (McKee, 2020). Her partner, Sara Canning, showed remarkable sensitivity in her reflections on that night, making the point that the young people rioting were of a generation who had been locked out of economic opportunity and the peace dividend that was promised to Northern Ireland in the aftermath of conflict (Canning, 2019); they were the same people, in search of a better life, for whom Lyra advocated in her writing.

All here in front of me in this landscape, viewed from the walls – the terrible legacy of the Northern Irish Troubles, the killings of young people at different points in time over the last five decades. It strikes me that, although by myself, I've not exactly been alone; Darran Anderson (2020) has observed that there are many different versions of Derry, to be glimpsed awry through our perspectives on its current incarnation, and all with their own ghosts. It is a 'thin place' of the kind reflected on by Kerri Ní Dochartaigh, a writer from the city who has also explored the hold that it has over her imaginatively and emotionally. Hers is a haunting account of Derry in which she defines place as a 'woven thread that never really loosens itself once we have been there and been held by it' (Ní Dochartaigh, 2021: 33). Her *Thin places* offers an emotionally devastating account of the landscapes she knows best, that cannot by themselves resolve the traumas of her own experience of the Troubles; nonetheless, this does not lessen her love of the city.

Scanning the city in front of me reminds me of John Wylie's writings about rethinking the relationship between landscapes and culturally engrained ideas of identity. Wylie (2009) argues that we tend to think about the relationship between people and place as anchored in ideas of immersion and connection. Instead, he argues for an understanding of landscape that is more spectral, especially those landscapes that are most cherished. Wylie goes further to suggest that landscapes characterised by absence (rather than immersion) and distance (rather than connection) might be thought of as 'geographies of love'. Moreover, he writes that it is 'within the tension of this openness and distance, perhaps, that landscape, absence and love are entangled' (Wylie, 2009: 275). The act of landscape-remembering, Wylie argues, articulates a love of place, rather than a mere sentimental attachment; looking out over the cityscape of Derry's west bank, a place I do not live in, have not lived in for more than thirty years, and yet know intimately, I feel the same.

Understanding

In his writings about geographies of love, John Wylie (2009: 284, 287) argues that acts of landscape-remembering involve a 'certain exposure to the other'; in fact, he goes further and considers landscape as 'sort of blindness'. As I continue walking the walls, I realise just how many blind spots the city holds for me, despite knowing it so well. Growing up on Bishop Street, just outside the City Walls, the most obvious blind spot is The Fountain, a Loyalist estate which runs parallel to where I lived and went to school. There is a wall separating The Fountain from Bishop Street: from Bishop's Gate, I can see how a series of barriers erected in the 1990s, including a gate that is locked in early evening to control access to the estate, dissect the city. Together, these barriers operate as a 'Peace Wall' protecting The Fountain's community inside from the much larger neighbouring Nationalist community.

Interviews with many residents of The Fountain stress the fear they experience living in the estate (Abdelmonem and Selim, 2019). Such fear is understandable, given the massive depopulation they have lived through in the late twentieth century: over 80 per cent of its Protestant population left Derry's Cityside from the beginning of the Troubles, with many people from The Fountain moving to housing in the city's Waterside, and not returning with the coming of peace. In their research, Gamal Abdelmonem and colleagues found a lack of basic amenities to support residents, which means they have little choice but to visit shops and food outlets in Nationalist areas; as one resident noted, 'kids here are hemmed in. They can't even use the shopping centre unless there's a group of them together. They can't use the corner shop unless there's a group' (Abdelmonem and Selim, 2019: 157). Above, I noted that I felt less constricted by geography than history when I grew up here, but it is obvious there are prisoners of geography in this city; indeed, my sense of (relative) ease in moving around the place was paid for in the ways in which others, living very close by, were confined by their environment.

I come down from the City Walls and wander around The Fountain. I am drawn towards a mural which offers a simple message to passers-by: 'LONDONDERRY WEST BANK LOYALISTS. STILL UNDER SIEGE. NO SURRENDER.' On the morning that I stand in front of it, the letters LONDON have been defaced by black spray paint. Residents have freely admitted to researchers a 'siege mentality' (Abdelmonem and Selim, 2019: 154). This phrase is in part a reference to the famous Siege of Derry in 1689, when Protestant residents living within the City Walls, and loyal to King William of Orange, barricaded themselves inside and refused to surrender the town to the Irish and Jacobite army led by King James II. Despite much suffering within the walls, caused by the Jacobite's attempts to starve the residents there into submission over 105 days, the city was held for the Protestant King, and to this day these events are the source of annual marches every August in the city. The siege has had a vast influence on narratives of Loyalism outside the city and across Northern Ireland more generally – especially the widespread adoption of 'No Surrender' as a mantra by generations of politicians representing Protestant communities. As I stand in front of the mural, I hear in my head the voice of another ghost, Ian Paisley, as he hammered home that phrase at many different marches in the 1980s and 1990s to contest various initiatives of co-operation between UK and Irish governments. In a contrast to The Undertones, Paisley's speeches formed a different kind of soundtrack to my youth.

The sheer weight of history within the mythic narrative of Loyalism has, for some, created concern about how Unionism defines itself now; Geoffrey Bell (2022) has noted the lack of understanding displayed by British politicians to the Unionist parties of Northern Ireland as a long-term problem for their constituents, and a threat to Northern Ireland's union with the rest of the United Kingdom. Walking around The Fountain, what strikes me most is the similarity between the housing here and for Nationalist communities elsewhere in the city; these are working-class places, regardless of the religious or political allegiances of their residents. I can't help but remember accounts of civil rights marches in the city in the 1960s where placards called for the organisation of working people along lines of 'class, not creed' (Bell, 2022: 121–3): the inability of working-class people across the city, and Northern Ireland more generally, to collaborate across ethnonationalist lines in their demands for better education, housing and jobs in the pre-Troubles period was one of the great tragedies of the last half century.

As I return up the steps to carry on my walk around the City Walls, I reflect again on the lack of easy movement in the city for residents of The Fountain, and the absence of places where people from all communities might mix. The newest building I see in my detour around the estate is the New Gate Arts and Community Centre. I'm writing this on the same evening as it hosts a tribute concert to Rory Gallagher, a musician from the South of Ireland defined by his love of the blues, but also known for his Catholic faith. Could spaces like these recalibrate our sense of place itself away from difficult heritage as the default, and something more generous and welcoming instead?

What's so funny…?

Throughout this walk, I have been thinking about the idea that remembering a landscape can act as an assertion of love for, and of, a place. I have cited the writings of John Wylie on this, and his arguments that we conceive of landscape in terms of a certain dislocation, rather than easy communion with, or communication of, that place. Wylie (2009: 280) asks his readers 'to let go, for now, of the urge to search for hidden depths, and even the axiomatic need to provide an "in-depth" account' of the landscapes we love. I think this helps to explain some of the ways in which I prefer to engage with narratives about Northern Ireland myself – all too often, I will turn off the radio when I hear politicians broadcasting their visions for the place, whereas I prefer to channel sounds and stories that are more generous in tone. We craft different types of memories, especially when thinking those that are shared or collective: some are rooted in first-hand accounts of lived experiences, whereas others are derived from what has been called 'technologies of memory' – the popular culture that informs our understanding of the past (Conway, 2003). This is, in part at least, where the power of a song like 'Teenage Kicks' resides for me. This is not a song about the Troubles, but in its focus on the everyday, it is not exactly apolitical. Rather, the articulation of everyday experience brings to light the remarkable qualities of mundane aspects of our social worlds (Back, 2020). There is also a parallel here with Les Back's (2017) reflections on how music can be a channel through which to acknowledge difficult histories and fine-tune our memories of lost lives in the urban cultures of the present. A song like 'Teenage Kicks' retraces memories of how I felt growing up in Derry during the 1970s and 1980s and articulates the 'value of returning' to politically charged traces of the past, on foot and immersed in the city – if only for a short time (Back, 2017: 35).

I'm still thinking about my own experience of the city – of its sounds, and of the 'small p' politics of dealing with conflict in graceful ways – as I come face to face with the celebrated mural of the *Derry Girls* cast on the gable end of a pub abutting the City Walls. What's so funny about peace, love and understanding? The *Derry Girls* writer Lisa McGee and the show's young actors seem to have hit on an answer, as the show demonstrates perfectly the benefits of levity in the face of collective trauma. Like those Derry boys in The Undertones a generation before them, *Derry Girls* presents a sympathetic portrait of the importance of ordinary experiences – friendship, family and fun – in the middle of extraordinary times and violent environments. The show offers stories about a political and physical landscape too often defined in media accounts by hard men and heavy weapons. To see the gender dynamics of Northern Irish popular culture flipped in this way is part of the 'small p' politics of the everyday. And, as in the scene in which the characters are invited to find similarities rather than differences between Catholics and Protestants (Channel 4, 2019), the scripts make it clear how important it is to keep things light when narrating landscapes of love and loss.

Acknowledgements

I would like to thank Les Back for sharing his work to help in the development of this essay, Dave Beer for his interest in the piece, and Nick Gane for his astute comments to sharpen its arguments.

References

Abdelmonem, Mohamed Gamal and Selim, Gehan (2019) *Architecture, Space and Memory of Resurrection in Northern Ireland: Shareness in a Divided Nation*. London: Routledge.

Anderson, Darran (2020) *Inventory: A Family Portrait of Derry's Troubled Past*. London: Vintage.

Back, Les (2017) Marchers and steppers: Memory, city life and walking. In Charlotte Bates and Alex Rhys-Taylor (eds) *Walking Through Social Research*. London: Routledge.

Back, Les (2020) Foreword: Making the mundane remarkable. In Helen Holmes and Sarah Marie Hall (eds) *Mundane Methods: Innovative Ways to Research the Everyday*. Manchester: Manchester University Press.

Bell, Geoffrey (2022) *The Twilight of Unionism: Ulster and the Future of Northern Ireland*. London: Verso.

Campbell, Julieann (2022) *On Bloody Sunday: A New History of the Day and its Aftermath – by the People who were There*. London: Monoray.

Canning, Sara (2019) Lyra McKee remembered by Sara Canning, *Guardian*, 15 December. Available at: www.theguardian.com/news/2019/dec/15/lyra-mckee-remembered-by-sara-canning [accessed 1 December 2024].

Capener, David (2018) Derry has a high suicide rate – but could redesigning the river help the city?, *Guardian*, 10 September. Available at: www.theguardian.com/cities/2018/sep/10/derry-has-a-high-suicide-rate-but-could-redesigning-the-river-help-the-city [accessed 1 December 2024].

Channel 4 (2019) The difference between Catholics and Protestants. *YouTube*, 13 March. Available at: www.youtube.com/watch?v=0j0OF-TlyAY [accessed 1 December 2024].

Conway, Brian (2003) Active remembering, selective forgetting, and collective identity: The case of Bloody Sunday. *Identity: An International Journal of Theory and Research*, 3 (4), 305–23.

Coulter, Colin and Shirlow, Peter (2023) Northern Ireland 25 years after the Good Friday Agreement. *Space and Polity*, 27 (1), 1–16.
Edensor, Tim (2013) Vital urban materiality and its multiple absences: The building stone of central Manchester. *Cultural Geographies*, 20 (4), 447–65.
McKee, Lyra (2020) *Lost, Found, Remembered*. London: Faber & Faber.
McLoone, Martin (2004) Punk music in Northern Ireland: The political power of 'what might have been'. *Irish Studies Review*, 12 (1), 29–38.
Ní Dochartaigh, Kerri (2021) *Thin Places*. Edinburgh: Canongate.
Wright Mills, Charles (1959) *The Sociological Imagination*. Oxford: Oxford University Press.
Wylie, John (2009) Landscape, absence and the geographies of love. *Transactions of the Institute of British Geographers*, 34 (3), 275–89.

8

Traces of industrial York

Nicholas Gane

While today the city of York in the north of England is a popular tourist destination known for the Minster, the Shambles, medieval buildings, and quaint tea shops, it was once an industrial city that employed thousands of workers in the North Eastern Railway carriage works and in factories that produced cocoa, chocolate and confectionery (see Rowntree, 1941: 9). With industrialism, however, came not only work and employment but also poverty. At the outset of the twentieth century, Seebohm Rowntree observed, in his classic study of poverty and town life, that about 12 per cent of 'working-class people in the city were living in comfortable and sanitary houses', while the 'housing conditions of many of the remaining 88 per cent left much to be desired' (Rowntree, 1941: 276). Rowntree revisited his initial survey with a volume on *Poverty and progress*, published in 1941, that found improvement in living conditions following the clearance of slum housing. And in 1951, in a final study of York, he made a case for the welfare state as a means for eliminating primary poverty. While these studies were once central to the analysis of social class within the discipline of sociology, they have now been largely forgotten. Together, however, they reveal a history of York that visitors do not normally see; a history that has become more important in the present day following the austerity politics of the post-financial crisis period, and, currently, a cost-of-living crisis that is 'disproportionately affecting people who are already on the breadline'.[1] Today, it is possible to revisit this history of poverty and class by walking along a former railway line that connects the Rowntree of the industrial past, embodied in its famous chocolate and confectionery factory, to the Rowntree of the present, in the form of Derwenthorpe; a mixed-tenure housing development through which philanthropy continues to be directed towards the home.

Starting at Haxby Road, the walk heads eastwards from the Rowntree factory, which has been disused for some time but at its height employed 6,000 workers. Built in the 1890s, it is hard not to be seduced by the fading beauty of this huge brick and glass building, which today is being converted into flats under the branding of 'The Cocoa Works'. The factory is a symbol of an industrial age that, in York and much of the UK, has now long gone. In its time, Rowntree was a progressive company: it introduced a retirement pension and holiday pay before statutory state schemes, a fund for widows, and established a charitable trust that benefitted more than just its workers. To avoid romanticising the past life of this structure, however, it is important to remember that progressive politics can be based on the exploitation of others. This factory was a site through which profits were extracted from the physical labour of people on an extraordinary scale. When Nestlé bought Rowntree in 1988, it was the fourth-largest chocolate manufacturer in the world and was valued at £2.55bn. This extraordinary accumulation of wealth was only possible through a colonial past, as the Rowntree family purchased plantations in Jamaica and Dominica in the late-1890s to supply the factory with sugar and cocoa. In 2021, the Rowntree's Board of Trustees issued a response to Catherine Hall's accusation that we are guilty of 'turning a blind eye' to the colonial histories of industrial wealth and power, and that this is 'a condition of "knowing and not knowing"; acknowledging the presence of empire but at the same time not confronting its meanings, especially its unsavoury ones' (Rowntree Society, 2021). The findings of the Rowntree investigation are shocking:

> the Rowntree story … includes histories and legacies of racial exploitation. Our initial findings show that the company was an active agent in colonial economies in Africa and the Caribbean across the nineteenth and twentieth centuries. They indicate that the Rowntree businesses benefited from unfree labour systems which caused harm to people of colour.

It is extraordinary to look at this building today and to think of the 'imperial chains' of power and exploitation that converged within it (Robertson, 2009), and which lay hidden within the seemingly benign commodities – sweets and chocolates – that it produced.

Walking away from the factory, the path follows a former railway line that used to bring freight to and from this site, as well as workers from South Yorkshire. The factory station, Rowntree's Halt, closed in 1988, and the platform has long since been removed. The only trace of the previous life of this path is a concrete-lined alley through which thousands of workers would have passed year after year on their way to the shop floor – the majority of them women. Today, little trace of this labour remains visible, but stately Victorian clocks have been left standing at the front and rear of the factory. In a brilliant essay entitled 'Time, Work-Discipline and Industrial Capitalism', E. P. Thompson (1967) describes time as an instrument of power in industrial factory settings. In a key passage of this essay, he refers to Werner Sombart's image of the 'Clockmaker', and observes 'If modern economic rationalism is like the mechanism of a clock, someone must be there to wind it up.' For Thompson, this 'time-discipline' was made possible by 'fines; bells and clocks; money incentives', and by 'preachings and schoolings' that insisted on punctuality that expressed 'respect for one's fellow workers'. These clocks remain on the public boundaries of the factory and have been maintained to keep time in the present, thereby leaving their moral histories intact.

Time might not still be discipline in the way documented by Thompson, but new technologies of measurement still contain moral imperatives that are more sophisticated than those embedded within the humble clock. My labour of walking this path is documented by a Fitbit, which rewards me for walking 10,000 steps a day. I have been seriously ill, and this device acts as a bridge between home and hospital as it monitors not only steps, but also resting heartbeat, active minutes, and sleep, among other things. The factory is located near to York Hospital, which was built in 1977, and today many NHS workers commute along this path on bikes and on foot. Their presence is a reminder of my illness, and I wonder what these workers will find when they arrive at their destinations. Seeing them outside of their occupational settings, as people with lives of their own, makes me feel more indebted and thankful for their care. Writing in 1951, in the wake of the National Health Service Act of 1946, Rowntree and Lavers (1951: 44) reflect that 'a great many of its beneficiaries would previously have gone without spectacles and without medical and dental help'. As I watch the NHS workers pass me on this path, I try to imagine the industrial York that Rowntree saw prior to the Second World War, in which those living 'life below the minimum' (see Rowntree, 1941: 82–4) would have had little, if any, medical care.

The path crosses Huntington Road over a former railway bridge and runs along the backs of houses and yards. On one side, there is a community garden for those living in back-to-back terraces who have little outside space of their own, and on the other, there is a 'fairy trail' that leads into central York along the banks of the River Foss. In between the old railway line and the fairy trail there is a fenced-off woodland with installations that encourage contemplation. There is a hand-built arbour with a carved inscription: 'Time to reflect'. And next to it, on a plaque mounted on a huge, rotting tree a quote from Einstein: 'Look deep into nature and you will understand everything better.' Along the length of this path, blue piping emerges at intervals, and takes the form of a public sculpture that mirrors the complex structures of the pipework that previously wove through the Rowntree's factory. The path approaches the centre of York through a deep, brick-lined cutting. Someone has planted roses alongside the bricks: an act of public kindness for walkers and cyclists to enjoy.

At James Street, the path opens onto a retail park: a new site for the convergence of global labour and supply chains. The sensory experience of walking changes, as the suburban landscape of gardens, yards and flowers gives way to the noise and smell of traffic. At this point, the path joins another former railway line, previously the privately owned Derwent Valley Light Railway that once brought freight into York. The Foss Islands Branch, along which the walk continues, was closed in 1989, and its holding company has since become Derwent London, a major property development and investment company that now has a commercial real estate portfolio valued at nearly £5bn. Foss Islands was, until the 1980s, the industrial heart of York, and was dominated by a power station, gasworks, goods yards and, where the rivers Foss and Ouse meet, one of the largest glass factories in the country. Today, there are few remaining traces of this industrial history except for a massive brick chimney built in 1899 as part of the York 'destructor': a power station that produced electricity by burning household rubbish. This chimney now stands next to a supermarket as an incongruous but largely unnoticed monument to an industrial and less environmental past.

Touching, briefly, on a busy road, James Street, the path weaves behind a council-run travellers' site built where York Layerthorpe train station used to stand. This station was closed to passengers in 1926 and to freight in the 1980s. James Street is one of two travellers' sites in York to be built upon former railway land. The duty for councils to provide accommodation for gypsies and travellers came from the 1968 Caravan Sites Act, key features of which were subsequently repealed by the 1994 Criminal Justice and Public Order Act. Judith Okely observes that such sites have tended to be built on 'marginal land' that is 'unsuitable for other uses' (Okely and Houtman, 2011), and this is, indeed, the case at James Street, as this site is prone to flooding. On one walk along this path, I witnessed flooding so severe that residents were forced to stand on the roofs of their homes while trying to remove their belongings as best they could.[2] It was impossible to help as the water was so high that the site could only be accessed by dinghy.

Beyond James Street, the path opens onto St Nicholas Fields, a nature reserve rewilded from a former rubbish tip. The noise from the retail park opposite recedes, and one is greeted by thick layers of vegetation, a brook, and a rich canopy of birdsong. In St Nicholas Fields, one can find refuge in an urban countryside, with bushes and trees obscuring any view into the distance. The path weaves towards Tang Hall, a social housing estate built from the 1920s onwards following the clearance of slums in Hungate and Walmgate nearer to the centre of the city. In 1941, Seebohm Rowntree wrote in *Poverty and progress* that prior to 1919, only thirty houses had been built by York City Council, but between 1920 and 1939 it built nearly 5,000, more than half of those built in the city through that period (see Rowntree, 1941: 224). Tang Hall and Clifton, beyond the hospital at the other end of this path, are two of the largest sites of this interwar social housing in York. The path weaves behind the gardens of houses built in Tang Hall, a neighbourhood designed upon a grid plan. Rowntree (1941: 234) vehemently opposed this design for 'working-class houses', and dismissed it as 'monotonous and wasteful'. Instead, he called for a layout that was 'more interesting and attractive', and included loops and cul-de-sacs that would generate a stronger sense of belonging and community. Even if the council houses built in this area of York were not 'in the front rank', Rowntree (1941: 234) concedes that they were 'immensely in advance of anything that proceeded them', not least because they had gardens that 'in summer are ablaze with colour'. The same is still the case today, although it is hard to see into the gardens of these houses as they are enclosed by high fences and obscured by a dense funnel of greenery that runs either side of the path. This makes for a rich sensory experience as there is more birdsong, and in the spring and summer the scent of wildflowers and the sight of butterflies dancing playfully on the wind.

In *Poverty and progress*, however, Rowntree (1941: 233) issues a cautionary warning: that 'houses last for generations' and are likely to outlive the layout and design of even 'the best modern practice'. In his final study of York, he asserted the importance of the welfare state for ensuring quality of life above and below the poverty line, or what he otherwise calls 'the minimum' (see Rowntree and Lavers, 1951: 67). Today, cuts to the welfare state coupled with an ageing and diminished council housing stock have led to pockets of deprivation in Tang Hall that are invisible to most visitors to York. The path arrives at Tang Hall by passing under two bridges. Before the first there is a community centre with volunteers working in vegetable gardens at the rear. This community centre is a striking illustration of the real-life effects of austerity politics and welfare reform (see Garthwaite, 2016). It has a canteen able to provide a family with a free meal, a cafe that reallocates food waste and a food cooperative or circle that offers cooking classes. A key section of Seebohm Rowntree's initial study of poverty in York addresses food poverty, and considers the function, quantity, kind and price of food, as well as the cost of cooking (see Rowntree, 1901: 103–6). The question posed at the outset of this study is more relevant than ever: 'How many families are … sunk in a poverty so acute that its members suffer … from a chronic insufficiency of food and clothing?' (Rowntree, 1901: vi). It is from the top of the bridge next to this community centre at Melrosegate that, in 1952, L. S. Lowry painted the then industrial landscape at Foss Islands, a visual depiction of working lives, smog, poverty and sociality in this part of York that is all but absent from other artistic representations of the city.

On passing the community centre and arriving at the second bridge, there is more blue pipework. This bridge, at Tang Hall Lane, is less noteworthy historically, but carries human traces of a different kind: graffiti. There are names and tags, but one isolated spray-painted line stands out: 'I miss you so much I could kiss your voice.' These words are new to me, and I have no idea if they come from popular culture, or, rather, are a deep expression of grief from the writer. I wonder about the experience and fate of its author. As I walk onwards, these words become ever more profound as I realise that my memory of those who have died whom I have loved is indeed a memory of their voice. This is the human quality through which I remember them: words spoken with a unique tone, quality and emphasis; never to be duplicated by anyone else; singular, unrepeatable and irreplaceable.

I continue along the path and reflect on my ongoing recovery from serious illness. The graffiti written on the second bridge is still in my mind, and I wonder whether everyone, especially in the move towards older age, is in some sort of recovery: from a life event of one's own or of a loved one? I try not to dwell on this thought as the path moves towards Osbaldwick and Heworth. Many students use this section of the path to access the university, and they stream past at speed on bikes and on foot, trying desperately to get to their lectures and classes on time. In so doing, they miss a mundane monument to the past at Fifth Avenue: an exit from the path that used to lead to a library. This library has recently been bulldozed, and, for the time being, only its concrete base remains as a trace.

I have learned from my experience of illness that the library is a place of refuge and one of the few remaining public spaces or 'community buildings' (Robinson and Sheldon, 2018) that offers shelter. There are churches, but these tend to be locked outside of service times, and in close proximity to this walk there are parks, holmes and strays,[3] but these places are weather-dependent, especially for bodies and minds that are frail. The library is a place of shelter and, indeed, the local council lists them first on its website as 'warm places' that one can go to 'free of charge, to spend time to keep warm if you're struggling to heat your home'.[4] The library is a rare communal space that offers sanctuary from the world outside for those struggling to keep above what Rowntree called 'the minimum'. It is also a place of education, sociality and connectivity, with spaces to meet, talk and access newspapers, magazines and the web. The library was a key site of interest for Rowntree in *Poverty and progress*, and he notes that while, historically, there were libraries connected to churches and working-men's clubs they were relatively underused, whereas 'the public library' was 'used by nearly a fourth (22 per cent) of York citizens (and of course a much greater percentage of those of reading age)' (Rowntree, 1941: 377). In an extraordinary survey, he observes that in 1938 the lending library in York had a stock of 2,719 sociology and 702 philosophy books, that together were issued nearly 12,000 times (see Rowntree, 1941: 380). Looking at the trace of the former library at Fifth Avenue, I wonder: what happened to these volumes, to the knowledge they contained, and to the people that read them?

The path leads, finally, to Derwenthorpe, a Joseph Rowntree Housing Trust development built in phases from 2013 onwards and named after the old railway line that began at Foss Islands. The plan for Derwenthorpe is far removed from the linear 'grid-iron' layout of Tang Hall that Rowntree (1941: 233–4) railed against, as instead it sought to create 'high-quality public space, with careful attention given to the design of streets, play areas, landscape and parking courtyards to ensure that all spaces were subject to overlooking and that play areas and recreational facilities were close to homes'.[5] This is a plan for a new garden village, a community without physical or symbolic barriers that discourage you from entering. And on arriving at Derwenthorpe, there is indeed an openness that is inviting, as private space, in the form of the home, is interwoven with public spaces – playgrounds, meadows, lakes, communal seating areas – that are designed for people to pause, reflect and meet without discouragement.

At the end of the path, there is one final installation of public sculpture constructed out of blue piping. Little is known about this piping and its significance, except that it was designed by the sculptor George Cutts as part of an installation that was commissioned in the 1980s when the railway tracks were lifted, and the line repurposed for walking and cycling. This sculpture is an allusion to the pipeline that would once have woven through the Rowntree's factory, but today leads from one end of this path, the factory, to the other,

Derwenthorpe. This walk across York reveals a colonial past built on the acquisition of land, labour and commodities that resurfaces in the present through the continued ambition to alleviate poverty at 'home'.

This walk across York is an act of discovery that calls for us to know more about the traces of the past and their bearing not only on the present but also on possible futures: from the colonial history of industrialism, through to the provision of social housing during the 1930s, the expansion of the welfare state after the Second World War, and its retraction following the 2008 financial crisis. Each site encountered on this walk demands sociological investigation through close historical analysis: from the factory and hospital at one end of the walk, to the travellers' site, the retail park, the 'destructor' that once supplied energy to York, the community centre, the library, and housing that is both public and private in form. These sites return us to the studies of poverty, class and the welfare state pioneered by Seebohm Rowntree, but at the same time invite us to move beyond them by reconsidering traces of history that can be revealed, encountered and reflected upon through the act of walking.

Walking is important because it is an act of physical labour, and perhaps even a method, for revealing such connections between past and present. Walking can be a time of companionship with others: a form of social support and care, and a time of conversation, friendship and love. But it can also be a solitary and silent activity – a time of attentiveness to the history of our surroundings that, in day-to-day life, for the most part go unnoticed. Walking is a slow time that makes reflection and inspiration possible. This connection between walking and inspiration is no accident, as through walking a recursive loop is set into motion between sensory experience and a conceptual mindset, and, with this, things become visible and audible in a different way. Walking is a physical activity and a sensory experience that makes possible a different kind of attentiveness, one that prompts curiosity and reflection about places and people, both in the past and in the present. Such curiosity, born not just from a pre-existing conceptual framework or mindset, but out of contact with the raw empirical and sensory experience of our surroundings (see Gane, 2009, 2011) is central to what C. Wright Mills (1959) famously called a sociological imagination.

Acknowledgements

I would like to thank my walking companions, Antonia, Arlo, Ava, Daryl, and Dave, for helping me get back on my feet, and Les Back, Roger Burrows, Lynne Pettinger and John Solomos for their encouragement from afar.

Notes

1 www.crisis.org.uk/ending-homelessness/the-cost-of-living-crisis/
2 www.yorkpress.co.uk/news/14443572.york-travellers-site-reopens-almost-4-months-after-devastating-flood/
3 Holmes are strips of land along streams and rivers that cannot be built upon because they flood periodically. Strays are areas of public or common land that date back to the time before the enclosures, where local people were able to graze their animals.
4 www.york.gov.uk/WarmPlaces
5 www.studiopartington.co.uk/derwenthorpe-masterplan

References

Gane, Nicholas (2009) Concepts and the 'new' empiricism. *European Journal of Social Theory*, 12 (1), 83–97.

Gane, Nicholas (2011) Measure, value and the current crises of sociology. *Sociological Review*, 59 (s2), 151–73.

Garthwaite, Kayleigh (2016) *Hunger Pains*. Bristol: Policy Press.

Okely, Judith and Houtman, Gustaaf (2011) The Dale Farm eviction. *Anthropology Today*, 27 (6), 24–7.

Robertson, Emma (2009) *Chocolate, Women and Empire:. A Social and cultural History*. Manchester: Manchester University Press.

Robinson, Katherine and Sheldon, Ruth (2018) Witnessing the loss in the everyday: Community buildings in austerity Britain. *Sociological Review*, 67 (1), 111–25.

Rowntree, Benjamin Seebohm (1901) *Poverty: A Study of Town Life*. London: Macmillan.

Rowntree, Benjamin Seebohm (1941) *Poverty and Progress*. London: Longmans.

Rowntree, Benjamin Seebohm and Lavers, George (1951) *Poverty and the Welfare State*. London: Longmans.

Rowntree Society (2021) *Statement on Rowntree Colonial Histories*. Available at: www.rowntreesociety.org.uk/currentprojects/rowntree-colonial-histories-and-legacies/statement-on-rowntree-colonial-histories/ [accessed 3 February 2025].

Thompson, E. P. (1967) Time, work-discipline, and industrial capitalism. *Past and Present*, 38 (1), 56–97.

Wright Mills, Charles (1959) *The Sociological Imagination*. Oxford: Oxford University Press.

9

A walk along Chester's canal: peeling back the past to rediscover colonial era Cheshire

Julia Bennett

Chester
January, 1775

My Dear George,[1]
At last some good news regarding the canal! We had a 'Grand Opening' Saturday last. It gave me great pride to be a part of the committee that had directed the construction of the canal as far as Christleton (you will remember passing through the village on the coach from London). We had commissioned the building of a flat barge to take us through the five locks from Northgate to the quarry at Christleton and back. It was tremendously exciting to be on board as people lined the banks to watch us pass. We celebrated with good Portuguese wine and there was a band on board playing music. Mrs Folliott accompanied me, as did the wives of the other committee members. They all seemed to use the occasion to have a new outfit made. I have enclosed a cutting from the *Courant* describing the celebration.

The digging of the cut continues apace, as the weather permits, and we hope to reach Nantwich by the summer.

I sincerely hope the situation in New York is stable. Please give my regards to Mrs Folliott.
Your brother,
James Folliott

* * *

The canal celebrated here is the Chester Canal, begun by Act of Parliament in 1772 and now a part of the Shropshire Union Canal. Chester's position in England's north-west on the River Dee, once the border with Wales, made it an important Roman port. However, by the start of the eighteenth century the Dee was silting up. The building of the canal was pursued by local merchants who were afraid of losing trade to Liverpool, on the other side of the Wirral peninsula. The original canal – due to problems with its construction and a lack of money – went only as far as Nantwich, a market town near the Shropshire border. This walk is along the original twenty-mile stretch, taking place in the present (2024) and, through some imaginary time-travel, over the course of the canal's early history.

Fictional or not, stories are a traditional way of presenting social research, indeed essential to its understanding (Richardson, 1997). Using historical data, as I do here, adds to the verisimilitude of the fiction, creating a story which 'tells the experience of a sociologically constructed category of people in the context of larger sociocultural and historical forces' (Richardson, 1997: 14). By assimilating elements from different data sources, I have tried to create a story of the canal that both humanises it and envelops it within the everyday life of the 1770s.

As a means of transport, often referred to as a 'navigation', the canal connects not only the places along its route but also, by joining to the port at Chester and through its financing, to the wider world, both in the past and the present. There are myriad continuing connections between the British countryside and colonialism, as Corinne Fowler (2024) has depicted through her country walks. She shows how much of rural Britain has been shaped by the colonial world, particularly through trade and economic activity. Any walk in Britain is likely to 'bring in half the world and a considerable amount of British imperialist history' (Massey, 1994: 154), and this route is no exception. All landscapes are palimpsests of past and present (Tilley, 2006: 7–8), which I have tried to illustrate here. Tracing the course of the canal across the Cheshire countryside draws together eighteenth-century merchants, international trade, the complex interrelations of the landed aristocracy, early industrialisation: in short, the raw materials of colonialism. A realistic understanding of how the current landscape evolved needs to include these global influences.

The walk begins beneath Chester city centre next to the grey-green waters of the canal below Northgate Street. A few disembodied voices drift down from the streets high above. The towpath is narrow; the Roman walls tower over this sunken section of the canal beneath the bustling city. This part, deep below the city walls, was formerly a trench dug by the Romans about 1,900 years ago, then filled with rubbish before being dug out again to allow the water to flow past. As horses pulled the boats round the bend the ropes dragged across the soft, red sandstone, the bedrock of the city, leaving their marks. I run my fingers along the smooth, cool grooves. The past is tangible here. On the opposite side of the canal bricked-up archways tell of cargoes of coal and iron unloaded straight into the cellars of merchants on Canal Street.

* * *

Canal Street, Chester
March, 1881

A colourful red barge is moored next to the arches of the cellars on Canal Street. A man and young boy, both blackened with coal dust, are hoisting bags of coal from the barge into the cellar.

'Where's this lot heading Mr Coppack?' calls the bargee.
'There's a ship leaving for Jamaica, it'll be good ballast', Coppack replies.
'Ain't it hot for coal fires in Jamaica?' asks the lad.
'It's to run the sugar mills, so you can have sugar in your tea.'

John Coppack, son of a widowed shoemaker, had attended the Bluecoat School, just along the canal. Thanks to this education and experience as an accountant with the Canal Company, he could now make a good living as a coal merchant.

* * *

Rather than the dusty smell of bags of coal, the disinfectant-like smell of Himalayan balsam assaults me. Apparently, some people find the smell pleasant; the plant itself is classified as an 'invasive alien species' due to its tendency to overwhelm native plants. Buddleia, too, grow abundantly, another vigorous plant introduced by the Victorians that the builders of the canal would probably not have known. The roots push apart the bricks in the walls of the canal, as the canal itself pushes its way through the farmlands of Cheshire.

Walking from Northgate avoids the crowded city centre, but past Cow Lane Bridge I'm dodging cycles and people as the towpath becomes a route into the city from the east and south. There are restaurants and pubs along this section which are particularly busy on Chester's historic and popular Race Days still held at the Roodee race course. The horse races have long been social and networking occasions as well as sporting ones.

* * *

Journal of Jane Harrison Folliott
New York
May, 1772

George received another letter from his brother today, discussing the progress of the new Navigation, the bill for which passed in March, I believe. Apparently, James met with Lord Kilmorey at Nantwich Races and persuaded him to invest £500 – a considerable sum. There was also some news about Kilmorey's son Robert having married Miss Frances Cotton. Of course, James did not mention who the guests were or what they wore! Miss Cotton's wealth, I know, comes from her mother's Stapleton family's estates in St Kitts and Nevis as her grandfather, I think it would have been, squandered the Cotton fortune. They have been fortunate to have made good marriages into the Anglo-Irish aristocracy.

* * *

Marriages into the gentry and aristocracy gave colonial estate owners a route into British upper-class society and boosted the finances of the aristocracy (Hall, 2020).

As a major transport route, the canal attracted industry to the outskirts of the city. A mill building is now office space. I scan the sky for peregrine falcons. The fifty-one-metre-high shot tower built in 1799 provides an ideal nesting spot.

Passing through Hoole Lock, the canal moves out past what is now suburban Chester. A small row of Victorian terraced houses known as Tollemache Terrace is squeezed between the railway and the canal – between, perhaps, the tentative start of the Industrial Revolution in Chester and its ending, with the railway allowing commuting from Chester to Liverpool for work. Still, the rows of Victorian terraced streets butting the edge of the towpath imply an expansion of the city's population in the nineteenth century. When the canal was built, this was open fields, the land purchased from the various landowners by the Canal Company.

* * *

Little Abbey Court, Chester
May, 1772

Mr Phillip Norbury, clerk to the Chester Canal Navigation Company, is working late. Candles are lit in sconces around the room and a half-burnt taper sits in its holder on the corner of the desk. Several used quills have been discarded on the floor. Mr Norbury is hunched over his work surrounded by sheets of paper covered in lists of names and amounts of money. Names, which the maid bringing in his supper might notice, if she could read, include Miss Eliza Trevisa and her brother-in-law Rev Edward Harwood. There is also a Mr Samuel Appleton, noted as being from Liverpool and Mr Robert Hesketh, who the maid knows is a sugar baker in Chester. These are all subscribers to shares in the new canal. Most, Mr Norbury notes, are Merchants, or deal in areas related to shipping, such as Mr Jonathan Whittle the ropemaker, as the canal will be of utmost benefit to these businesses. There are also subscriptions from physicians at the Infirmary and a colleague of theirs from London. Norbury overheard that Dr Fothergill has just sold his Nevis estates, including over one hundred slaves, and was looking for sound investments. Mr Norbury's own physician, Dr Currie, is not on the list, despite being set to make money from selling his land along the route.

With his supper of bread and cheese on the table, along with a decanter of Portuguese wine, Norbury gathers the various lists into a neater pile, puts the lid on the inkpot and retires to the fireside.

* * *

Traversing what was once Dr Currie's land, the red brick terraces of Great Boughton give way to fields by the side of the busy A55 road and adjacent to the Chester to Crewe railway line. Past the Old Troopers pub, now a drive-thru Costa coffee shop, large mid-twentieth-century houses line the opposite bank, with gardens stretching down to the water, some with boat moorings. Weeping willows trail bright green leaves into the murky green of the canal. Ducks are often welcomed onto wooden decks. Moorhens peep and rummage among the reeds on the far bank, chicks straggling along behind. Today, it is hard to believe that the residents of Christleton had multiple disputes with the Canal Company regarding the building of the canal.

* * *

Christleton
July, 1775

A group of men on horseback are gathered outside the Troopers Inn on the Whitchurch Road just south of Chester. The canal, cut here eighteen months previously, is bordered by muddy paths. Morris' Field has been chopped clean in two by the canal. The owner, Mr Thomas Brock, Chester's Town Clerk and Lord of the Manor at Christleton, has insisted on a bridge behind the Inn to join the two halves of his field. This is in addition to Quarry Bridge at the southernmost end of the field to access the stone quarry, bought by the Canal Company. The men are inspecting the bridge to ensure the repairs agreed upon have been carried out satisfactorily. Mr Hall, the solicitor dealing with the complaints from the Christleton landowners, dismounts, along with another two men and they walk over the bridge, talking animatedly.

Mr Clowes and Mr Moon, the canal engineer and his assistant, remain on horseback watching the proceedings. As Mr Hall and his companions, Justices of the Peace sent to settle the disputes, return to their horses, Mr Clowes nods at Mr Moon, relieved that the bridge has passed inspection. They will ride back post-haste to give the news to the committee.

* * *

The houses taper off and there are open fields and a golf course on the opposite bank, although the busy A41 road (the Old Coach Road to London) is never far away. Passing quickly through the village of Waverton the canal becomes rural again and the towpath narrows. The asphalted section through the outskirts of the city has long ended and for most of the route it is trodden grass, muddy after rain. As I walk, I am aware of my own bodily presence in the landscape but also of those who walked, rode and barged their way here previously. Those who worked on the canal are a constant absent presence haunting the route. Some are noted in the company minutes.

Canal Navigation Company Accounts 1772–73

> To Henry Bullock and Robert Mason for building of Northgate Bridge the sum of £82/10/-
> To John Grindley, wheelwright, for locks …
> To John Leigh, bricklayer for building locks …
> To Thomas Rabey for building bridges …
> To James Laithwaite for hammers, picks, Shovels &c. …
> To Mr Yoxal of Nantwich for Wheelbarrows …

With no other people around, I can hear cows munching grass on the other side of the hedge. A chaffinch 'wheep wheeps' continuously, but is well hidden. The hedgerows here include crab apples, sloes and damsons. Passing Davies Bridge and Salmons Bridge, named after the farmers of 1773, is a path, bordered by gnarled oak trees, leading past a field and up to St Peter's Churchyard. Some of the people buried here would have seen the canal being built.

* * *

Waverton
September, 1776

Two small and slightly grubby children are chasing each other, laughing, along the path from the new canal towards the church. Esther is carrying a basket of purple fruit. Benjamin is kicking among the carpet of brown leaves from the oak trees lining the path. He stoops to gather up the acorns he finds and stuffs them in his already bulging pockets. He plans to give some to the pigs later on to make them fat and tasty. The church bells are ringing and a group of people cluster around the lychgate. As the children near the church they slow to a walk, bowing their heads but unable to refrain from catching each other's eyes and giggling.

* * *

The graves in the churchyard include Benjamin Dutton, who died in 1779 at only 10 years old, and Esther Hill who died in 1852 at nearly 80 years old.

It is quiet and peaceful here. A long way from what might be expected of an industrialised landscape. And yet, that is what this is, or was. Canals were essential to the improvement of transport infrastructure that heralded the Industrial Revolution in Britain. And the funding was from subscribers who earnt their money, directly or indirectly, through colonial trade. In other words, extractive capitalism funded Britain's Industrial Revolution. And like much of Britain's industrial past this is now hidden through the bucolic images of tranquil waterways traversing the countryside. As Fowler (2024: 114) points out, celebrations of the landscape can obscure the history of the place.

At Golden Nook farm there are permanent moorings. Boats are tethered to the far bank, some with miniature gardens or sheds, mini-wind turbines and solar panels. Names give some indication of the owners: 'Survivor' is how Tony and Sue from Shropshire greet us, 'Lady Mags' is from Beaumaris, on Anglesey, a destination for coasters carrying coal from Chester in the past. Cargoes arrived at Chester from many European destinations and some from further afield. Incoming and outgoing ships and their cargoes were listed in the local papers.

* * *

Chester Chronicle
August 14th 1775

On Saturday last this city began to shew an agreeable prospect of an extension of its commerce; about eleven in the morning the *Juno*, Capt. Eagles, equipped by Thomas Cotgreave and Co, sailed initially for Africa and thence to the Americas.

AMERICAN WHEAT

Being just arrived and to be sold by John Rogers and Co.
Who have also for sale,
Baltic Rye, Riga hemp, Fine scale sugars from Antigua and Tobago, Carolina Indigo, Malaga Raisins.

* * *

The towpath here is a narrow line of trodden grass bordered on the canal side by a variety of wildflowers: great willowherb, vetch, white field bindweed, nettles, hemlock, meadowsweet, grasses and reeds. On the land side a thick hedge contains brambles and thistles along with hawthorn, honeysuckle, dog rose and ivy. Walking past I am enveloped in a cloud of gatekeeper butterflies. I've never seen so many butterflies at once before. There are some larger peacock butterflies too, their red wings and large blue 'eyes' standing out from the orange-brown of the gatekeepers. Past the moorings all is quiet again for a couple of hundred metres until a heron flies low straight along the canal, its wings seeming to almost touch the banks – and me – before landing in the top of a tree. Herons symbolise good luck and I feel lucky as it is rare to see one in flight here. It is hard today to imagine the forty men who were employed to dig the cut here: the mud, the noise and the general disruption to the slow pace of rural life.

The canal now follows the course of the River Gowy to Nantwich. Another sharp bend to the east and Beeston Castle comes into view. Beeston Castle was built by Ranulf, Earl of Chester, in the 1220s, five hundred and fifty years before the canal. Beeston was the terminus of the canal for a time, when money ran out in 1775.

* * *

Adams's Weekly Courant
4th September, 1775

CHESTER CANAL NAVIGATION

Notice is hereby given
That a special meeting of the Proprietors of the said Navigation will be held on Thursday next, at the Canal Office near the Eastgate, at 10 o'clock in the forenoon, in order to determine upon, the most eligible method of carrying on and completing the undertaking, agreeable to the powers granted by act of parliament for making and maintaining the same.

By order of the general meeting,
J. MOON
Clerk to the Company of Proprietors

* * *

Before the canal was, eventually, fully opened Mersey flats – wide shallow barges – ran from here several times a week carrying passengers and light goods to and from Chester. Behind Beeston Castle, less visible among the wooded hills, is the nineteenth-century Peckforton Castle.

* * *

Journal of John Tollemache
Helmingham Hall, Suffolk
January, 1842

Today I have commissioned Anthony Salvin Esq. to design a medieval-style castle to be built on land in Cheshire that I recently purchased from Sir Thomas Mostyn. The money received from the Slave Compensation Commission for grandfather's Antiguan estates will more than cover Mr Salvin's fees. I'm sure my new home on Peckforton Hill will give splendid views overlooking fields and the canal. I remember stories of how Great Uncle Wilbraham invested £1,000 in the canal but saw no return on it. I believe the canal fell into disrepair until it was extended to join the River Mersey by the renowned engineer Mr Telford. Now I expect it will give a pleasant outlook from my battlements with the colourful boats sailing past!

* * *

The two castles dominate the skyline on the sandstone ridge above the otherwise flat Cheshire plain. The Chester to Crewe railway runs close to the canal, both making their way through the gap in the north–south ridge. Skirting the base of Beeston Crag I pass the busy Shady Oak pub, and then Wharton's Lock. With the River Gowy not much more than a ditch, another ideal spot for Himalayan balsam, I reach the unique Beeston Iron Lock, now a Grade II listed building.

* * *

24 Abingdon Street, Westminster
May, 1824

Sirs,
Thank you for your letter of the 15th inst. I have considered the problem of the collapsing lock at Beeston and have, I think, devised a solution, albeit one that will cost a considerable sum and take some time to implement.

I enclose drawings for a lock with walls of cast iron plates. These will provide a firmer barrier than the current stone walls and prevent the leakage of water. As I have previously explained, building the canal close to the riverbed always ran the risk of being left unsupported by the sandy substrate. I am willing to supervise the construction of the new iron lock according to the attached plans at a suitable remuneration to be agreed.
Yours &c.
Thomas Telford Esq.

* * *

The next stretch is a muddy path after rain. A flash of blue out of the corner of my eye, but when I turn my head the air is empty again. A kingfisher. I wait, but it doesn't reappear. The occasional boat meanders past, with waves, nods or shouts of 'hello!' Trains rush past on an embankment, the railway crossing over the canal just before Bunbury staircase locks, the final locks before Nantwich.

* * *

Houghton Hall,
Bunbury
December, 1787

Sirs,
It has recently come to my attention that the locks at Bunbury have collapsed due to the poor craftsmanship employed in building them. I have £100 of shares in your company but have as yet seen no return whatsoever. I would be willing to support the enterprise by transporting my cheeses to the Cheese Wharf at Chester via the canal if this were a reliable means of transport. However, until the state of the canal is improved I cannot risk delays to my shipments to the Royal Navy, who will not wait on the vagaries of your canal locks!
Yours faithfully,
George Garnett Esq.

* * *

At Calveley, I pass the mill where artisan cheeses are made today, but no longer supply the navy. A man passing on a boat lends me a pole to ward off some aggressive swans on the footpath who are protecting their cygnets. The canal runs next to the busy main road and the towpath shows little sign of being used. The hedges are up to eight feet thick, reducing the noise and pollution. They seem to be sheltering a variety of birds which I can hear but not see. A little further along, at Barbridge, I cross the junction with the Middlewich branch connecting to the Trent and Mersey canal. This was planned as part of the original canal but not built until 1827 due to lack of funds.

Past Hurleston Reservoir, built to keep a reserve of water for the canal, is the lock joining the narrower Llangollen Canal. Most of the land the canal passes by from here to Cuckoo Lane, Nantwich, was owned by the influential Tomkinson family of Dorfold Hall, who invested in canal shares.

* * *

Dorfold Hall, Nantwich
March, 1778

James Tomkinson, attorney, and his son Henry are standing by the mullioned windows of a large sitting room overlooking extensive lawns where Henry's sons are playing with their mother, Anne, while their grandmother, Katherine, looks on.

'Henry, I have good news regarding the Canal. As you know, I've had some considerable correspondence with the Company and they have at last agreed to reroute the Navigation around our estate, rather than cutting through it. I'm sure you'll agree this is a very pleasing outcome for us as we have seen the disruption that the work causes. I now hope that we will eventually get some return on the investment in the company that we made six years ago!'

'Yes Father, that is good news. We should, perhaps have heeded Lord Bridgewater's warnings, relayed through his agent Uncle William, that this was an ill-considered and amateurish undertaking. No matter – once completed the canal will prove a useful trade route to Chester and beyond.'

* * *

Skirting around the Dorfold Estate, I arrive at the comparative noise and bustle of Nantwich marina where the original route of the Chester canal ends. Although the industrial beginnings of the canal are celebrated by the Canal and River Trust, the histories of trade and commerce, exploitation and the violent regimes of colonialism and slavery that provided the finance are not described on the information boards.

This story of the canal has resurrected voices of ordinary, although largely relatively wealthy, people. People who – as far as I can ascertain – took for granted the economic order of the time, not questioning the morality of slavery or colonial exploitation. The acceptance of the status quo is what makes them ordinary. Nevertheless, the wide-ranging networks of the financers of the canal and landowners show how the infrastructure of the United Kingdom is even today dependent on its colonial connections for much of its historic foundations. The entangled roots of Britain's wealth are an integral part of the canal's story leaving inalienable traces of a largely forgotten and ignored past in the landscape.

Note

1 All the people referenced in the fictionalised letters and historical sections of this essay are real people and the key facts noted are historically accurate. Facts are taken from *Adams's Weekly Courant* (1770–79); Chester Canal Navigation Company (1771–1813); Cheshire Archives and Local Studies (2024); Craig (1964); Aylett (1987); English Heritage (n.d.); The Chester Bluecoat Charity (n.d.); Centre for the Study of the Legacies of British Slavery (2024).

References

Adams's Weekly Courant (1770–79) Mf 343/6; Mf 343/7; Mf 343/8; Mf 228/2 [microfiche]. Storyhouse, Chester (Cheshire Archives and Local Studies).

Aylett, Philip (1987) Attorneys and clients in eighteenth-century Cheshire: A study in relationships, 1740–1785. *Bulletin of the John Rylands Library*, 69 (2), 326–58.

Centre for the Study of the Legacies of British Slavery (2024) Legacies of British Slavery Database. Available at: www.ucl.ac.uk/lbs/ [accessed 16 October 2024].

Cheshire Archives and Local Studies (2024) *Cheshire Tithe Maps Online*. Available at: https://maps.cheshireeast.gov.uk/tithemaps/ [accessed 9 August 2023].

The Chester Bluecoat Charity (n.d.) *History of The Bluecoat building*. Available at: www.thechesterbluecoatcharity.co.uk/history-of-the-bluecoat-building/ [accessed 21 February 2025].

Chester Canal Navigation Company (1771–1813) *Minutes of the Chester Canal Navigation Company (1771–1813)*. The National Archives RAIL 816.

Craig, R. (1964) Shipping and Shipbuilding in Port of Chester in 18th and Early 19th Cent. *Historic Society of Lancashire and Cheshire*, 116. Available at: www.hslc.org.uk/journal/vol-116-1964/attachment/116-4-craig/ [accessed 4 October 2025].

English Heritage (n.d.) *History of Beeston Castle.* Available at: www.english-heritage.org.uk/visit/places/beeston-castle-and-woodland-park/history/ [accessed 11 July 2024].

Fowler, Corinne (2024) *Our Island Stories: Country Walks Through Colonial Britain.* London: Penguin.

Hall, Catherine (2020) The slavery business and the making of 'race' in Britain and the Caribbean. *Current Anthropology*, 61 (S22), S172–82.

Massey, Doreen (1994) *Space, Place, and Gender*. Cambridge: Wiley.

Richardson, Laurel (1997) *Fields of Play: Constructing an Academic Life.* New Brunswick, NJ: Rutgers University Press.

Tilley, Christopher (2006) Introduction: Identity, place, landscape and heritage. *Journal of Material Culture*, 11 (7), 7–32.

10

Walking the line: search practices, environment and the practice of care in mountain rescue work

Robin James Smith

Rendezvous

It is already dark as we gather at the control vehicle, on the area of loose-packed stones forming a car park of sorts, nestled in the valley at the foot of the Pen y Fan horseshoe. After the rush of the call-out being triggered, and the rush to get there – to base to collect team vehicles, or in individual cars 'going direct' – we wait to be tasked. Team members hurriedly but smoothly retrieve rucksacks and kit from boots of cars, zip-up thick Gore-Tex waterproof jackets, or pull on the more permeable but more comfortable Páramo smocks. They tie boot laces, put on headtorches, check for spare batteries. They turn on radios. Two party leaders are called to the control vehicle and the incident controller briefs them. There is not so much to go on. The mispers are likely somewhere on the ridge. A couple with a child. No names at this point. Not much by way of description either. The police have passed on a grid reference from a SARLOC on one of the misper's phones, but contact has been lost, and that was some time ago. They had passed the trig point at the top of the ridge, but beyond only a very general direction of travel their whereabouts remain unknown. The party leaders gather their party members. Two groups of six. Each to split the various bits of kit, the medical pack, the casualty bag, between them. We set off.

* * *

This essay follows a party of volunteers of the Central Beacons Mountain Rescue Team as they search for walkers who have lost their way somewhere along a high ridge, in the Bannau Brycheiniog (or Brecon Beacons) in Wales. The sociological interests and themes that their work brings to view include the relationship between movement and perception, the production of work practices and work sites and the practical enactment of care *as* movement. In this sense, the essay describes aspects of mountain rescue and the production of landscape, as a specific instance in which perception, landscape and mobility are mutually shaping.

The team, as with all other mountain rescue teams in England and Wales, is entirely staffed by volunteers. They come from varied walks of life and backgrounds, although the demands of time and the expense of kit and petrol means the membership is somewhat self-selecting after the period of initial training. What connects the architects, engineers, academics, police officers, social workers and mechanics of the team is a love for the outdoors and a commitment, largely unspoken, to helping others who find themselves in various troubles and in need of assistance to get off the hill and down to safety. The team's practice and work are intimately tied to the locations in which they operate. Less dramatic than the rocky crags of Eryri and the Lake District, the rolling slopes of 'the Beacons' (as they are commonly known) are, consequently, home to less dramatic rescues. Yet, largely due to the accessibility of Pen y Fan, the highest mountain in South Wales, the team is one of the busiest in the country. In addition to numerous lower limb injuries, the team's bread and butter is searching for missing persons or 'mispers' who are either lost or not wishing to be found.

The team's active engagement with place and environment is the business of search and rescue – work in which walking figures as necessarily *vital*, in both senses. Walking figures as a practical engagement with place which, in turn and in combination with other sensorial, embodied, perceptual practices, produces a given environment as a *worksite* in which the work of mountain rescue gets done. There is, then, a reflexive relationship between patch and practice, between knowing and going (Hall and Smith, 2014).

Sociologically, then, we find walking as not only a mobility practice taking place in a particular space but, rather, as a fundamental practice of the social organisation of the environment as a perceptual field.

Walking does not figure here as a professional method of the social scientist, but as a members' practice which yields a reflexive relation between movement, knowledge and landscape. This knowing engagement is not, of course, the preserve of the search and rescue teams that have 'made an art of finding and science of how people get lost.' (Solnit, 2017: 10). Solnit muses on how those who become lost lack the possible 'art of attending to the weather, to the route you take, to the landmarks along the way, to how if you turn around you can see how different the journey back looks from the journey out, to reading the sun and moon and stars to orient yourself, to the direction of running water, to the thousand things that make the wild a text that can be read by the literate.' (2017: 10).

In another register, in which the landscape is not treated as a text to be read but as an achievement, we might consider how the phenomenal field is itself a conglomeration, a *gestalt contexture*, of practice, of movement, of perception, and of the shifting saliency of material features, of foreground and background. Ways of walking are inextricable from ways of seeing and ways of knowing. Movement is reality (Bergson, 2007); no movement, no vision. Nothing to see, and no means of seeing it (see Noë, 2004). Yet, the world is not just perceived but shifts with movement and with the particulars and contingencies of the task at hand. The environment does not contain mountain rescue work: rather it is animated, accomplished, in and through it. Despite all the senses in which walking is a generic and ubiquitous human practice, it is not to be understood through its generalities. Walking on the hill, for the team, is attended to as a specific instantiation of practice that in turn generates configurations of landscape and environment (Smith et al., in press). It is here that literary metaphors fall short.

* * *

We walk briskly down past the long-abandoned pumphouse buildings. Exposed beams, highlighted in the torchlight, break the night sky. Our party, moving ahead, walks down a short steep bank, always slippery due to traversing tree roots worn smooth. We walk in single file across the narrow bridge that spans the run-off canal from the reservoir before making a short ascent up another bank, on a muddy track to the grassed top of the dam wall itself. We settle into a rhythm, moving well. Bodies and lungs and hearts and legs adjust to the work and to the weight of the packs. Some chat passes back and forth about the possible whereabouts of the mispers, about how they got there. Talk of just how often people manage to miss the turning down to the car park. It is a working theory born of experience. There are comments about the conditions. And the time. And about how they'll be getting very cold by now.

The settling-in to the night's work continues en route. Adjusting of kit, tightening of straps, a lengthening of stride. Those of us with a radio, and notably the party leaders, make sure we have communications with the control vehicle:

> Morlais Control, Morlais Control, this is 536 requesting radio check, over.
>
> 536, this is Morlais Control, receiving loud and clear, over.
>
> You also, Control. 536 out.

The track has been recently worked on by the park authority, producing a more 'walkable' access to the ridge. Landscaped, as it were. A winding gravelled path provides a gentler ascent of the first short climb. While we are not in any sense rushing, the party moves purposefully, cutting a line straight across the bends in the path. We follow the familiar track, through a gate which separates the land owned by the water company from the open access land of the valley basin.

* * *

Rescue searches are planned activities. Yet searches are only ever accomplished on the ground, with feet and eyes, and hands and ears and nose. Their walking is coordinated through methods for the management of environmental contingencies. Not, then, an abstract notion of perception and not, then, an environment in general, but perception organised and accomplished in and for *this* environment, on *this* night, on *this* occasion. What is known about the misper is the primary consideration managed in relation to the visual availability of objects, signs and clues, in situ. How tall is the misper? Are they wearing bright or dark clothing? A hat, perhaps? Do they have a rucksack? What size? What colour? Do they have a dog with them?

Headtorches or just mobile phones? Is it light, dark or in between? Is it raining? Is the 'clag' down (a colloquial UK term for mountain cloud and mist)? Is the terrain open? Long or short grass or heather? Are we going into forestry? Dense bush? How many team members do we have for the size of the search area? These are the contingencies of any search's occasion.

Up to the ridge

The ridge looms above us, the ridgeline itself just visible, silhouetted against the night sky. No stars, just clouds sketched in relief by what moonlight there is. At once familiar yet seen again for another first time. We are not just getting somewhere but attending to our surroundings as we go. We reach the start of the climb proper. The 'improvements' continue here. A smooth path replaces the old slog up the boggy lower slopes of the basin. We tread steps of local yellow-grey stone, giving way to the distinctive red-orange bedrock of the ridge itself. The steps are not so old to have been worn by passing boots, but signs of previous walkers lie to each side where people have stepped off the path, wearing tracks in the grass. Any chat drops away as the pace quickens. After twenty minutes or so we reach the foot of the ridge itself, breath steaming.

I look up at the now steepening steps, glistening wet with water running in small channels and conduits. Pools in worn and natural recesses, highlighted by the sweeping light of the torch. Stiff-soled boots slip back a fraction on smooth wet stone, making the next step a little further away. We move to our own paces, beginning to spread out as the ascent progresses. No sense in rushing. You'll only arrive tired. But we want to get there, to them. You can feel a quiet urgency. Those at the front stop every so often, turning to face down the hill, checking on the distance to the swaying headtorches of those further down the incline, and to catch their own breath. I glance across to the contoured ridge, scanning the skyline for flickers of light, from a torch or phone screen, for silhouettes. The depth of the steps increases as the ridge steepens. The depth of the breaths with them. Alternative tracks open each side of the steps caused by the coursing of water off the top of the ridge. Scooped out bowled corners as the path switches back on itself, depositing the detritus of the mountain. It is steep enough now that I place my hand on a step further up as I turn with the path and feel the cold wet stone through my glove.

The first members of the party reach the top of the steep track and stop for a moment's rest. We lean against the peat side of the deep cut path that runs the east side of the ridge and catch our breath. 'Jeez, you're hardly blowing are you?' says one member to another, laughing. Warmed from the effort of the ascent, we undo jacket zips to vent air, remove gloves. Everyone knows not to remove too much clothing though; standing still generates no warmth and the wind is blowing strongly along the ridge, stripping away heat where it can.

The party leader radios Control to log that they've reached the ridge top and to check if any further information has been received on the mispers. 'Wait one' says Control. The party regathers as its remaining members summit the final steps of the ridge. We dim torches and angle them towards the floor so we can talk without blinding one other. And then we wait. There is no point rushing off until Control has updated our briefing – the mispers could have been found or found themselves by now. The wind and rain make communication difficult even when stood close, and we organise ourselves along the narrow track so that we can stand with our backs to the worst of it. The party leader holds the radio handpiece inside his hood as he's hailed by Control. No further information on the mispers. Proceed to original search area. The party leader checks if everyone is ok and ready to head off.

Without a firm location for the missing walkers, we build a plan for the search tasking. We will walk up the short track to the trig point on top of the ridge and spread out to form a line search heading south-east. The eastern arm of the line will drop slightly off the top of the ridge. The western side will stretch as far as the overlapping visual range between the team members allows. We arrive at the trig and assemble ourselves into the line. Two members with radios are positioned at the far ends of the line, and the two party leaders space themselves in the centre. A compass bearing is taken and passed along.

We walk the line. We have all been on the ridge numerous times but in the dark and by torchlight the terrain can be deceiving. I check the mapping app on my phone. The ridge drops away to my left and rises gradually to my right, its folds and valleys produced by ancient forces of water and earth. We walk on its shoulder on undulating, chossy ground. Boggy, mostly. Rough scrub and dense tufts of spiked grass known as 'babies' heads' that push you off balance. Large steps of peat, with shallow petroleum-like glistening pools at their foot. Patches of exposed smooth stone. You try not to focus on where you are putting your feet and it's hard to keep your head up, scanning. You remind yourself to focus, a conscious effort to really attend to what the senses can produce. I scan along the line and check the spacing of the team. It looks good. Well drilled. There's a sense of pride at how we fall into our pattern without much chatter and minimal faff.

* * *

The search is at once 'open' in that the eye should be snagged by objects and silhouettes and movements, but focused, too, in searching not for *anyone* or *anything* but for signs of the mispers in question. Novices will be excited by any potential indication: litter, discarded clothes, footprints. Old hands will filter out possible 'false finds' through experience; the labels of packages faded, pine needles atop the sodden hat, the footprint too fresh or not fresh enough. Searches, typically, are done by members forming and moving in a line, a line calibrated via a method to determine the 'range of detection' (ROD) in the current conditions. The team will spread out only so far as the object concerned – a person, a jacket, a rucksack, a wallet – can be visible between any two team members. If the method is known in advance, the distance cannot be proscribed, and cannot even be assured from the start of the search to its hopeful conclusion. And the line is not walked rigidly. A compass bearing is taken, but only as a guide for the direction of the search and its parameters. Straight lines walked produce less coverage than those that meander. The team call this 'purposive wandering'.

* * *

We weave as we go, stopping every now and then to turn around completely or to shout the names of the mispers into the dark and the wind and the rain. We think we hear something in the wind.

A shout. It's hard to make out and even harder to locate where it is coming from. The contours of the ridge and the whipping wind work against us. The voices sound like they're coming from below us, further down the ridge. '515 party hold positions' is passed over the radio, and 'HOLD!' is shouted down the line, arms raised in the air until everyone has come to a halt. And we listen again. Voices again. And sounding as if rising from below, again. The PLs have a quick conversation, reasoning that it's unlikely that the mispers would have tried to climb off the ridge down its steepest side, but, equally, that there's relative shelter from the wind down there. Two members already on that side of the line are tasked to drop further down, off the side of the grassed, steepening slopes to make sure we don't overshoot the source of the voices. The line adjusts accordingly. 'MOVE OFF' is passed along the line and we continue our wandering.

Before not so long 'HOLD POSITIONS' is heard again, followed by 'FIND'.

'Morlais Control. Morlais Control. This is 515. Mispers located. Grid reference to follow. Over.'

Off the hill

We find the couple and their child huddled in a dip, just off the shoulder of the ridge, three hundred metres or so further downhill from the trig point. They are, thankfully, wearing what look to be thick jackets with layers underneath, but the woman is in leggings that must be soaked through. We quickly unpack a shelter and place it over the family along with a team medic and scribe. We crack self-warming heat packs and pass them in. We pull out gloves and hats from the hypothermia pack. A team member unpacks his waterproof trousers and helps the woman pull them on. It's a smart idea as removing the windchill from wet clothes will make a difference, despite minimal warmth being generated from her body. The family are assessed. No injuries, no disorientation, just cold. The child seems to be fine and is in good spirits that hide being a little scared. A team member is talking to him, calling it an adventure, talking about how we'll soon be back at the truck where there'll be a hot chocolate with his name on it. The man is fine too, again just cold.

But it's the woman that's causing the concern. She's so cold she's in pain: legs and hips and back seizing up from the cold and the huddled position they've been sitting in. She's not sure how far she can walk.

Outside the tent we talk about getting off the hill. Will we call for a stretcher? That's another thirty minutes to wait in the cold. Let's try and get her moving and see how she does. Just trying to move will generate warmth. Better than just sitting there. Yep, let's walk them off.

We go back to the tent and explain the evacuation plan. We'll walk off. Slowly. At your pace. We'll stay with you and help you down. If you want to stop, just say. But it'll be good to keep moving. The team vehicles aren't so far away and it's warm down there. Shall we go?

We update Control and start to walk, although that description of our movement might be stretching things a little. The woman is struggling to move even with support from me on her right-hand side and a team member on her left. Her steps are painful, her hips and lower back protesting with each lift of the foot. Still, we are moving. We eventually make our way back up to the trig point and take a pause. We check in with each other, and with the family. She's doing ok, but still in a lot of pain. Still cold and still shivering. It's all downhill from here, we say cheerfully. She's apologising for dragging us out on a night like this, for being so slow, for getting lost in the first place. I know better than this, she says. We reassure her, tell her we didn't have any plans for the evening anyway, nothing better to do, nowhere we'd rather be than on the hill. And there's some truth in that.

* * *

Walking together is a common enough phenomenon, but here it becomes a primary mode of care and of assistance. Indeed, 'contexts of care similarly harbour a wealth of situations where care recipients and carers need to engage in joint mobility.' (Cekaite et al., 2021: 470). Walking together figures here both as a movement towards further care, but also as care itself. The coordination of bodies and feet in relation to the terrain emphasises the often-overlooked inter-relation of both. The environment, then, produces its own challenges, intertwined with the bodily state of the casualty and the efforts of the team to get them to safety. If searching is one mode of engagement with and production of the environment, then the evacuation is another. A different line is walked, one drawn between speed and safety. Surfaces, friction and capacities of the body provide for a heightened attention to each step.

* * *

The gentle descent from the trig point down to the edge of the ridge continues. The woman is finding it easier moving downhill, relatively speaking. We arrive at the top of the rough deep steps that lead down to the gravelled path below. We pause, knowing this is the crux of the walk off. Rich and I have a quick chat, deciding that it's best if only one of us directly assists her. The other will go in front and protect against any slips becoming trips becoming falls. Here we go then mate, there's a few steps to get down but then it's smooth sailing. Lean on me as much as you need. There's no rush, ok?

The woman is a good deal shorter than me and I stoop to have my left arm around her back and up under hers. Braced together like this we take the first step down. She's wincing in pain, telling me her back is totally seizing up with the change in angle, the steps too deep. We stop and I rub her lower back trying to get some warmth and circulation going. It's not much, but it's something. We take the next step with the same result. The woman is apologising again. I tell her it's fine again. Let's try the next one mate, ok?

And we do. Step by step. Our world shrinks to the limits of the headtorch and the next step. One at a time. Move, stop. Rubbing of the back, which seems to be helping in some way. Let's try and keep moving, ok mate?

The slope gradually eases, and the steps become shallower as we descend. She is moving a little more freely and we make our way off the stone path and on to the gravelled track. She's asking again about her kid – long gone, I say cheerily. He'll be sat in a truck drinking that hot chocolate by now! He's absolutely fine. We'll be with him soon. And eventually we are. We get the woman sat in a vehicle with her family, heating on, more warm clothes on offer. More medical observations, more good-humoured chat. She's still apologising for getting lost, we're still telling her it's fine. It's what we do.

References

Bergson, Henri (2007) *The Creative Mind*. New York: Dover Publications.

Cekaite, Asta, Keisanen, Tiina, Rauniomaa, Mirka and Siitonen, Pauliina (2021) Human-assisted mobility as an interactional accomplishment. *Gesprächsforschung-Online-Zeitschrift zur verbalen Interaktion*, 22, 469–75.

Hall, Tom and Smith, Robin James (2014) Knowing the city: Maps, mobility and urban outreach work. *Qualitative Research*, 14 (3), 294–310.

Noë, Alva (2004) *Action in Perception*. Cambridge, MA: MIT Press.

Smith, Robin James, Smith, Thomas and Pehkonen, Samu (in press) The senses-in-action: Visual and haptic encounters with occasioned environments. In William Gibson, Natalia Ruiz-Junco and Dirk vom Lehn (eds) *Sensing Life: The Social Organisation of the Senses in Interaction*. London: Routledge.

Solnit, Rebecca (2017) *A Field Guide to Getting Lost*. Edinburgh: Canongate Books.

11

Walking through waves: technology, the Thames and urban development

Alex Rhys-Taylor

Pre-amble

Drop a pebble in a body of water, and watch its waves ripple outwards. In London over the last two millennia, technological revolutions have also acted a bit like pebbles, sending ripples outwards, leaving residues – buildings, infrastructure, culture – in layers around the city. This walk chases those waves through the cross-section of the city cut by the Thames, sifting through the enduring sediments that each technological surge deposited.

Wind

Just west of London Bridge, about twenty-five gulls hunch into their plumage as they bob on the rusty river. A spring shower blows over from west to east, the direction showers have moved across London for millennia. With even more predictability, the full moon has pulled the river away from its bank. Poking up from the muddy foreshore in front of Fishmongers Hall, are a series of damp blackened stumps. These are remnants of the old quays running westward from London Bridge: Coal Wharf, Timbre Wharf, Three Cranes, Steel Yard Wharf and Queenshithe (Rocque, 2013). Most of the remaining infrastructure is from the nineteenth century, but archaeology shows these quays in use from the initial Roman settlement (Waddington, 1934). For much of first thousand years of London's history, Queenshithe, in particular, was the most important port on the river (Ayre and Wroe-Brown, 2015).

A twin-hulled river taxi chugs past, chasing the shower eastward down river. Its wake laps at the exposed shore of Steel Yard Wharf. During their centuries of use, many of the products passing through The London Pool (the collective name for these quays) came up through the Thames from nearby coasts around the British Isles and Western Europe. Over time these goods came from increasingly further afield, aided by the growing hulks of sea traders (Marsden, 1994). By 1300, the products of a myriad windmills, watermills, fisheries and farms from across northern and eastern Europe made their way in and out of Queenshithe and the neighbouring quays. Immediately beside the Queenshithe port, London's Steel Yard is an especially important location, the westernmost point in a chain of Hanseatic docks extending east through Bruges and Hamburg to Lübeck and Tallinn to Novgorod. By way of the innovatively high-sided Hanseatic 'cogs' and 'hulks', cargos of pelts, salt, cloth, wines and grain from across Europe moved via these wharfs (Unger, 1980: 138, 184). London grew especially fat on the barrels of silver-scaled herring arriving with Hanseatic traders (Harreld, 2015: 212). The city's finances also thrived on the gold and silver these traders exchanged for the wool, cloth and metals exported from London (Mucklow, 1932; Marmefelt, 2013). Through this period, London's population went from around 18,000 in 1000 CE to 30,000 in 1300 CE (Mount, 2015).

As London moved into the Middle Ages, the inflow via its fluvial oesophagus caused the city to strain at its old Roman girdle. But not to burst through it. Walking a little further east, towards the Tower of London, the name of one historic quay denotes the assemblage of technology, ideology and labour that would see London fatten beyond its medieval bindings. Sugar Quay. The first large dock after the Tower of London, and therefore the easiest to access by incoming merchants, the prestigious quay had previously been used for one of the Isles' biggest exports: wool. Wool Quay, was also known as Customs House Quay because the taxation of wool exports was central to building monarchic power in the Middle Ages (Rose, 2017). In this respect, Wool Quay had been a central location in establishing monarchic power and modulating the emergence of proto-capitalism across Europe. Finally, the site was eventually renamed Sugar Quay following its association with sugar, treacle and molasses that was offloaded from the fifteenth century onwards. By the sixteenth century, Sugar Quay burned white hot with world-changing intensity. A maritime historian might note that this transformation was enabled by the development of ocean-going carracks, caravels and galleons, as well as the invention of the pivot-mounted dry needle compass (Unger, 1994). But all of these would be nothing without the combination of muskets, fetters and excusatory theology (Gerbner, 2018: 31–49) that enabled the transatlantic trade in humanity and the profits it brought to London.

By the 1970s this stretch of inner city quays ceased to import or export anything much. This is when Sugar Quay became the headquarters of cane sugar refiners Tate & Lyle. More recently, the site was refined into luxury apartments by the property developers Nick and Christian Candy. Across the UK, a Black Lives Matter-inspired decolonial movement has resulted in statues toppling or being removed from Bristol, Cardiff, Edinburgh and Liverpool, along with several institutional name changes around London itself. Decolonial campaigners are also currently at work to remove the name Sugar Quay entirely from the area (Reclaim EC1, 2022). However, the association appears particularly sticky here, as it is elsewhere. For all the reworking of memorials, many other homages to the entwining of 'sweetness and power' (Mintz, 1986) can still be found within a mile of this quay. These include statues of Robert Geffrye, Thomas Guy and John Cass, each a staunch patron of the transatlantic slave trade. Institutions founded in this era still persistently thrive, unashamed of their origins. A five-minute walk up the alleys lining the riverbank beside Sugar Quay brings you to the current headquarters of Lloyds of London. Currently encased in a future-facing 'structural expressionist' shell, the foundations of the famous insurance market are entangled with slavery and colonial conquest (Williams, 1994: 105).

Not all local monuments look back at the wreckage of the past with as blind an eye as global finance. On this brief diversion away from the river, sat between pick and mix shapes of twenty-first century office blocks, you might have passed through a maze of petrified sugarcanes. Michael Visocchi's sculpture, the Gilt of Cain, sprouts from the site of St Gabriel's Fenchurch Street, commemorating The Reverend John Newton, a slave-trader turned preacher and abolitionist. The sculpture is inscribed with a poem by Lemn Sissay, including the line 'The Truth. Cash flow runs deep but spirit deeper / You ask Am I my brother's keeper?'

Back down the prehistoric slope to the riverside walk. Another cloud is following with a drizzly breeze, nudging the narrative eastward. Tourists clot around the Tower of London, a messy military palimpsest with layers that go back to the Roman era. The riverside fort was originally the starting point for the city wall. Parts of that old wall were revealed through demolition in the 1840s and can still be seen nearby (*Illustrated London News*, 1843: 442). That the wall had to be 'revealed' at all lies, in part, because by the 1700s the fortification was redundant. By this point, gunpowder and cannons could embarrass most city walls. But perhaps more significantly the steady evolution of technologies of surveillance and urban management meant that walls were increasingly obsolete. The wild lands beyond city boundaries could instead be tamed by the promulgation of propriety and policing.

Much more interesting than the city wall itself is the newly industrial metropolis that herniated it, assimilating the ancient fortification into new buildings and metabolising neighbouring hamlets into a new colossus. Much of the eastward expansion of the city from the eighteenth century was catalysed by the increased centrality of the Thames to the global economy. Walking under Tower Bridge – an engineering marvel shrouded in butterscotch Jacobethan icing – we reach Saint Katherine Docks. With large boats increasingly unable to navigate the congested main artery of Georgian London, the early industrial age offered an assortment of machines for solving the problem. Employing an assemblage of steam-driven cranes and diggers, various initiatives were undertaken to carve a series of basins out of the riverbank further east of the Tower of London and the old wall. These included West India Dock, East India Quay, The London Dock, East Dock and Shadwell Basin. Each of the new off-river ports was lined with cavernous brick and wrought-iron warehouses. The smallest of the new off-river quays, St Katherine Docks, was only in operation for 140 years. Its last major tenant was the General Steam Navigation Company whose boats carried goods and people around Europe. In the 1970s, St Katherine Docks was among the first of these off-river basins to see its industrial moorings replaced with a post-industrial marina, jetties lined with gin palaces, warehouses flipped into retail and office space.

Steam

Strolling along the river path beyond St Katherine Docks, the imminent arrival in London's historic 'sailor town' – Wapping – is accompanied by a chorus of sea shanties. The auditory apparition turns out to be pseudo-salty types taking part in a workshop at the Hermitage Community Mooring. Unlike the St Katherine yachts, the boats at the Hermitage are grungy restorations and rustic replicas from a more seafaring age. Their swaying spindle of masts alludes to a lost riverscape and obscures the waterside view from the newer residential columns behind them. A few steps further east, and the riverside path is pushed inland by buildings pressing right against the riverbank. Along this inland path are a string of old institutions: The Prospect of Whitby, The Town of Ramsgate, Turner's Old Star, The Dockers Inn, all erstwhile hubs in Wapping's knot of sailmakers, sex workers and dockers. But, as tempting as their warmth might be, being pushed inland and into pubs is not where we want to be. In this respect, it would have been worth hopping on that river taxi that passed earlier. From the river, passing through Wapping, you can still see the face of a much older city. Starting with the old headquarters of the marine police, the journey by boat takes you past a wall of warehouses and factories. An assortment of widths and heights, these mismatched warehouses are united only by their bricks' hue, which they also share with the river. Every now and then, the multi-windowed old warehouses are punctuated by a set of mud-slicked steps running from shore to street. One set (beside Execution Dock) has gallows, complete with a noose. Above eye level hang cast iron winches and cranes that once serviced third-storey loading doors. Far from functional, these vestigial protrusions are, at best, concessions to conservationists. More realistically, the historical texture helps create a marketable sense of place for the offices and residential units that fill the old warehouses.

Wind remained the primary power source driving boats across seas to the Thames, for a remarkably long time, with the last wind-borne cargo arriving in 1966. The advance of steamboats started in the early nineteenth century with the 'inland shipping routes', such as from London to Lieth, or Calais or Rotterdam (Chatterton, 1910: 215–33) before the later nineteenth extension of steam-powered cargo routes across the Atlantic and, via the new Suez Canal, to Calcutta (Bordo et al., 2007: 35). Coal and steam also lay behind the weaving of iron rails around the country, and the propulsion of carriages along them, enabling increases to the volume and reach of goods pulled out of the docks. Crucially, steam also powered the machines processing the various imports and exports throughout industrial London. The fabrics, the furniture and the tools produced along this stretch of the river were often products of coal-powered steam engines. Up to at least the 1880s, most factories or workshops had their own individual, and labour-intensive, steam engines to power their local machines (Donnachie, 2008). The multiplication of these furnaces through the city inevitably came with an increase in noise and pollution. A key location of this sooty humidity, Wapping was also home to an innovative effort to alleviate the sensory misery of industrial east London. Just over the road from the Prospect of Whitby, sandwiched between the Shadwell Basin and the Thames, sits the Wapping Hydraulic Power Station. Now a Grade II listed building, the Wapping plant was the largest of five tasked with drawing water and coal from the river to fuel giant centralised steam engines. These, in turn, were designed to channel highly pressurised water through a 186-mile network of thick cast iron pipes to anyone who subscribed to the hydraulic service. Replacing a myriad of localised steam engines, the hydraulic network

> operated the Safety Curtains at the Drury Lane and His Majesty's theatres ... raised the cinema organ at the Leicester Square theatre ... [The] Savoy hotel was extensively 'wired' for hydraulic power – even the vacuum cleaners depended on it ... At the height of its fortunes, in 1930, the London Hydraulic Power Company supplied 8000 machines with power' (Donnachie, 2008)

The centralised hydraulic service continued right through subsequent revolutions in electricity, petroleum and atomic power. Its valves were only finally closed in 1976 (Turvey, 1993). With the hydraulic powered city, a forgotten vision of the future, the turn of the millennium saw the power station rebirthed as an art space, cocktail bar and restaurant before once again closing. Current plans for the space revolve around stuffing its shell with apartments.

Electricity

As the enduring presence of the river police in Wapping suggests, a complex nocturnal economy had evolved around the docks. For centuries, pilfering from the port was widespread, and the retrieval of unpaid wages in the form of 'stolen' cargo was a tolerated part of port life (de Sena, 1986). Abetted by moonlight and smouldering oil lamps, it is unlikely that the dock's cast of smugglers, runners and fences would have welcomed the changes wrought by mechanical illumination. London's first public gas lights, achieved through the treatment of coal, appeared in the West End in 1807 (Matthews, 1827: 32). When lighting arrived around the docks, it introduced the docks to a process that was not only colonising space, but also the terrain of the urban night (Koslofsky, 2011). In the mid-nineteenth century, a gas lamp-lined pedestrian tunnel opened, connecting Wapping to Rotherhithe on the south bank of the Thames (Drew, 1852: 244). With attractions all along its length, from 'Egyptian necromancers' and 'dancing monkeys' to 'toyshops with polished marble counters' (Drew, 1852: 246–7), the tunnel was initially a pay-to-enter tourist attraction. The subterranean bazaar would not have been possible were it not for gas illumination, which filled the space with 'brilliant' light (Drew, 1852: 246). This tunnel was later given over to trains that now run along the Windrush line, accessible via Wapping Station.

As much as gas lamps increased access to the nocturnal life of the city, it was electricity that accelerated this process. A succession of 'bulbs' complete the colonisation of the city's night: first the blue-white crackle of arc lamps, followed by the yellow candescence of early twentieth-century bulbs, and by the mid-twentieth century the fog-penetrating orange corona of sodium lamps. Only recently have the latter been replaced by the permanent daytime glare of LEDs. Lighting up the docks, and the city behind them, electrical power also propelled the extension of the city into new suburbs. Electricity was particularly effective in animating commuter settlements. Residential clusters and new public amenities emerged all round the city's newly energised outer rim. From Ealing and Wimbledon to Barking and East Ham, Edwardian suburbs rarely had space for cars. Rather, they relied on a network of electric trams and the trains of the London Underground Electric Rail Company for their viability. Also typical of the early electric age were the first substantial waves of London County Council homes. Interrupted only by war, many more fully electrified three- and four-storey 'homes for heroes' were constructed from Wapping though the Isle of Dogs to Greenwich, and are still visible from the river walk.

A little further east past Wapping, into Shadwell, it is possible to see traces of an early source of this electrification. Visible from the river, where the mouth of Regents' Canal meets the Thames, there is a jetty jutting into the water that seems to serve nothing more than a row of houses. This was once a coal pier serving Stepney Electrical Power Station. Alongside its bigger siblings Bankside (now Tate Modern) and Battersea (now a retail complex), Stepney Power Station was an exemplar of elegantly functional Edwardian design. This family of powerhouses lining the Thames would use coal furnaces and river water to drive their turbines which, in turn, defibrillated the increasingly soot-congested city.

Petrol

As much as it marked a departure from steam power, the electricity produced by the Stepney Power Station was created by burning coal offloaded at its pier. The end of this power station's comparatively short life came with a new generation of turbines and power stations that increasingly relied on oil for heat. The provision of oil was part of the transformation of the city, and its infrastructures, by the increasingly dominant petroleum oil industry. Further down the Thames north bank, maybe a couple of hours on foot and just beyond the reach of the river taxi, is perhaps the most iconic institution of the diesel age. With its famous elliptical blue logo overlooking the river 'Ford of Dagenham' comprises a sprawling brown factory complex covering 475 acres. It is located beside the river because, when it first opened in the 1930s, road infrastructure was insufficient for industry (Hudson, 2009). By the 1950s, however, the diesel age had enabled commuter expansion right into the city's erstwhile rural surrounds, to the extent that it is unimaginable that this factory was ever poorly served by road. Marked by the migration of middle-class communities out of the city (Gamsu, 2016) and into the world of school runs and trips to out-of-town shopping centres and retail parks, the car gave birth to *sub-urbanism as a way of life*. With Fordist expansion, suburban highways were widened to encompass multiple lanes of traffic and industrial estates were redesigned prioritising access by lorries. At the same time, the footprint of suburban houses extended to contain garages and driveways. In the metropole's outer edges, roads still take longer to cross, and trains run less frequently. At the time of writing, only 3 per cent of households in 'inner London's Hackney have access to more than one car. In suburban Havering, however, the number soars to 39%' (London Assembly, 2022).

But you don't have to travel miles down its tarmacadam tentacles to dead-end cul-de-sacs to see the impact of petrol on the metropolis. At any point along the Thames, from its start in the rolling hills of the Cotswolds, right through to its gaping North Sea estuary, the world granted by petrol is entirely discernible. Just listen. The baritone rumble of vans. The Brownian roar of overhead planes. The whiny cackle of mopeds. The sonic backdrop of the early twenty-first century is an artefact of the diesel age's long tail.

The twentieth century birthed two notable waves of technological revolution, the first driven by advances in electrical engineering and a second fuelled by petrol. But in its dying breath the era unleashed a final technological shift that would once again transform the material, culture and economy of the city. Over the course of a fifteen-minute walk beyond the ghost of Stepney Power Station, you can follow the Thames around its iconic bend. In the middle of this meander is where the East India and West India companies carved out their larger downriver docks. These too were made redundant by the mid-twentieth century 'containerisation' of global shipping. Near abandoned for at least four decades, the obsolete docks were finally repurposed as water features beside new gargantuan columns of high finance. The second outpost of London's financial quarter, the Canary Wharf development, is a typical post-industrial 'reurbanisation' initiative (Butler, 2007) grounded in digital technologies and associated with seemingly dematerialised global 'flows' in information (Castells, 2011). Populated by institutions like HSBC, JP Morgan

Chase, Barclays, KPMG and Citibank, today's entire urban economy is interwoven with the district through a web of optical fibres. Which is not to say that the institutions in Canary Wharf have any allegiance to the city in which they are embedded. Rather, they exist as a relay between the locality and the global economy. As such the flap of a panicked trader's arms on the other side of the world instantly registers its effects in the financial machinery of Canary Wharf. More precisely, the issuing of mortgages to Americans with poor credit can level an entire bank based beside the Thames. The 2008 bankruptcy of Canary Wharf-based American bank, Lehman Brothers, started a chain reaction that cost the entire British economy at least five years of growth (Loh and Scruton, 2018). Ironically, the local finance sector emerged from the crisis relatively unscathed. At the same time, many residual industrial and manufacturing industries that remained in London from previous eras were devastated by the 2008 'credit crunch' and never recovered (Harris, 2016).

Aside from tying Londoner's real-time finances to events around the world, the digital revolution has also had other profound effects on the city. In one vision of the future, the digital revolution was supposed to have led, ultimately, to a sort of deurbanisation. Networked technologies were supposed to afford both spatially and temporally more flexible types of working. The 'space of places' (a society grounded in physical spaces), we were once told, was to be displaced by the 'space of flows' in information and culture (Castells, 2011). This prediction certainly fitted with the general trend. Up to the end of the twentieth century, successive waves in sociotechno innovation had driven economic activity, urban cultures and communities, further and further from the historic urban core. Technological advances throughout the twentieth century thinned the city out, with the inner ten London boroughs population dropping from 2.5 to 1.7 million between 1961 and 1981 (Brown et al., 2020), while outer boroughs grew. But with the final loss of industry from the city and the digitalisation of the economy, a renaissance of urban cores has occurred. Rather than triggering a final 'fade to black' for urbanism, the digital revolution has seen waves rebounding off suburban limits, coursing back up the river like a tidal bore. As these waves crashed back onto the shores of the city's innards, they coughed up a jetsam of tech workers, creatives, bars, gyms and coffee shops, once again inflating the population of London's ten inner boroughs to 2.6 million residents (ONS, 2014).

In the ages of its industrial expansion the city had a proletarian core surrounded by a crust of petit bourgeois suburbia. Today's city has seen that model increasingly inverted. The twenty-first century digital economy and its technocratic operatives have thrived on inner urban space. They have been drawn, of course, by the consumable spectacle and residues of urbane culture (Zukin, 1995, 2020). But it is also clear that urban space continues to afford opportunities for agglomeration. As dematerialised as the digital economy might sometimes seem, it still requires the physical clustering of amenities for its operation. This is manifest in more ways than simply the hyperbolic clustering of artisanal bakeries and arthouse cinemas in the '15-minute' pedestrian city. It also pertains to infrastructure. If we follow the river around the idiosyncratic knee that Canary Wharf sits on, just past the Radisson Hotel, there is a strange windowless cuboid overlooking the river. This is Telehouse South. It is the first in a chain of blocky buildings stretching a quarter of a mile north from the river. Comprised of Telehouse South, West, East, North and North Two, the cluster is owned by the Japan-based KDDI organisation. With their own purpose-built power substations and advanced cooling facilities, these anonymous boxes' tenants include Amazon Web Services, Microsoft Azure, Google's Cloud Platform and the London Internet Exchange. The entire digital economy is facilitated by these very real, very large, power-hungry cubes. Their proximity to one another and to necessary infrastructure is not a coincidence. From clusters of coffee shops, bars and gyms that reproduce knowledge workers, to centralised server farms and power substations, the digital economy thrives on the spatial efficiencies that historic inner cities offer (Giuliano et al., 2019).

Floods and frozen rivers

In an important and often overlooked essay, historical sociologist Norbert Elias cautioned against late-modern sociologists' tendency to retreat into the present (Elias, 1987). A focus on immediate problems and short-term solutions, Elias argued, risked an underestimation of the gifts that the past makes to its futures. A myopic focus also tended to overlook the connections between processes taking places across disparate regions. Arguing along similar lines, early twentieth-century Russian economist Nikolai Kondratiev argued that, as much as orthodox economics tries to understand the world through the short-term cycles of boom and bust, we would do well to look towards longer-term trends. In particular, he argued that we could understand economic, social and cultural change better when looking at the forty to sixty year-long waves of activity concurrent with accelerations in technological development (Kondratieff and Stolper, 1935). Notoriously difficult to identify in quantitative data, at worst, evidence of longer-term economic cycles might simply be the hallucination of patterns amid reams of otherwise confounding information (Nurkse, 1953: 12–13). But as urban sociologists, from Louis Wirth (1938) and Georg Simmel (1997) to Thomas Bender and Ignacio Farías (Farías and Bender, 2012) have argued, technological changes have had an especially profound impact on urban life. Accordingly, if we look towards the materiality of cities as well as the social and cultural life historically entangled with it, we might be able to more clearly identify the deposits left by longer-term waves of change. It is these technologically mediated waves of development that we have been trying to follow through a cross-section of the city's growth rings.

A more universal flaw in Kondratiev's cyclical model of social and economic evolution, shared with familiar theories of shorter-term cycles, is its hubristic infinity. As many have argued over the last half century, the cyclical growth and mutation of economies is not necessarily endless. Nor are cities immortal. As long as economic activity is extractive, then each successive wave of development builds towards the moment wherein no more waves are possible (Meadows et al., 1974; Daly, 1993). The wisps of condensed hot air ventilated from the cooling systems at Telehouse are a timely reminder that the digital age too is environmentally extractive. Around 80 per cent of the world's energy is still derived through the burning of gas, oil or coal (British Petroleum, 2024). Aside from transforming cities, the consequence of all this combustion is an increase in the atmosphere's capacity to trap heat. This continual heating has many consequences for cities, especially those that emerged – as many have done – out of tidal waters. As you might notice if you walked along the Thames at full tide on a new or full moon, the oscillating river is often mere centimetres away from bursting its banks. Any rise in sea levels increases the risk of catastrophic flooding in the city. Our walk ends with London's effort to delay that apparent inevitability.

Travelling ten minutes further east, past Telehouse, and slightly along the Thames Path in Silver Town, an astonishing piece of engineering straddles the river. Catching the sunlight as the clouds drift out to sea, stand nine titanic silver-hooded sentinels. Since 1982 the piers of the Thames Flood Barrier have stared out to sea, shoulder to submerged shoulder, daring storm surges to test it. Designed to protect the city from everything up to one-in-a-thousand-year weather events, the Thames Flood Barrier has, thus far, proved to be very effective, guarding from flood damage 221 times (Environment Agency, 2024). The most serious incidents it responds to involve increased fluvial flow and a spring tide, combined with a storm surge driving southward down the North Sea coast. Were a perfect storm to raise the river above the hydraulic behemoths, a very real (neither metaphorical nor abstract) wave could cause a potential £300 billion worth of damage (Environment Agency, 2024). The server farms at Telehouse, the towers of high finance and subterranean shopping malls at Canary Wharf, the generous front rooms of Edwardian suburbs, the lamp-lit Victorian subway tunnels, the banks and insurers of the Old City and much more beyond, could be inundated by unforgivingly silty water. This is not an end-of-days disaster fantasy but an increasingly likely possibility. As the Environment Agency notes, 'the defences were not built to withstand the higher water levels expected in the future'. While the flood barrier is predicted to still be functional in 2070, 'in some places, sea levels will be high enough for waves to go over some defences and cause regular flooding by 2040' (Environment Agency, 2023).

Such floods would be the short-term impact of climate change. Longer term, the effects might be even more transformative. Were, for instance, the Gulf Stream to weaken or collapse – as many models of global warming suggest it could – then the wider climatic impact on the Thames Estuary would be profound. No longer would the prevailing wind blow from the balmy west, but from the icier north-east. Whenever this has happened for anything longer than the occasional cold spell, such as during the eighteenth century's

Little Ice Age, the Thames has frozen solid (Hopkin, 2006). But these cold spells can last even longer than an 'ice fair'. In the last epochal period of global warming, the lead up to peak warmth was interrupted by thousand-year-long glaciations (National Research Council, 2002). It might be a lonely post-apocalyptic ice-skate down river to Dagenham.

References

Ayre, Julian and Wroe-Brown, Robin (2015) The eleventh- and twelfth-century waterfront and settlement at Queenhithe: Excavations at Bull Wharf, City of London. *Archaeological Journal*, 172 (2), 195–272.

Bordo, Michael, Taylor, Alan and Williamson, Jeffrey (2007) *Globalization in Historical Perspective*. Chicago, IL: University of Chicago Press.

British Petroleum (2024) *BP Energy Outlook 2024*. Available at: www.bp.com/content/dam/bp/business-sites/en/global/corporate/pdfs/energy-economics/energy-outlook/bp-energy-outlook-2024.pdf [accessed 6 January 2025].

Brown, Jack, Gariban, Sara and Belcher, Emma (2020) *Central London in Focus*. Centre for London. Available at: https://centreforlondon.org/reader/central-london/central-london-in-focus/ [accessed 6 January 2025].

Butler, Tim (2007) Re-urbanizing London Docklands: Gentrification, Suburbanization or New Urbanism? *International Journal of Urban and Regional Research*, 31 (4), 759–81.

Castells, Manuel (2011) *The Rise of the Network Society*. Hoboken, NJ: John Wiley & Sons.

Chatterton, Edward Keble (1910) *Steamships and their Story*. London: Cassell and Company Limited. Available at: www.gutenberg.org/ebooks/72045 [accessed 16 October 2025].

Daly, Herman E. (1993) Steady-state economics: A new paradigm. *New Literary History*, 24 (4), 811–16.

de Sena, Peter (1986) Perquisites and Pilfering in the London Docks, 1700–1795. Master's thesis, Open University. Available at: www.proquest.com/docview/2334693079?pq-origsite=gscholar&fromopenview=true&sourcetype=Dissertations%20&%20Theses [accessed 26 December 2024].

Donnachie, Ian (2008) Hydraulic Power Company. Talk given to the Lambeth and Southwark Archaeological Society, 1979. Available at: https://web.archive.org/web/20080127230807/http://www.vauxhallsociety.org.uk/Hydraulic.html [accessed 26 December 2024].

Drew, William A. (1852) *Glimpses and Gatherings During a Voyage and Visit to London and the Great Exhibition in the Summer of 1851*. Augusta, GA: Homan & Manley.

Elias, Norbert (1987) The retreat of sociologists into the present. *Theory, Culture & Society*, 4 (2–3), 223–47.

Environment Agency (2023) *Thames Estuary 2100: Why we Need it.* Gov.uk. Available at: www.gov.uk/guidance/thames-estuary-2100-why-we-need-it [accessed 2 January 2025].

Environment Agency (2024) *The Thames Barrier – protecting London and the Thames Estuary for 40 years.* Press release, 8 May. Gov.uk. Available at: www.gov.uk/government/news/the-thames-barrier-protecting-london-and-the-thames-estuary-for-40-years [accessed 2 January 2025].

Farías, Ignacio and Bender, Thomas (2012) *Urban Assemblages: How Actor–Network Theory Changes Urban Studies.* Abingdon and New York: Routledge.

Gamsu, Sol (2016) Moving up and moving out: The re-location of elite and middle-class schools from central London to the suburbs. *Urban Studies*, 53 (14), 2921–38.

Gerbner, Katharine (2018) *Christian Slavery: Conversion and Race in the Protestant Atlantic World.* Philadelphia, PA: University of Pennsylvania Press.

Giuliano, Genevieve, Kang, Sanggyun and Yuan, Quan (2019) Agglomeration economies and evolving urban form. *Annals of Regional Science*, 63 (3), 377–98.

Harreld, Donald (ed.) (2015) *A Companion to the Hanseatic League.* Leiden and Boston, MA: Brill.

Harris, James (2016) *Business Activity, Pay and Declining Jobs in Manufacturing in London, 2015.* Office for National Statistics. Available at: www.ons.gov.uk/employmentandlabourmarket/peopleinwork/employmentandemployeetypes/compendium/earninglearningandbusinesschurning/revealinglondonsindustrialeconomyin2015/businessactivitypayanddecliningjobsinmanufacturinginlondon2015 [accessed 21 February 2025].

Hopkin, Michael (2006) Gulf Stream weakened in 'Little Ice Age'. *Nature.* https://doi.org/10.1038/news061127-8

Hudson, Paul (2009) 80 years of Ford at Dagenham, *Telegraph*, 15 May. Available at: www.telegraph.co.uk/motoring/classiccars/5318900/80-years-of-Ford-at-Dagenham.html [accessed 7 January 2025].

Illustrated London News (1843) Nooks and Corners of Old England, *Illustrated London News*, 24 June. Available at: http://archive.org/details/sim_illustrated-london-news_1843-06-24_2_60 [accessed 26 December 2024].

Kondratieff, Nikolai and Stolper, Walter F. (1935) The long waves in economic life. *Review of Economics and Statistics*, 17 (6), 105–15.

Koslofsky, Craig (2011) *Evening's Empire: A History of the Night in Early Modern Europe.* Cambridge and New York: Cambridge University Press.

Loh, Velma, and Scruton, James (2018) *The 2008 Recession 10 Years On*. Office for National Statistics, 30 April. Available at: www.ons.gov.uk/economy/grossdomesticproductgdp/articles/the2008recession10yearson/2018-04-30 [accessed 6 January 2025].

London Assembly (2022) *London Car Ownership – London Travel Demand Survey*. Available at: www.london.gov.uk/who-we-are/what-london-assembly-does/questions-mayor/find-an-answer/london-car-ownership [accessed 31 December 2024].

Marmefelt, Thomas (2013) Hanseatic monetary arrangements and the functional separation of money. Paper prepared for the EAEPE Conference 2013: Beyond Industrialisation: The Future of Industries, Paris, 7–9 November.

Marsden, Peter Richard Valentine (1994) *Ships of the Port of London: First to Eleventh Centuries AD*. Swindon: English Heritage.

Matthews, William (1827) *An Historical Sketch of the Origin, Progress, & Present State, of Gas-Lighting*. London: Rowland Hunter.

Meadows, Donella H., Meadows, Dennis L., Randers, Jørgen and Behrens, William W. III (1974) *The Limits to Growth: A Report for the Club of Rome's Project on the Predicament of Mankind*. New York: Universe Books.

Mintz, Sidney Wilfred (1986) *Sweetness and Power: The Place of Sugar in Modern History*. New York: Penguin Books.

Mount, Toni (2015) *Everyday Life in Medieval London: From the Anglo-Saxons to the Tudors*. Stroud: Amberley. Available at: http://archive.org/details/everydaylifeinme0000moun [accessed 18 December 2024].

Mucklow, Walter (1932) Herrings and the first great combine, part II: The Hanseatic League in England. *Journal of Accountancy*, 53 (5), article 6.

National Research Council (2002) *Abrupt Climate Change: Inevitable Surprises*. Washington, DC: National Academies Press.

Nurkse, Ragnar (1953) *Problems of Capital Formation in Underdeveloped Countries*. Oxford: Basil Blackwell.

ONS (2014) *Historical Census Population*. London Datastore, London Assembly. Available at: https://data.london.gov.uk/dataset/historic-census-population [accessed 7 January 2025].

Reclaim EC1 (2022) 'When will the City Of London revert the name of Sugar Quay to the less contentious Custom House Quay?', *RECLAIM EC1* [blog post], 11 August. Available at: https://reclaimec1.wordpress.com/2022/08/11/when-will-the-city-of-london-revert-the-name-of-sugar-quay-to-the-less-contentious-custom-house-quay/ [accessed 6 January 2025].

Rocque, John (2013) *Rocque's Map of Georgian London, 1746*. Old House Books.

Rose, Susan (2017) *The Wealth of England: The Medieval Wool Trade and its Political Importance 1100–1600*. Oxford: Oxbow Books.
Simmel, Georg (1997) *Simmel on Culture: Selected Writings*, ed D. Frisby and M. Featherstone. London: Sage.
Turvey, Ralph (1993) London lifts and hydraulic power. *Transactions of the Newcomen Society*, 65 (1), 147–64.
Unger, Richard (1980) *The Ship in the Medieval Economy, 600–1600*. London: Croom Helm.
Unger, Richard (1994) *Cogs, Caravels, and Galleons: The Sailing Ship, 1000–1650*. Annapolis, MD: Naval Institute Press.
Waddington, Quintin (1934) Vestiges of pre-Roman London. *Journal of the British Archaeological Association*, 39 (2).
Williams, Eric (1994) *Capitalism and Slavery*. Chapel Hill, NC: University of North Carolina Press.
Wirth, Louis (1938) Urbanism as a way of life. *American Journal of Sociology*, 44 (1), 1–24.
Zukin, Sharon (1995) *The Cultures of Cities*. Oxford: Wiley-Blackwell.
Zukin, Sharon (2020) *The Innovation Complex: Cities, Tech, and the New Economy*. New York: Oxford University Press.

12

In the Big Yin's footsteps: class, belonging and the long walk home

Les Back

In 2010, Billy Connolly, known affectionally as The Big Yin, was awarded The Freedom of the City of Glasgow, Scotland. This is the highest recognition that is in the municipality's power to offer any person and it is conferred by the Lord Provost of Glasgow. Born on 24 November 1942 at 65 Dover Street, in working-class Anderston on the north bank of the River Clyde on the western edge of the city centre, the world-renowned comedian, banjo player, actor and artist is inextricably linked to his beginnings there.

Nelson Mandela, another recipient of this honour, congratulated the Lord Provost of Glasgow, local Councillor Bob Winter, commending this 'freedom-loving part of the world' for choosing Billy Connolly. Mandela wrote: 'On this special occasion, I wish Mr Connolly my congratulations on the high honour being bestowed on him today. Welcome to a very special club indeed!'[1] Through his stand-up routines that lovingly portray the absurdities and realities of everyday life in the tenements and shipyards, Billy Connolly has done more than perhaps anyone to tell the city's story.

When I was a child in the 1970s, the only person on TV who described a world that I understood as a young working-class kid growing up in the suburbs of London was Billy Connolly. Now fifty years later as a 'new Glaswegian' in my sixties, his city has become mine. The trace of Billy Connolly is everywhere, and he is beloved in the city. I have met Glaswegians who find his close association with the rich and famous film stars hard to take and feel his acceptance of a knighthood in 2017 is at odds with his working-class credentials.

Stories of home often contain ambivalent attachments (Blunt and Dowling, 2022). It can be something that we yearn to find or reach, an allusive peaceful place of being in the world that is comfortable, even if you've not moved, even if you stayed in the same place. At the same time, Billy Connolly made his name as being of this place of Glasgow. He worked as a welder in the shipyards, but like one of the ships on the Clyde he had to leave and get out of Glasgow, even though it was his 'home'. One of the things he reveals in his autobiography, *Windswept and interesting* (2021), is the damage wrought in that place and the sexual abuse that he experienced at the hands of his father. He escaped it when they were moved out of the Glasgow tenements to the new homes of the public housing schemes on the fringes in a place called Drumchapel. In an almost matter of fact way, Billy writes: 'Finally, I could sleep soundly in my own bed without interference' (Connolly, 2021: 100).

He hasn't lived in the city since the late 1970s, but has returned to the city routinely in the fifty years since leaving and has said of Glaswegians: 'I belong to them, and they belong to me'.[2]

Connolly is a magpie storyteller who is unflinchingly honest, but so many of his tall tales were shared with him by the people of Glasgow and then retold and embellished in his stand-up routines. He often introduces them by saying 'Please let this be true'. Those stories, lovingly told, were vivid and full of life, and neither romantic nor cruel. They had texture. They felt close to me even though I was four hundred miles away living in a council estate in Croydon, south London. Billy Connolly documented a specific experience which also resonated beyond conveying what Raymond Williams called a *structure of feeling* within working-class communities (Williams, 1977).

Connolly described the elaborate forms of Friday night pub singing that would happen at the parties that were true of working-class communities throughout Britain – something that Richard Hoggart called 'club singing' ballads of the 'feeling heart' (Hoggart, 1957: 166). He was part of a generation of young working-class voices that were coming of age at that moment and who were giving working-class life a new voice expressed on its own terms, from musicians like Gerry Rafferty, with whom he played in the folk duo The Humblebums, to painter and filmmaker John Byrne and authors Val McDermid and Agnes Owens.

During his 2010 visit to receive the Freedom of the City of Glasgow, Billy Connolly was asked where he would take a visitor if he were showing them around the city. He replied:

> There are two places I would take people who came to Glasgow ... you could go for a walk up Buchanan Street from the bottom right up away to the top to the bus station to see Glasgow at its busiest most thronging pedestrian, wise-cracking self. That's one Glasgow and it's a very, very worthwhile Glasgow. But my favourite is the peaceful Glasgow ... Kelvin Way.[3]

I want to walk these streets as a way of contributing to this book on what we learn about social life when we get out into their ebb and flow and move through them. I have used walking as a way of accessing the secret life of cities in much of my previous work, from the migrant experience to understanding the trace of political and musical histories (Back, 2017; Back and Sinha, 2018). Walking in Billy Connolly's footsteps I hope to learn about the cultural and political forces that formed the Glasgow he knew, but also how this story is implicated in the stories of other cities. It is through wandering that we hold the past, present and future in a relationship with each other.

* * *

It's late afternoon in central Glasgow in January 2025. Freya Hellier has her sound recording equipment to document a 'soundwalk' through Buchanan Street. This recording provided both a way of documenting the sounds of the street and an opportunity for us to work together and generate ideas that we are imagining as a future podcast. So, the sound walk is both an 'empirical' writing resource and a medium in its own right.

Our starting point is just a short walk from Glasgow's Central Station, which was opened in 1879. Behind Buchanan Street is St Enoch subway station and the Bank of Scotland. Looking north, the Royal Concert Hall looms above this wide pedestrian thoroughfare – a place to wander, shop and exchange both goods and ideas. Buchanan Street is named after the wealthy Tobacco Lord, plantation owner and former Lord Provost of Glasgow, Andrew Buchanan, of Buchanan, Hastie & Co., who was one of the first

Scots to speculate in tobacco. The street was bought with the blood money made from his tobacco empire in Virginia, which was reliant on the Atlantic slave trade (Mackenzie and Devine, 1999). While Glasgow was not a slave port in the sense that very few slave ships docked on the Firth of Clyde, it was a major destination for the ignominious fruits of slave plantations in the form of tobacco, sugar and cotton. (Mullen, 2009). The American Revolution of 1776 forced the Buchanans to change direction, as all their plantations in Virginia were seized. They moved their money into textile manufacturing and industrial capitalism. The street name is a reminder of the deep implication of Glasgow in plantation slavery and colonial expansion, second only to London as a metropolis born out of empire (Devine, 2015).

Walking up Buchanan Street today is very different to the city that Billy Connolly would have grown up in, which was forged by the ship-building industries on the River Clyde. You can almost see it from here, and the banks of the Clyde were the centre of the city's industry, its coal- and oil-based economy. The fortunes of the city floated on the Clyde in many ways as the city's main artery in the industrial and imperial eras (see Gibbs, 2022).

Immediately to the left is the department store, Frasers, and on the other side of the street the brands of today can be found in Zara and a Nike superstore. It's a mixture of the grandeur of the high streets of now, and the Victorian buildings that climb up on either side of this beautiful thoroughfare. It is a wide-open street, with pedestrian walkways five paving stones wide, reminiscent of the sidewalks of New York. In the nineteenth century it was a street for horses and carts, but then in the twentieth century for the motor car. The movement to pedestrianise Buchanan Street began in the 1970s, initially focusing on the southern end, and by 1978 the street was made entirely pedestrian.

To the right, as I walk up the hill, is the beautiful Argyle Arcade. Built in 1827 in the Parisian style, its shopfronts glittering with expensive jewellery and watches, the L-shaped arcade cuts through an old tenement linking Buchanan Street with neighbouring Argyle Street. Walter Benjamin wrote that a guide to any city can be other cities that we have known (Benjamin, 1997: 298). I feel that Glasgow today is a guide and an uncanny reminder of the post-industrial London of my childhood. Benjamin was fascinated by the arcades because they embodied an archetype of urban modernity, ideal for the wandering flâneur to lose and find himself (Benjamin, 1999).

A middle-aged man in a 'top hat' approaches us. 'You can't film in here without permission', he says in a disapproving tone. 'We're not filming, it's just sound recording', I say, pointing to Freya's microphone covered by a 'dead cat' wind protection device that is aptly named. I realise further explanation is required. 'I teach sociology at the university, and I'm writing a piece about Billy Connolly's walks through Glasgow, and Buchanan Street is one of them.' The top-hatted security guard immediately softens at the mention of the Big Yin's name. 'So you are not filming?' 'No, we won't do any damage', I say jokingly. He nods approvingly. I imagine what Billy would have said to the geezer in the top hat.

The thing I love about this street is that it opens to the sky; there is a strong sense of being in a city, but also the city doesn't crowd you in. It's a place for any kind of public communication – and lots of music, the many buskers are often joined by enthusiastic passers-by, keen to dance or have their turn on the mic. It feels unregulated, perhaps except for the arcade. Billy says that this street has the finery of the grand shops but also some of the tackiness – the best and the worst of human commerce. I hear a passing American tourist say, 'It's a very nice city'. How right they are. James Pringle Weavers, established in 1750, a place to buy tartan scarves and all things Scottish, is right next to Urban Outfitters and an Apple Store – contemporary global brands being housed in these classical Victorian sandstone buildings. Another busker, this time a trumpeter performing the second movement from Haydn's Trumpet Concerto to a backing track, at deafening volume. This contrasts with my favourites, who are usually electric guitar players performing punk and classic rock anthems a little further up the street.

To the right is Queen's Street train station. Just opposite is Nelson Mandela Place with St George's Tron Church in the middle with its beautiful, tall spire – quiet, compact, angular and steep.

Nelson Mandela stood trial multiple times and spent over twenty-seven years in prison in South Africa. While he became a global symbol of resistance to South Africa's white minority oppression of the Black majority, it is easy to forget that the Conservative establishment – including in Scotland – long viewed him as a 'terrorist'. The Scottish anti-apartheid movement was strong, and included people like Brian Filling who had been campaigning since the 1960s. In 1981, Glasgow's Labour Council decided to award Mandela the Freedom of the City while he was still in prison. Then, because of anti-apartheid campaigning and lobbying, the City Council changed the name of St George's Place in the city centre to Nelson Mandela Place in 1986. It was a bold provocation because the South African consulate was based here on the fifth floor of the Stock Exchange building. Mandela would be in an apartheid prison for four more years, but throughout that time, the South African consulate in Glasgow was located at an address that bore his name.

Mandela was given the freedom of nine cities and regions during his imprisonment, but on his release he chose Glasgow as the place to formally receive these honours at the City Chambers. In his acceptance speech on 9 October 1993, he said: 'While we were physically denied our freedom in the country of our birth, a city 6,000 miles away, and as renowned as Glasgow, refused to accept the legitimacy of the apartheid system, and declared us to be free' (Brocklehurst, 2018). Written into this street is not only Glasgow's complicity with imperialism and racial capitalism but also its contribution to global struggles against racism for freedom.

Further up the hill is the cheap side of what Billy Connolly talked about in the street's economy – the Tartan House of Scotland. Bagpipes are blasting as we walk close by; the T-shirts are magnificent. There is a black one with Victor and Jack from the BBC Scotland sitcom *Still Game*. The t-shirt says 'Two pints, ya prick'. There's something about the profanity of the culture in Glasgow that I just love. A place to swear and laugh in equal measure. In 2010, Connolly commented:

> The thing that undoubtedly stands out about Glasgow, beyond all other cities, is its humour. There's a warmth and humour which I think comes of immigration: Jewish, Italian, Highland Scottish, Irish – all mixed in together in the Victorian times, and has come through as this Glaswegian thing. Edinburgh's lovely and it's got lots of dead things that are very nice … Glasgow's lovely and has lots of live things that are even nicer. I am honestly confused sometimes, and I meet people in America and they say 'I've just been in Glasgow, what friendly people', which hasn't always been my experience because I have lived here and I have met people who are friendly and I have met people who are not very friendly, but I am so immensely proud of the tourists' impression of Glasgow. Glasgow likes outsiders.'[4]

It's one of the things I've noticed as an outsider trying to make a sense of home in Glasgow. Everyone I meet has a story about London – of having lived there or visited. 'I went to London once. How you could live there with all that hustle and bustle?' There was a famous street trader named Dick Lee, known as 'Cockney Jock', who sold dolls, toys, towels and bedding, and is remembered for gathering the largest crowds with his funny jokes and gags at the famous Barras Market in Glasgow's East End. London in Glasgow: Glasgow in London. I have not experienced anything approaching hostility here as a cockney. But you must be able to take a joke, and you must not take yourself seriously.

We pass Buchanan Street subway station, another Glasgow institution. It only has one circular line – with trains going in either direction – so if you miss your stop, you can just stay on and come right around if you need to. It's referred to as the Clockwork Orange by Glaswegians. And then, across the street, there is the largest Victoria's Secret women's underwear store I have ever seen. Glasgow is a cheeky and saucy city – it's alive on Saturday night when droves of youngsters converge on the city, often in fancy dress or various states of undress, bound for clubs on dark, cold winter nights. They have a word for it – 'Gallus' – meaning naughty, mischievous or bold. It is in the humour of life, a profane kind of playfulness, and it is in the sophisticated swearing too that has been a hallmark of Billy Connolly's stand-up routines.

At the top of the street is Glasgow's Royal Concert Hall, a boxy twentieth-century modernist structure next to the John Lewis department store. There are many gigs in the Royal Concert Hall connected to the Celtic Connections folk festival, which takes place in January. There is a beautiful sign beside the staircase featuring the figure of St Mungo with his open hand raised. Below him is Glasgow's crest, which includes two fish, a bell, a tree and a scroll bearing the words of the city's motto: 'Let Glasgow flourish'. This year – 2025 – marks 850 years of Glasgow. At the bottom of the stone steps leading up to the concert hall is a statue of beloved Scottish politician Donald Dewar. He was Scotland's first First Minister, and on the plinth is a simple message of self-determination: 'There will be a Scottish Parliament'. It is unmarked by graffiti or vandalism.

This is the view that I love, and you can see the thoroughfare of Buchanan Street past St Enoch subway station. You can't see the river, but you know it's there. The sun is going down. It's a beautiful pink sky. And you can see on the other side, in the distance, the hills beyond. There's another busker with an impressive voice singing Olivia Newton-John's hit 'Hopelessly Devoted to You'. A man is dancing halfway up the concert hall steps. I find myself involuntarily shouting: 'Yes, geezer'. We exchange grins. He is swaying his outstretched arms, fists clenched like an aeroplane tipping its wings in time with the music.

* * *

The light is starting to fade as we arrive at the second walk in what Billy Connolly called 'peaceful Glasgow'. The West End, in many ways, is the centre of science and culture in the city. It is also a beautiful green space, as Billy describes: 'Kelvin Way runs through the middle of Kelvingrove Park to the East of the art galleries. Walk up there over the River Kelvin and just have a lovely peaceful wee walk to yourself. Glasgow University is to your left, the tennis courts are on your right, and if you want more just turn right into the park and there's a lovely walk along the Kelvin, feed the ducks … happy as a clam. That's what you need in your life.'[5]

Billy Connolly's eldest sister Florence would sometimes bring him here, to the imposing Kelvingrove Museum, as a boy: 'It made a huge impression on me. Some of the art there was amazing. I was completely blown away by Salvador Dali's *Christ of Saint John of the Cross*, which I thought was the greatest painting I had ever seen … I also loved the Kelvingrove because it had these fantastic slippery marble floors, and I could take my shoes off and run and slide at great speed between its many artistic masterpieces' (Connolly with Gittins, 2018: 137). Kelvin Way is another hill, and to our left is the spire of the University of Glasgow's Gilbert Scott Building.

As a boy, Billy Connolly lived in the neighbouring district of Partick (see essay 6 by Kirsteen Paton). He went to school on the south side of the river in Govan. The museums and libraries were places of refuge for him. It was the same experience for working-class kids around the country for whom the public library was a place to think for yourself and become more than the world had decided for you. It is another resonance between Billy Connolly's life and my own (see Back, 2016: 195–200). Connolly comments in his memoir: 'When I was young, people used to have all kinds of advice as to how the working class could free themselves from factory life and all of that frustration, but for me the true secret tunnel, the hidden escape route, was in the library, reading books.' (Connolly, 2019: 7). Kelvin Way is on my journey to work at the university every day. It has a feeling of peace and calm. It is mostly a pedestrian space, only partially accessible to cars. As we go up the hill, there's a burger van parked there permanently called MacTassos. It boasts of providing Glaswegians and visitors to the city with authentic Greek food since 2017.

We approach the bridge that crosses the River Kelvin. When the weather is bad, the river flows wildly – brown and furious, its surface patterned with eddies and swirling currents.

On each of the corners of the Kelvin Way Bridge stand a pair of magnificent bronze sculptures representing Peace and War, Commerce and Industry, Philosophy and Inspiration and Navigation and Shipbuilding. Each pair is like a totem of Glasgow's past. Two female figures stand back to back; one wears an apron and holds a ship and mallet, while the other places her right hand on a boat's tiller and gazes out to the horizon, symbolising Clydeside's shipbuilding and imperial exploration. My favourite pair is Charles Darwin holding a skull underneath his elbow as he looks down, stroking his beard philosophically and contemplating big thoughts while a female figure looks out, searching for inspiration, holding a lute.

Completed in 1914 by the artist Paul Montford, who was born in Kentish Town, London, and studied in his father's studio and then at Lambeth School of Art (1884–85). Between 1893 and 1919, Montford received several commissions, including sculptures for Battersea Polytechnic, Battersea Town Hall, and the bridge at Kelvingrove – another example of the close artistic and cultural connections between London and Glasgow. The bridge was hit by a Nazi landmine during the Clydebank Blitz in March 1941, and ironically the Peace and War statues ended up falling into the River Kelvin. The sculptures were restored and repaired by Estonian-born sculptor Benno Schotz after the war.

The sun is starting to go down. It's the magic pink light. The spire of the university has been illuminated as the light fades. Students are wandering down the hill after a day of study. To the left, as we walk up the hill, there is a small park and a statue of Lord Kelvin holding a book in a patch of green encircled by wrought-iron benches.

A murder of crows surrounds the scholar as if they are cross-examining him in the twilight. Along the iron fence are lines of Christmas trees that have been discarded after the festivities. The council shredding teams have gone home now. The steaming pile of mulched Christmas trees gives off the moist smell of freshly cut pines as they decompose – the smell of winter.

The hill on the other side is home to the exclusive Park Circus, with its beautiful mansions and famed residences of professional footballers like Steven Gerrard, who lived there while managing Glasgow Rangers. In Alasdair Gray's novel *Poor things*, the reanimated heroine Bella Baxter is also described as living there with the scientist Dr Godwin Baxter (Gray, 2002). The trees are bare tonight, and a thick carpet of decomposing leaves covers the path. It gets steeper as we climb toward University Avenue. In the summer, it is a lush green woodland boulevard, but tonight it is a wintery and aptly austere path leading to the place of knowledge, enlightenment and learning. No surprise that a young boy looking for the outside, looking for an escape route, looking for a life beyond the one that he knew, would be enchanted by the peace in this place.

There is an award-winning tree too, just off to the left at the top of the hill. The Hungarian oak tree was the Scottish tree of the year in 2015, but it looks a little battered today. It is known as the Suffrage Tree, and was nominated by the Glasgow Women's Library. The plaque next to the tree explains that it was planted on 20 April 1918 by women's suffrage organisations in Glasgow to commemorate the granting of votes for women (see King, 1993). In October 2017, the Suffrage Tree was severely damaged by Storm Ophelia, which ripped a large tear in its trunk, and this historic tree lost 30 per cent of its canopy. To save it and make it safe, Glasgow City Council had to perform tree surgery to amputate and balance the branches. The offcuts were gifted to the Glasgow Women's Library, which used the storm-damaged wood to create and sell items celebrating the efforts of the suffragettes. These included earrings, chopping boards, coasters, magnets and trinket boxes crafted by local artist Annie Graham.

So here we are at the top of Kelvin Way, just on the edge of the university campus, a place where the students, sometimes, when they're out for their runs, stop to catch a breath, and where I turn to climb the hill of University Avenue. There are two sets of pillars at the entrance, and both entrances have Victorian lights on them. There's a pink light over Park Circus. I feel the ghost of Alasdair Gray looking down on us thinking, 'What in the world are you doing?' Three boys emerge, full of furtive mischief, from a smashed telephone box covered in graffiti, which at nightfall looks like an ancient ruin from another time.

To end this stroll in the Big Yin's footsteps, I want to return to Billy himself, who will be 83 years young this year. He reflected in 2012:

> Glasgow is my city of conflict. The views, the sounds, and the smells of these streets are jammed with memories of being cold and warm, in love and broken-hearted, crying with laughter and regret. I loved Glasgow, but that love has always been matched with an urge to leave, to see over the horizon, and that pull has made me a proud citizen of the world. Yet there has always been a string in my heart that I am glad pulls me back to where I am from to all the things good and bad that made me.[6]

Glasgow is a place to laugh and find solace. Perhaps, like him, we are all losing and finding our place in the world. He has told the city's story, and the accolades he has received are part of that long walk home.

Notes

1 This letter is available at the Nelson Mandela Memorial Foundation: https://mandelascottishmemorial.org/nelson-mandelas-letter-about-billy-connolly-receiving-freedom-of-glasgow#:~:text=On%2028%20July%202010%2C%20Nelson%20Mandela%20wrote,strong%20connection%20to%20the%20people%20of%20Glasgow%2C
2 Quoted from *The Adam Buxton Podcast* 114, 14 December 2019.
3 Quoted in *Glasgow: Scotland with Style*, interview 2010 on the receipt of the Freedom of the City, by Glasgow City Marketing: www.youtube.com/watch?v=-7iaSuTbEg8
4 Quoted in *Glasgow: Scotland with Style*, interview 2010.
5 Quoted in *Glasgow: Scotland with Style*, interview 2010.
6 *Billy Connolly: Made in Scotland*, BBC Two, directed by Mike Reilly, series producer Jacqueline Houston, 7 Wonder Productions. Broadcast 28 December 2018.

References

Back, Les (2016) *Academic Diary: Or why Higher Education Still Matters*. London: Goldsmiths Press.

Back, Les (2017) Marchers and steppers: Memory, city life and walking. In Charlotte Bates and Alex Rhys-Taylor (eds) *Walking Through Social Research*. London: Routledge.

Back, Les and Sinha, Shamser (2018) *Migrant City*. London: Routledge.

Benjamin, Walter (1997) *One-Way Street*. London: Verso.

Benjamin, Walter (1999) *The Arcades Project*. Cambridge, MA: Belknap Press.

Blunt, Alison and Dowling, Robyn (2022) *Home*. London and New York: Routledge.

Brocklehurst, Steven (2018) Why did Nelson Mandela thank Glasgow? *BBC News*, 9 October. Available at: www.bbc.co.uk/news/uk-scotland-22976781 [accessed 31 January 2025].

Connolly, Billy (2019) *Tall Tales and Wee Stories*. London: Two Roads.

Connolly, Billy (2021) *Windswept and Interesting: My Autobiography*. London: Two Roads.

Connolly, Billy with Gittins, Ian (2018) *Made in Scotland*. London: BBC Books and Penguin Random House.

Devine, Tom (ed.) (2015) *Recovering Scotland's Slavery Past: The Caribbean Connection*. Edinburgh: Edinburgh University Press.

Gibbs, Ewan (2022) Glasgow, Clydeside's carbon capital, *Drouth*, 6 November. Available at: www.thedrouth.org/glasgow-clydesides-carbon-capital-by-ewan-gibbs/ [accessed 21 January 2025].

Gray, Alasdair (2002) *Poor Things*. London: Bloomsbury.

Hoggart, Richard (1957) *The Uses of Literacy*. Harmondsworth: Penguin.

King, Elspeth (1993) *The Hidden History of Glasgow's Women: The New Factor*. Edinburgh: Mainstream Publishing.

Mackenzie, John and Devine, T. M. (eds) (1999) *Scotland and the British Empire*. Oxford: Oxford University Press.

Mullen, Stephen (2009) *It Wisnae Us: The Truth About Glasgow and Slavery*. Glasgow: Glasgow Anti-Racist Alliance.

Williams, Raymond (1977) *Marxism and Literature*. Oxford: Oxford University Press.

13

Under a hawthorn tree or thoughts about Nightingales and war

Vron Ware

In the spring of 1917, the painter Paul Nash was stationed in northern France. Recalling his experience after the war had ended, he wrote of his despair at walking through what had once been a wood, now reduced to 'a place with an evil name, pitted and pocked with shells, the trees torn to shreds, often reeking with poison gas' (Gough, 2010: 135). Weeks later he had revisited the same battlefield. To his astonishment, this 'most desolate ruinous place' was drastically changed. It was now 'a vivid green'. In a letter to his wife he described the scene that confronted him: 'the most broken trees even had sprouted somewhere and in the midst, from the depth of the wood's bruised heart poured out the throbbing song of a Nightingale. Ridiculous mad incongruity! One can't think which is the more absurd, the War or Nature.'

* * *

Enfield Lock train station is on the northern edge of London's Zone 6, the final point at which I can use my Freedom Pass. The exit to Ordnance Road takes you on to a busy thoroughfare lined with shops and houses that could be anywhere. Checking the sun, I set off to the east. If you're looking for military history, then the word 'ordnance' is a pretty big clue that you're on the right track.

My actual destination is the Lee Valley Country Park, which is located a couple of miles north of the M25, and spans the border between Hertfordshire and Essex. I had chosen this route so that I could join the towpath that leads all the way from the Thames to Waltham Abbey, where the park begins. The raucous chatter of

Sparrows competing with heavy traffic bodes well, I think, as I mentally prepare myself for much sweeter sounds. June is a little late in the year to hear Nightingales, but it seems an awfully long time to wait for them to return next April and I am hoping to catch a straggler.

Sometimes I assess the quality of life by counting how many different species of birds I can hear from my bed in Zone 2. It depends on the season of course. Parakeets are common all year round in north London, and Robins too. One early morning in April we heard a passing Cuckoo, which must have taken a rest just outside our window. Blackbirds sometimes sing exuberantly in July. By the end of the month it goes very quiet and you'd be lucky to hear anything from inside the house, at least until the Tawny Owls get going in the autumn. But in November it is not uncommon for a Thrush to start up as dawn breaks, clearing its throat and practising until it's ready for full throttle in January.

When I was growing up in rural Hampshire in the fifties and sixties, visitors were either enthralled or disturbed by the dawn chorus that swelled every year with the first signs of spring. From April to July, they might have been kept awake by a Nightingale singing in the garden, or so I was told. I have no memory of that, but I do recall the incessant call of the Cuckoo, which always seemed to arrive on 17 April. Since birdsong was taken for granted in our household, I did not realise until much later that these sounds were diminishing year by year.

Now I would go anywhere to hear the sound of a Nightingale, day or night. My dream is to stay in a place where they are singing so I can drift in and out of sleep as I listen. It is still possible to do that, as long as it is within their range: south of a line from the Severn to the Humber. According to the British Trust for Ornithology, the numbers of UK Nightingales declined by 90 per cent between 1967 and 2022, although in some parts of Kent, Sussex and Essex they are holding steady thanks to conservation attempts to preserve the scrubby woodland areas where they nest.[1] The males generally begin to arrive in early–mid April, flying from their wintering grounds in The Gambia and Ghana to scout possible nesting sites in England. Once they have paired, they lay an average clutch of three to five eggs. After their young have fledged, they set off on the return journey in July.

Because of their reputation, people often think that they only sing at night, but this isn't actually true. You can be lucky at any time of day. But it's hard to hold on to that particular sound when you have to pack up and head home.

* * *

In 1889, the year in which Paul Nash was born, William Morris published a short essay called 'Under the Elm Tree', which he composed while lying on the side of a road in the Ashdown Forest, in Sussex, surrounded by grass and wildflowers. He begins by luring the reader into a languid, sensory state as he describes the colours, scents and sounds of a summer's day in the English countryside. But as he shields his face from the sun, he finds himself thinking about the state of the country. His next paragraph begins, 'What is that thought that has come into one's head as one turns round in the shadow of the roadside elm? … A country-side worth fighting for if that were necessary, worth taking trouble to defend its peace' (Morris, 1889: 212–13).

Barely moving his head, Morris reflects on the conversations and encounters he had enjoyed over the past few days, using his 'socialist ears' to bear witness to the abject plight of the agricultural labourers. His concluding words shows how much his mood had changed as he allowed his mind to wander:

> Yet think I to myself under the elm-tree, whatever England, once so beautiful, may become, it will be good enough for us if we set no hope before us but the continuance of a population of slaves and slave-holders for the country which we pretend to love, while we use it and our sham love for it as a stalking-horse for robbery of the poor at home and abroad. The worst outward ugliness and vulgarity will be good enough for such sneaks and cowards.

Interpreting the work more than a century later, historian Peter Linebaugh (2014: 124–5) noted that 'In a mere four and a half pages, the essay moves from impressionistic natural impressions through working-class oral testimony to an exposition of the systemic structure of capitalism in both town and country … all this while lying on the side of the road!' But, he concluded, although the writer begins by depicting 'the conventional summer scene of the poet', what he actually sees is war.

* * *

Morris was born in Walthamstow in 1834 and spent part of his childhood in Woodford, barely a mile away on the fringes of Epping Forest. He would definitely have been able to hear Nightingales from his bedroom. And although he was living in Hammersmith by the time this essay was published in *Commonweal*, he might have written the same kind of reverie much nearer to his childhood haunts: beginning with the sights, smells and sounds of his immediate environment, contemplating the conditions of working-class servitude nearby, and also ending with the question: is this still worth fighting for?

It occurs to me as I walk along Ordnance Road that by 1889 Morris would have been well aware of the world-famous Royal Small Arms Factory at Enfield Lock. Founded seventy-five years earlier, this was more than an innovative industrial operation mass-producing some of the most lethal tools of mid- to late-nineteenth-century warfare.

At the beginning of the nineteenth century all European infantry-men were expected to use a muzzle-loading musket which fired only seven out of ten times, and not at all in damp weather (Headrick, 1981: 85). During the Napoleonic Wars, the combination of faulty design and uneven production rates – leading to high fatalities among British soldiers – had demonstrated beyond doubt that the private sector was neither efficient nor reliable when it came to equipping men for battle. In 1813 the Board of Ordnance, a governmental body dating back to the Tudor period, decided to take responsibility for both the design and manufacture of small arms, or rifles.

Enfield Lock was the perfect location. The Lee navigation system, a complex arrangement of channels that had rendered the River Lea navigable as far north as Hertford, ensured that there was sufficient water pressure from the lock to power the new machines, and the artificial island between the new canal arm and the river made an ideal setting for the workers' living quarters.

The construction of the millpond, factory and cottages was completed in the autumn of 1815, shortly after the Battle of Waterloo. For the first four decades, Enfield Lock operated as a site for research and development in an attempt to standardise the parts for existing weapon design. The situation changed, however, by mid-century when the Royal Small Arms Factory began issuing the Enfield Pattern

1853, or the Enfield P53 for short. This was a muzzle-loading gun, also known as a repeating rifle, and it had several features that made it more effective than previous models (Smithurst, 2011). Most schoolchildren will have heard of this particular weapon without knowing anything about why it was so important in changing the course of history.

In her book *Empire of guns*, Priya Satia (2018: 16) has explained how 'war did not trigger every aspect of industrial revolution, but it was the context in which that revolution took shape'. While Florence Nightingale and Mary Seacole were busy caring for the sick and wounded in the Crimea, Enfield Lock was attracting visitors from far and wide to marvel at modern machine tools – mostly imported from America. But what made the Royal Ordnance site different from the gunsmith foundries that had put cities like Birmingham and Leeds on the map was the fact that the War Office, the predecessor of today's Ministry of Defence, had introduced the system of open competition as a means to acquire new weapons, and this had helped to end the monopoly of the private gun trade.

Learning about British weapons manufacture is like opening a cupboard in a darkened attic. As you grope for the door handle (for the information is not exactly easy to find), prepare to be flattened when the contents spill out and threaten to overwhelm you. Facts and figures involving geography, physics, chemistry, economics and, of course, politics; complex relations between state control and private sector; and an unruly domain where competition, commissions, corruption and criminality result in the proliferation of ever more ruthless and efficient ways to kill. *Just how did the world become so full of guns?*

* * *

I had been reading about this history before I came within sight of Enfield Island Village, today all that remains of the factory site. Although the towpath that would take me directly to the Country Park passes to the west of the island, I decide it would not take long to cross over and simply have a look. It is just two in the afternoon and the sun is high. I have plenty of time to explore, even though I suspect that there is not much to see. I am not thinking about writing, or even Nightingales, but war is on my mind too.

There is no chance of lying down here to contemplate the current state of the country or indeed its role as a global arms supplier. First there's the A1055 which meets Ordnance Road at right angles, taking most of the traffic with it. The only way to access the island on foot is to cross over two waterways. It is all very confusing. But as I come over the second bridge I see a tall, unmistakably industrial building that once housed the factory water tower.

The structure is not simply an industrial relic. It stands as a symbol of the strong community bonds that developed on the island over more than 150 years. In 1988 the government announced the sale of the factory, along with other Royal Ordnance sites at Waltham Abbey and Leeds. The buyer was none other than British Aerospace (known today as BAE Systems, one of the world's largest arms companies, employing around 100,000 people in more than forty countries). This was just two years after the UK and Saudi Arabian governments signed the notorious Al-Yamamah arms deal with British Aerospace as prime contractor.

Spotting another opportunity to cash in, the arms company then joined up with property developer Trafalgar House under the name Lee Valley Developments, and submitted an application for a residential development. This prompted the National Audit Office to carry out an inquiry into fiscal irresponsibility on the part of the Ministry of Defence.[2] The Ministry was cleared of any wrongdoing, but it would not have been the first time – nor the last – that they had missed an opportunity to restore money to the public purse.

As various proposals for the site's regeneration came and went, the Grade 2-listed machine room began to deteriorate. Any residential development was further complicated by complex planning issues that were causing costly delays. For instance, the island was technically within the Epping Forest district of Essex, and it was unclear whether it fell inside the designated green belt. In 1996, Lee Valley Developments gave up and sold the site to a local firm, Fairview New Homes. The planning disputes continued, not least over the presence of toxic materials in the soil, but the Island Lock Village, now transferred to the Borough of Enfield, was finally completed as a 'model brownfield development' in 2003.

The Village Centre, which opened in 2001 after extensive restoration of the factory buildings, seems quite deserted as I approach. A poster on the community noticeboard announces that the Big Lunch is taking place today, but there is no sign of it. Apart from the supermarket in the same complex, I notice the Empire Sports and Performance Studios ('the first and only acrobatics and urban sports facility in the borough of Enfield, dedicated to delivering expert training across disciplines such as cheerleading, acrobatic dance, tumbling, and more'). But the most impressive building is the original machine room which has been converted to a small museum, known as the Interpretation Centre.

I peer through the window, but it is firmly closed. As it's a Saturday I had gambled that it might be open to the public, but curiosity had already led me to their website, which said it all.[3]

* * *

> The resulting rifle, the 1853 pattern musket, was a very accurate weapon which also benefited from Standardised parts. However, its new paper cartridges, combined with an indifference towards the concerns of Indian soldiers by the East India Company, led to the Indian Mutiny of 1857. This rifle was produced in private factories across Britain, and despite the Royal Small Arms factory not selling to either the US Army or Confederate states, was very popular in the American Civil War.
>
> Throughout the latter half of the 19th Century, rapid development of breech-loading weapons saw the factory converting most Pattern 1853 rifles into breech-loading Snider rifles, to be used alongside Martini-Henry rifles, which saw service most famously in colonial wars in Africa, such as the Zulu and Boer wars.
>
> The culmination of this development was the Lee Enfield rifle – featuring a .303″ calibre barrel and five-bullet magazine. The Bolt action firing mechanism allowed soldiers to cock and reload their weapons whilst still prone. This rifle remained in service for over 60 years, seeing action in the First and Second World Wars, as well as the Korean War.

* * *

A map indicating the layout of the island shows that I can easily access Gunpowder Park by crossing a footbridge just a few streets away. Before I get there, I hear a Reed Warbler in a clump of reeds in a narrow waterway, and stand for a moment listening to its crazy song. That would bring me joy if I lived next door, although I might worry that a Cuckoo had laid its eggs in its nest.

Seeing the green expanse of the park, I quicken my pace. Although I am probably going in the wrong direction, I reason that if I just follow the river going north, it will eventually lead to the same destination. Besides I've had enough of military heritage. I'd rather be thinking about Nightingales.

But just as Nash discovered in France, Nightingales can be very evocative creatures with an uncanny ability to reveal just how absurd humans can be. Just a few years after his epiphany, the English cellist Beatrice Harrison persuaded Lord Reith, founder and director general of the BBC, to broadcast a live recording of her playing a duet with a Nightingale in her garden in Surrey. Despite his reservations, on 19 May 1924 over a million people across the British Empire were able to tune into the first outside recording to be broadcast in real time. The joint performance was repeated the following week, and thereafter became an annual highlight.

While Harrison had initiated the magic of relaying the ambient sounds of an English spring to a homesick anglophone audience, she was not responsible for what happened next. On 19 May 1942, BBC technician Sam Bonner set up his equipment to record a solo concert by Nightingales on what would have been the eighteenth anniversary of the first live broadcast. Two minutes after he had authorised the break into the late-night dance programme, he realised that the distant sound of planes was audible in the background. Although he abruptly ended the broadcast in the interest of security, he kept the microphones on and the Nightingale sang for a full six minutes, accompanied by the swelling and ebbing drone of the Bomber Command force as it passed overhead.

It transpired that this was the sound of 197 Wellington and Lancaster planes heading for Mannheim where they would carry out (what was considered) a relatively ineffective raid. The tape was then stored in the archives and later released commercially by HMV, along with Harrison's performance.[4]

Perhaps Nash had expressed it best with his rant about 'ridiculous mad incongruity' because he knew what war was like. David Rothenberg, a philosopher who writes about birds and music, was more measured. This juxtaposition created 'a strange soundscape of menacing bombers and incessant Nightingales, singing as they always do, even in the midst of human destruction and the violence that come with civilization' (Rothenberg, 2005: 143). He cites the media historian, Iain Logie Baird, who expresses a similar thought: 'the coincidence of these two things being heard, broadcast, and recorded so close together resembled a divine intervention; a triumph of light over darkness; Nature's defiance of the affairs of Man'.

* * *

I've thought a lot about how to interpret Nash's shock at witnessing the simultaneous forces of destruction and regeneration on the killing fields of northern France. The devastated trees showed no sign of life, evoking the pulverised landscapes in Gaza, Ukraine and other war-torn countries that we witness on our screens today. But revisited in spring, 'a few weeks later', the same trees were bursting with new growth, and the birds were simply returning to a suitable habitat where they could nest on the ground. It was not Nature that was absurd after all, only War.

Gunpowder Park is lusciously green and quite wild in contrast with the tidy streets of Enfield Island Village. Paths wind between bushes and brambles inviting me this way and that. I start looking out for Whitethroats, another dwindling family of summer migrants once associated with farmland. It's lovely to see them fluttering up a few metres and then to hear their scratchy voices as they dive back down. Like Nightingales they are inconspicuous little brown birds with a second home in Africa. I wish I'd brought my binoculars. I wish I'd brought my beloved. I'm aware I mustn't stray too far west, or I'll never reach my destination.

The sun is surprisingly strong, so I look for a spot to sit down and rest. I have my own associations between Nightingales and war that still haunt me. The first incident was on 21 April 2016, my second year of pilgrimage to the Lee Valley Country Park. After a disappointing expedition on the previous Friday evening, we had returned on the Sunday at midday, as good a time as any to hear them sing.

No sooner had we reached the zone than we heard that distinctive voice cutting through all the other sounds – runners, dog walkers, Chiffchaffs, gulls and warblers, and EasyJet planes glinting in the sky. We stopped in our tracks, transfixed by the sheer genius of the

Nightingale's repertoire and the contagious quality of its aliveness, joyfully reassured that the migrants had returned.

As the clouds passed in front of the sun, the voice went quiet. I remember the sky turning to steel grey and the temperature dropping. We strolled on in silence, still listening but totally unprepared for what happened next.

It began with an ugly noise growing louder; then the sight of two grotesque aircraft flying too low, their upright propellers making them look like giant drones, snarling engines drowning all other sound. We stood open-mouthed to watch them pass overhead, and then they were gone.

Later we learned, thanks to a plane-spotting site, that these were MV-22 Ospreys ferrying President Barack Obama to Air Force One in Stansted. A quick check shows that Ospreys have 'the speed and range of a turboprop, the manoeuvrability of a helicopter and the ability to carry 24 Marine combat troops twice as fast and five times farther than previous helicopters'. The President may have been on a diplomatic mission to allies in Europe, but his mode of transport radiated business as usual rather than an aspiration to keep the peace.

Strangely this would not be my only experience of being interrupted by the noise of war machines while straining to listen to a Nightingale. The following year I was visiting a nature reserve in Cambridgeshire, happily listening to a new arrival as it obliged from the top of a tall tree. I became aware of a distinctive growling in the background, and looked around to see what it was. My companions recognised it immediately as a Spitfire, the small plane that symbolises the heroism of the Battle of Britain in 1940. The bizarre coincidence of hearing these two sounds simultaneously was explained by the fact that the former RAF station in Duxford, a couple of miles from the reserve, is now owned by the Imperial War Museum.

There was no triumph of light over darkness, no sense of Nature's defiance. Just a reminder of the banality of war heritage as it intruded into the tentative evidence of a spring day. How then to interpret the simultaneous acts of listening to and hearing these different worlds of life and death? That was the question that had drawn me to the old gun factory in the hope that I might be uplifted by the precarious survival of endangered species nearby. A different kind of incongruity, one that rests on a determination not to forget the perpetual violence that continues in plain sight while remaining open to the disrupted rhythms of organic life.

* * *

Sitting in the shade of a hawthorn tree, I wonder if I have the energy to continue with my journey as I have not covered much ground so far. I realise the irony of resting in a place called Gunpowder Park, where the soil itself is saturated with traces of war. Before I left, I had read about the Royal Gunpowder Mills in Waltham Abbey, a small town that lies on the other side of the M25 in Hertfordshire, and had half a mind to visit that as well. One of only three such sites in the UK, the location has been used to manufacture various types of explosives since the seventeenth century. It was closed in 1944, but repurposed the following year as a government research base. Today it functions as a digital archive and heritage centre set in 170-acres of parkland, an area that is 'shaped by 300 years of making explosives and propellants'.[5]

The historic link between the gunpowder mill and the small arms factory is that they were both integral to the development of British firepower that helped to expand and maintain the empire. In this part of the world, that same military heritage, apparently purged of all sense of absurdity, now offers family entertainment enhanced by the aspiration to conserve wildlife. A thought occurs to me: perhaps the Nightingales would not have survived here without this public interest in the history of mechanical violence. And then, can we imagine a world in which war itself is consigned to museums as evidence of human folly?

I had originally hoped to pass by the Mills on my way north to Fishers Green, so, rising to my feet, I resolve to make my way back to the towpath. As I orient myself back to the river, I find myself entering a new estate, with spacious modern housing bounded by cast iron railings. I wonder what it's like to live on the edge of London with open parkland as your back garden. I wonder what it costs. But I am not ready to leave the brambles and bushes and turn my back on this anonymous place.

The official exit to Gunpowder Park, which I soon see in the distance, consists of a strange edifice built to commemorate its 'explosive past'. I later learn that this section was once a munitions testing range owned by the Ministry of Defence. The gateway brings me out onto a busy ring road and I suddenly lose my sense of direction. That's the thing about walking with your ears and eyes open. You never know where it's going to lead. But I seem to have wandered into another kind of warzone.

Walter Benjamin (1979: 213) once wrote that the further we emerge from the inner city, the more political the atmosphere becomes: 'Outskirts are the state of emergency of a city, the terrain on which incessantly rages the great decisive battle between the town and country.' Not for the first time I wonder if he ever travelled on a ring road. I try to maintain the same sense of curiosity that led me astray, but there is nothing to see except flattened drink cans; nothing to hear except wheels.

Eventually I come to the tunnel under the thundering M25, London's orbital motorway, the last barrier before reaching Waltham Abbey and the entrance to the country park. It feels even more odd to be on foot at this point, and passing underneath I am half terrified by the noise. But now I've officially left London behind. I'm walking a tightrope between a world city and a hinterland that has lost the will to fight back. I glimpse a building ahead and quicken my pace. But my heart sinks when I see the word 'Poundland' written in large red letters.

* * *

I finally reach the main road that runs through Waltham Abbey, but instead of relief at being nearer my destination, I am disoriented by having left the city, stranded beyond Zone 6 in a place where I don't seem to belong. Demoralised, I decide to abandon my mission, and accost a passing family for advice on how to get to the nearest station. They seem to sense that I am lost and do their best to reassure me. Hearing their accents I wonder if they were perhaps propelled here by war or the threat of war in their own land. I begin to feel more at home and, at the same time, quite foolish for having allowed myself to meander so far from my planned route.

Yet while losing my way on foot I have had time to pause and to listen. One of the joys of following the rhythm of bird migration is that it offers the chance to contemplate life on non-human scales. By deferring the chance to hear a Nightingale today, I allow myself to submit to the planetary energies that govern the movement of living things, along with currents, tides and other phenomena beyond our control. There is always next year, or so we can hope. In the meantime, there will be other arrivals and departures as well as the constancy of Sparrows and other non-migrating species. And, at a time when our lives seem to accelerate, passing much too fast, walking can help to slow us down, to bring us to our senses. Even, or perhaps especially, on ground that bears the imprint of war.

Notes

1 See the British Trust for Ornithology website for more details: www.bto.org/understanding-birds/birdfacts/nightingale
2 British Aerospace and two of the other bidders, GKN plc and Trafalgar House plc, assured the National Audit Office that they had been interested in purchasing Royal Ordnance as a going concern, not for property speculation (NAO, 1989).
3 'The Interpretation Centre is a small exhibition of the Royal Small Arms Factory's history, a vital part of the industrial past of the Lee Valley. The centre was established to tell the story of the factory, its workers, technology and products. Though small, it is a valuable memorial located at the factory itself and is used as a resource by local schools.' https://rsaf.org.uk
4 The recording, 'Nightingales sing as RAF bombers fly', is available on YouTube, as well as the campaigning website: Nightingale Songs http://nightingalenights.org.uk/celebrate-in-song/
5 www.walthamabbey-tc.gov.uk/community-directory/the-royal-gunpowder-mills-waltham-abbey

References

Benjamin, Walter (1979) *One-Way Street and Other Writings*. London: NLB.
Gough, P. A. (2010) *A Terrible Beauty: British Artists in the First World War*. Bristol: Sansom & Co.
Headrick, Daniel R. (1981) *The Tools of Empire: Technology and European Imperialism in the Nineteenth Century*. Oxford: Oxford University Press.
Linebaugh, Peter (2014) *Stop Thief!: The Commons, Enclosures and Resistance*. Oakland, CA: PM Press.

Morris, William (1889) Under an elm-tree or thoughts in the country-side. *Commonweal*, 5 (182), 212–13.

NAO (1989) *Ministry of Defence: Further Examination of the Sale of Royal Ordnance plc*. London: HMSO.

Rothenberg, David (2005) *Why Birds Sing: A Journey into the Mystery of Bird Song*. London: Allen Lane.

Satia, Priya (2018) *Empire of Guns: The Violent Making of the Industrial Revolution*. Richmond: Prelude.

Smithurst, Peter (2011) *The Pattern 1853 Enfield Rifle*. London: Osprey Publishing.

Recompose

Exercise 3: Stillness and movement

Find somewhere to sit and spend ten minutes observing the place you are in
Now spend another ten minutes observing while moving around
What did you notice?
How did stillness and movement compose and recompose your observations?

14

The rhythms of walking and doing sociology on The Street

Dawn Lyon

Heading out onto The Street

It's windy at the end of The Street, whatever the weather. Today, in the early spring, it's blowy but not too fierce, and there's some weak late-afternoon sunshine. Surrounded by water and the light showing the movement of the sea's surface, I wobble a little. The ground is a claggy combination of sand, shell and gravel. The Street is a shingle spit that emerges at low tide up to half a mile long and is concealed again as the tide turns. I'm in Whitstable, a small town on the north Kent coast in south-east England where the River Thames and the Swale meet the North Sea.

The Street is a big draw locally and has become something of a tourist attraction for visitors from further afield (Cool Places, 2025; Tripadvisor, 2025). At low tide at the weekends, and especially when the sun is shining, lots of people walk out on this shingle spit apparently to wonder at the sense of being both on land and at sea at the same time, and to experience themselves in this place (Urry and Larsen, 2011). The landscape of the estuary more generally has recently been recognised for its particular allure as well as its environmental importance (Lichtenstein, 2016; Hubbard, 2022).

There's a thrill to walking out on The Street, standing somewhere that was covered by water, metres deep, just hours ago. Land and sea fluid, fluctuating. It's characterised by in-betweenness as mudflats and marshland merge at the physical level, but it's different from the intertidal zone of an ordinary beach which is repeatedly revealed afresh then concealed again according to the rhythms of the tides. It's also a liminal spot culturally as the interstitial zone between land and sea offers a space of pleasure, danger, freedom and possibility (see Shields, 1990). On The Street, especially at its tip, the experience is of being surrounded by the sea but not quite; being immersed in the water but on firmish ground. There is a near illusion of walking on the water when that's all that the eye can see and the waves are close to the feet. This makes it distinctive and feels eerie. The sense of almost walking on water is reinforced when looking at The Street from the slopes behind the beach. In some lights, it really does look as if people are wandering out as if on the water, with improbable confidence and capability.

The first experience of walking The Street is heading towards the open sea. The mouth of the shingle strip is wide as it emerges from the beach at low tide, perhaps fifty metres across. I run towards it from the concrete path that separates the beach huts from the shingle heading between the wooden, sea-worn groynes that hold the beach in place at repeated intervals. The Street lures the walker, inviting this rush of enthusiasm. Slipping on the shingle adds to the momentum of arrival. As it extends, the strip narrows, sometimes forming a sharp point cutting into the water at its tip. I slow to a steady pace. I like the sound of the wet shingle underfoot – something between a squelch and a scrape – made from the simple repetition of one foot in front of the other. My steps are heavy, as if the waterlogged ground is pulling me down into its sodden mass or the unseen sea is seeping into my boots and feet. The boundaries of the body feel more porous here than usual. The seabed is uneven with patches of sand, mud, rocks and sticky clumps of London clay. At some times of the year, algae create stretches of bright green which stand out from the wet brown of the mud.

The Street is as much a line in the sand – quite literally – as a destination. Arriving *at* The Street is embarking on a walk *along* The Street, feeling and hearing it underfoot, and enjoying a fleeting escape from life on land. It can take a good ten minutes or so to walk its length when the tide is low and the spit extended. I always want to reach the end of The Street, but am in awe, fearful even, of the mass of water ahead and around as I get close. There are days when the wind, indifferent to whatever is in its path, feels strong enough to push me into the sea. The movement of the water is quite different on each side of the strip. To the west, the current is visibly strong as waves hit the small mound of shingle. To the east, the sea is calm, often clear and appealing to paddle in. A couple of summers ago on a particularly warm evening, I was walking with my partner on The Street and came across a couple preparing to swim from halfway along it. They were excitedly changing out of their clothes, leaving their bags at the water's edge. I felt compelled to intervene: 'I wouldn't do that if I were you!' – and this was before the extent of sewage pollution in the area was known (SOS Whitstable, 2024). 'The tide is actually coming in and you'll lose all your stuff.' The repetition of walking and noticing lays down new knowledge and understanding. To the newcomer, the shingle strip appears as land. However, even if the Kentish flats are relatively shallow, the incoming tide can move quickly and unevenly, and it is soon returned to its watery state.

So being on The Street brings the relational qualities of walking to mind. It takes a combination of feeling your way and some keen observation, sensing your step and looking out for others. It involves turning around repeatedly to ensure that the path remains open and checking what the tide is doing by attempting to read the level, direction and speed of the water. This is always an imprecise mission, despite my love of reading tide times in advance. The figures never seem to quite tally with the movement of the sea. On that summer evening, the tide was coming in faster than we realised, and the walk back involved hurriedly traversing newly formed puddles with an ominous sense of the water rising. We were not actually in danger, but that's not to underestimate the risk of getting cut off, or for fishers just off The Street, being swept into deeper water by strong currents. Indeed, those working at the border of sea and land often are at risk. I frequently think of the terrible drowning on the evening of 5 February 2004 of at least twenty-one undocumented Chinese migrants picking cockles close to Morecambe Bay as the unseen incoming tide moved rapidly around them in the dark.

The return to shore

The water of the incoming tide makes us all turn around sooner or later. The Street is a back-and-forth path, without other options. Walkers cross one another on their way out or when they head back, all doing the same thing. Looking back to the shore, there's a row of beach huts and a couple of holiday homes. Some are available for day rentals, and in the summer passersby can hear the sounds of joy and tension from get-togethers that did or didn't go to plan. Privately owned and carefully curated huts now sell for multiple tens of thousands of pounds. Further back and higher above sea level, there's a line of houses visible at the top of the grassy slopes. They are large, mostly detached properties with hefty price tags as gentrification based on what Hubbard (2022) terms 'oysterfication' has taken hold here. Although famed for centuries for its native oysters – once the food of the working poor – it's only in the last twenty years or so that Whitstable has been perceived and developed as an attractive location for visitors and second homeowners, especially DFLs (Down from Londons). Local cultivation is carried out by the family-run Whitstable Oyster Company on trestles at the Pollard Ground, a large area to the west of The Street, which benefits from the tidal flow in the estuary and across the flats – also a site of contest, especially for recreational use. The repositioning of the oyster as a gastronomic delight is key to the transformation of the town (Hubbard, 2022). As Hubbard discusses in *Borderland*, a book about this 'edge of England', Whitstable (2022: 33) offers 'a distinctive imagination of the English seaside' which celebrates a middle-class vision of 'the *authenticity* of coastal living'.

Walking out along The Street, I feel the freedom that striding away from the mundane and into the unknown sparks. It's the kind of walk that nourishes dreams and imagination (Gros, 2023: 79). When I turn around to retrace my steps, I'm always slightly surprised that the slopes and the houses are still there, and close by too. The distance is confusing though. To the eye, the built environment seems nearer than my senses imagined it. But for the feet, it's a different story. The walk back can sometimes feel like quite a hike. It's a process of reconnection, albeit an ambivalent one. Getting back to life, with its comforts and assurances, but leaving behind the magic of that spot where who knows what might have been possible. I'm sure that the other day when the sun was out and the pale blue of the water felt as if it would be warm, I could see the shimmer of sand beneath the surface on the shallow banks several miles out. Could I have reached those wind farms on the horizon if I'd just kept going?

Re-viewing The Street

If The Street is a space for playfulness and wonder, residents in the luxury houses above appear to survey it. Indeed, another experience of The Street is viewing it from the top of the slopes that sit alongside the beach, a sort of sloping, slanting angle along the line of the shingle spit towards the horizon. It's a different way of knowing it, not least for those for whom it's not an accessible space. There are a large number of benches that invite people to stop, rest and look. I have a favourite one that is situated at the foot of Whitstable Castle Gardens, across the road from the castle itself and at the top of a green bank overlooking the sea. As I sit and look out at The Street, I think of Lefebvre's (2004) discussion of seeing and listening from a window or balcony, in his case in Paris, to perceive rhythm. The bench offers a kind of balcony perspective. There's no central point to fix on from here as my gaze traces the line of the shingle spit, up and back, along and down. Sitting still helps me tune into the rhythms of the walkers out there, feeling their pace as they walk out to sea, getting smaller from my vantage point, and I wonder about whatever it is that makes them stop and look about from time to time. Dogs seem energised by The Street; children too, cavorting in the wind. It's just as Lefebvre (1991: 205) describes: 'rhythms in all their multiplicity interpenetrate one another', especially in and around the body. If some rhythms 'operate on the surface' though, others 'spring from hidden depths' and must be tracked 'through indirect effects' (Lefebvre, 1991: 205).

Indeed, this spot has its own particular history, once the centre of the local copperas (green vitriol) industry, where the mineral alum was mined to be used to fix dyes in cloth – there's a worn information panel in the Castle Gardens that tells a little of this story. Still, it's hard to imagine now that mining and an early chemical industry were thriving here from the late sixteenth century for around two hundred years – albeit one that took its toll on workers who had little protection from toxic fumes. Or that it was a site both exploited by smugglers and used for defence. There's a curious juxtaposition today between the emphasis on recreation in the town and along the coast, and the 'working beach' with fishing and asphalt production at the harbour. This makes for a heady olfactory experience too as the odours of bitumen combine with the smell of seaweed from the fishing boats and chip fat from the nearby eateries.

On a clear day, the Maunsell Sea Forts directly to the north serve as a reminder of the political significance of the Thames Estuary during the Second World War, when they were operated by the Navy to deter German air raids and protect this vital supply route. The contours of buildings in Southend on the Essex coast are barely visible to the north-west; if the city feels close on some days, a hundred years ago it was directly connected to Kent with a ferry service between Southend and Sheerness on the Isle of Sheppey. To the west of The Street, the eastern coast of Sheppey is just a few miles away where the shell spit of the Swale National Nature Reserve gleams in the sunshine. To the east, it's open sea dotted with ships and wind turbines – and a sense of mystery and possibility. I am endlessly fascinated by the changing formations of sea and sky here, especially when their meeting points are indistinguishable in cloud, mist or rain, as in some of Hiroshi Sugimoto's seascape photographs taken around the world, or in J. M. W. Turner's paintings of the sea, sky and light, some inspired by Margate, just a few miles along the coast. The North Sea may be small in global terms, but it offers a 'powerful horizon' in Elspeth Probyn's words, a way into a more-than-human sensibility or 'an inspiration for new forms of being' (Probyn, 2016: 40, 38).

Whether or not I walk The Street on any particular day in Whitstable, or sit on a bench to wonder at it, I often look from the grassy slopes above the beach at the movement of the sea across its surface and just how far out it goes according to a particular tide. I am mesmerised by its there and not-there properties as it surfaces and disappears with the rhythms of the tides as well as the outflow from the Thames. It's different each time. It's still The Street, but never quite the same Street. It varies in width as well as length, and changes with the light and moisture in the air, at times wet and muddy, at others brighter and sandy looking. Whatever the water level, the shingle strip isn't only there where it's visible. Its effects are conspicuous underwater as it alters the patterns of the waves on the sea's surface. It creates a sort of wandering seam that stretches out to sea, a connection to an unknown elsewhere. I can't help but think of the parallels to the sociological imagination here, wondering about hidden undercurrents and where power lies as social relations move in and out of view, and the time it takes to notice and understand. Sometimes things become apparent on the move; at other times, it's necessary to 'stay put' (Gandy, 2024) to grasp what's going on.

Imagining The Street from afar

It's October 2024 and I find myself in Canberra in the Australian Capital Territory. While far from the coastline, the city was designed with water in mind. The artificially constructed Lake Burley Griffin is its focal point, formed by damming the Molonglo River and filling its flood plain. It looks familiar, probably because the planners deliberately sought to evoke the British picturesque style (Weller, 2001). But the trees, especially the large eucalyptus, some several hundred years old, and the sounds, especially the chatty kookaburra birds, are different from what I'm used to. They help me to notice what's strange here as well as familiar and to think afresh about The Street.

At first I miss the sea, and struggle to adjust to the stillness of the lake, even though the wind sometimes picks up the water on the surface and it almost looks as if it's going somewhere. Signage around the lake proposes different interconnecting loops or circuits. Wherever you start from, there's no option but to return there. I generally like a loop and often find myself trying to create circular paths where the landscape invites more linear movement or back and forth along a strip, just like on The Street. I rewalk my walk along The Street in my mind as I wander around the lake and think about the ways in which walks are constantly being remade and reworked – as the 'Recompose' section of this book evokes. I imagine the to and fro along the length of The Street. But the rhythm of walking in lines just doesn't fit. I start to realise how the rhythms of the sea in Whitstable are a marker for my movement, something to keep time with (Gros, 2023) – for instance, listening for the whoosh of a breaking wave as water hits shingle or the calls of seagulls in the early evening. Instead, in Canberra, rhythm emerges from the walking itself and sometimes feels intensified by the tranquillity of the water. I come to realise how walking in one place – and imagining another – sensitises me to the polyrhythms of both. I am also aware of walking on the land of the Ngunnawal (Ngunawal) and Ngambri peoples, indigenous to Canberra – originally, Kambri – who have lived in the region for over 20,000 years, before being displaced by European settlers. There's a limit to what can be grasped directly by walking, but the act of walking does stimulate connections across time and space (Ingold, 1993; Vergunst, 2010), including to the deep history of this land and the different lives that continue to take shape here.

I'd arrived in Canberra depleted by the sheer volume of work and anxiety associated with job losses and restructures in higher education in the UK at the time – and soon learned there were to be deep cuts in the academy here too. Back in Kent, many of my closest colleagues had already left the university and everyone was uncertain about their futures in the institution and the sector. When I walked in the late morning in Canberra, nine hours ahead of the UK, I was briefly free of the 'frenetic digital timescapes' that underpin academic life and overwhelm the everyday (Manathunga et al., 2022). It was more than a welcome escape. It offered a renewed temporal sense, both about the rhythms of the everyday that are conducive to academic labour, and a longer view on the recalibrations of the sector.

Coming back to The Street

It's winter by the time I get back to The Street. Did anyone miss me, I wonder? There are instances of spontaneous conversation between strangers on The Street and a sense of being somewhere together as walkers cross or share paths (Shields, 1990). On my last morning in Canberra, I did my usual loop but in reverse. I headed along the side of the lake first, then up the road to the apartment as I prepared to leave. I wanted to take it all in, to be able to hold it in mind, and rewalk this walk back in Kent. I looked up to see someone walking the walk I usually did in the opposite direction. We smiled as we crossed paths. I had seen this woman before. It's her walk too, I suddenly realised. I like the idea that she will keep reproducing this path while I get back to the rhythms of The Street and recall the lake, making new spatial connections.

The sea seems vast after those landlocked weeks in Canberra. I had become used to that scaled back horizon, reckoning only with the space from one side of the lake to the other and the reverberations between them. I am overcome, visually flooded by the image of the water, and the sense that my energy will dissipate into space. I've arrived from a place of boundaries to a landscape that seems to have no edges. I'm struck too by all the movement in the water. Now I miss the stillness of the lake. I long for one of those moments when the tide is about to turn on a calm day, and it's easy to think that there's not much going on. But the water and the land are in a constant process of rearrangement or recomposition here, whatever the surface suggests.

I stride out on the pathway of The Street, as I now think of it. I feel that familiar instability, a kind of wobble underfoot as the ground slowly shifts. The spit is emerging and disappearing as I walk, waves gently lapping one side and landing with more force on the other. It seems wider than I remembered and I feel a sense of abandon and the impulse to leap about. There is space to walk here, to be at sea and contained on land. It's a cold day but dry without much wind. I head towards the narrow point of the spit at which the water is only faintly divided by that wandering seam that ripples along the surface. At the end of The Street I put my arms out to steady myself and to absorb the moment. I turn and retrace my steps. Behind me, the tide is already coming in, wiping out any trace of my footprints on this chilly morning, preparing a renewed space for other walkers at the next low tide.

Acknowledgements

Thank you to Phil Hubbard for helpful comments and suggestions on a draft of this essay.

References

Cool Places (2025) *The Street: Tankerton Beach*. Available at: www.coolplaces.co.uk/places/uk/england/kent/whitstable/1767-the-street# [accessed 10 February 2025].

Gandy, Matthew (2024) Attentive observation: Walking, listening, staying put. *Annals of the American Association of Geographers*, 114 (7), 1386–404.

Gros, Frederic (2023) *A Philosophy of Walking*, 2nd edition. London: Verso.

Hubbard, Phil (2022) *Borderland, Identity and Belonging at the Edge of England*. Manchester: Manchester University Press.

Ingold, Tim (1993) The temporality of the landscape. *World Archaeology*, 25 (2), 152–74.

Lefebvre, Henri (1991) *The Production of Space*, trans. D. Nicholson-Smith. Oxford: Basil Blackwell. First published 1974.

Lefebvre, Henri (2004) *Rhythmanalysis: Space, Time and Everyday Life*. London: Continuum International. First published 1992.

Lichtenstein, Rachel (2016) *Estuary: Out from London to the Sea*. London: Hamish Hamilton.

Manathunga, Catherine, Black, Alison L. and Davidow, Shelley (2022) Walking: Towards a valuable academic life. *Discourse: Studies in the Cultural Politics of Education*, 43 (2), 231–50.

Probyn, Elspeth (2016) *Eating the Ocean*. Durham, NC: Duke University Press.

Shields, Rob (1990) The 'system of pleasure': Liminality and the carnivalesque at Brighton. *Theory, Culture & Society*, 7 (1), 39–72.

SOS Whitstable (2024) Home page. Available at: www.soswhitstable.com/ [accessed 2 December 2024].

Tripadvisor (2025) *The Street*. Available at: www.tripadvisor.co.uk/Attraction_Review-g503922-d3701728-Reviews-The_Street-Whitstable_Kent_England.html [accessed 10 February 2025].

Urry, John and Larsen, Jonas (2011) *The Tourist Gaze 3.0*. London: Sage.

Vergunst, Jo (2010) Rhythms of walking: History and presence in a city street. *Space and Culture*, 13 (4), 376–88.

Weller, Richard (2001) The National Museum, Canberra and its garden of Australian dreams. *Studies in the History of Gardens & Designed Landscapes*, 21 (1), 66–84.

15

Territory and temporality on the university campus

Katherine Quinn

Watching my steps

> 21 August 2023
> Smiling round the bend of the stairs but distance moving, growing, expanding. 'How are you?' 'Yeah fine! How are you?' 'Good.' 'Good!!' Swapped places, swapped angles – up-to-down, down-to-up – navigating the corner of oblivious stone steps while navigating interactional levity. Gritting grins and gripping the buffed grey of the curved handrail, etched Portland. I pinch it like I'm checking solidity, mitigating evaporation, finding an anchor. Exhaling out of the revolving doors I ponder the quick work I think I do here. Avoiding, shortening, making light, insubstantial, harder to grip than the curved blocks of the building. Few impressions are good impressions. (100)

Pannier dumped, bottle filled, emails refreshed. With dithering tactics exhausted, I move my small – too small to be very useful – notepad from desk to bag. The notebook is slight but weighty, overlaid with questions, scribbles, notes hoping to be meaningful. I'm moving with it. On one level I am walking away from one site on Cardiff University's campus in the capital city of Wales and towards another, a site where I am involved in a short, barely funded ethnographic project concerning the relationship between built design, collaboration and the university's future. On another, I am rescoring steps I hope will finally stick: moving from research student to fixed-term lecturer, from supervised to trusted, from solo to team. Static or mobile, at this time I am never far from thoughts about my contract ending. I pack my staff ID card in my bag: the object I need to open doors in the research site building; the card I will come to wear, tethered to a lanyard around my neck, to demonstrate appropriateness while there. It reads: 'Expires 31/08/2024' in red text next to a photo of my first-day face. It seems to suggest that I will expire with the card (Quinn and Lewis, forthcoming).

> 14 June 2023
> Lanyards flourish from Cathays to Innovation. Never seen in Glamorgan, at SPARK they are worn by all. Red for Cardiff, grey for SPARK-SPARC, too-wide too-garish green for 'VISITORS', visibly needing to be escorted. Needed to move from the public first floor, past the 'no tailgating' signs, into the office space, the lanyard sifts and sorts. Furtive glances behind while holding the door to verify I'm safe. After a few days of observations, I root around at home for an old lanyard, needing to feel innocuous. My staff card gains new prominence to me: first-day photo, contract expiry date: tethered, ticking. (100)

I am watching my steps. Over the course of this project, I oscillate between loud discomfort and quiet bravado about doing 'insider research' at the university I hope will continue to employ me. The project relates to my interests in the territories and temporalities of higher education, of classificatory practices, of design. Alongside two sociology colleagues the research seeks to engage with the advent of a 'purpose-built' Social Science Research Park, called SPARK, at Cardiff University. SPARK opened in spring 2022 and is situated on what is (colloquially if not wholly accurately) understood as the opposite side of the main university campus to the School of Social Sciences where we are based. We want to understand what SPARK – and its emphasis on various new forms of collaboration, commercialisation and innovation – means in practice for those – often employed on a fixed term as funded project researchers – working within the walls of the building. Engaging with the turn to materiality in cultural sociology (McDonnell, 2023) and with a Live Methods (Back and Puwar, 2012) orientation, we consider how SPARK's material and conceptual design, and those working within it, accommodate, reframe and in some cases contest the broader imperatives of the 'funded project' paradigm (Fred and Godenhjelm, 2023) in the contemporary university.

The project's shape is fortuitous in some respects: walkable, cheap, collaborative and enthusiastically received by supportive gatekeepers at

SPARK. Its rhythms promised to fit in among the new schedules that being an early career lecturer demand. These schedules were overlaid: I navigate new responsibilities while checking my (rapidly named) 'anywhere sociology' saved search on jobs.ac.uk daily; preparing lectures for the first time weekly; renting privately during a housing permacrisis monthly; wondering where my life will be in three years, regularly and throughout. My experience of time, space and location while completing my PhD just a few years earlier was different. Back then, I lived in unusually secure yet flexible affordable housing (a radical housing co-op), and was enmeshed in constellations of care beyond any academic attachments. Writing time then felt mostly circular, often spacious, unusually privileged, helpfully meandering. Writing space was meaningfully tied to a locality and a community. While there was the inevitable 'exit velocity' (Dakka and Wade, 2019: 189) of the final six months' 'crescendo' of 'writing up', there was also time for ambiguity and meandering.

Walking this project through, then, was inspired a little more frantically, a little more graspingly, by the symptoms of untethered, short-term academia. Like so many others pursuing careers in contemporary academia, I had been swept up onto the conveyor belt of fast academia (O'Neill, 2014; McKnight, 2020). On getting a fixed-term teaching and research post that had been tacked on to the end of another fixed-term research post I had been advised, like so many others – and not unkindly – to 'make myself indispensable'. It's a strange positioning, and weighs on my movements. To be unable to be dispensed with I need to become unmovable, fixed, tethered. To pin my ephemerality down I am told to do other movements: over and above; above and beyond. Writing became truncated, and I turned to a creative practice of writing, *100s*, to unlock writer's block. Popularised by Lauren Berlant and Kathleen Stewart's (2019) book, *The hundreds*, I have grown to appreciate this flash format – of writing in 100-word multiples – as a way of tricking myself into writing (Quinn et al., 2020, 2025). *100*-ing helped me catch an idea, observation or reflection un- or less-aware, with a rapid but unrushed rhythm. In the *100* that opens the essay I express these contortions and how I sought private, material reminders of solidity while feeling as if floating. I describe bumping into a senior colleague at work and (wonder whether I) work to appear acceptable, amenable, through miniaturised small talk. Mapping the shifting territories of my own anxiety connected the personal and social, situated and relational, individual and sectoral.

Office to park: the circulating academic body

> 13 June 2023
> I like the first fifteen – Queen Street station to Glamorgan (Google Maps: 14 minutes). Sun but not yet scorching, busy but not yet harried. The second is Glamorgan to the Business School – building on Column Road (Google Maps: 13 minutes). I use a radiating wheelie bin as a rest for my headphones and get my sunglasses out of my bag. The view from the Business School – my third stop for the day – SPARK (Google Maps: 13 minutes) – thuds through slowing steps. Six storeys looming visible and distant over the railway line but not navigable by the promised – abandoned – public footbridge. (100)

It is June 2023 and the beginning of a near heatwave. Walking down its wide stone entrance steps at 10 a.m., my office building creaks into warmth; the morning sun makes the air thicker and brighter. This building, my academic home base, asks you to 'look up' while recognising its depth of foundation, its permanency. Grey Portland stone columns divide Cardiff University's Glamorgan Building's frontage, dramatic and ostentatious statues frame its iron-cordoned steps, evoking Greek myths combined with Welsh industry. The edges of the building's grandeur have been knocked off with light neglect and are faded all over with time and weather, yet it stands solid and imposing. It is a building with little external description but one which anchors the university's School of Social Sciences, and the School of Geography and Planning. Its changing historical functions meld permanency with temporariness, too. Though a building that conjures the image of this civic university, the go-to location for hat-tossing graduation photos, and prospectus covers presenting the gown of Cardiff's town, it was not purpose-built for Cardiff University. Rather, the Glamorgan Building was built in 1912 as the headquarters for Glamorgan County Council, and was only acquired by the university in 1997. A sense of civicness needing a home, a projected permanency, links both proprietors, the city and the university, then and now.

Alternative pasts and possibilities of the 'idea of the public university' (Holmwood, 2011) haunt the campuses of British universities today. Fifteen years ago, the Browne Review accelerated the shift from higher education being a publicly funded social right to being a private investment in human capital (Holmwood and Bhambra, 2012). While students were repositioned as customers (Cruickshank, 2016) they also – particularly international students paying higher fees – became responsible for the financial health of their institutions through revenue raised by individualised debt (Dolton, 2020). Today, many universities – not least Cardiff University – stand at 'the brink' of bankruptcy due to having been 'buffeted by too many market forces and too much government control' (Davies, 2024). The transformation of the idea of the public university has spatial, material and temporal implications. While studying libraries for my PhD I experienced how 'the reforms to British HE bring with them a cultural complexion of boundaries, distinctions, permissions, and memberships. What the university means for civil society and how it is experienced by those "outside" it has, by consequence, shifted' (Quinn, 2022: 3). Technically public buildings, security gates emerge in front of university libraries to communicate the priorities of the fee-paying student (Quinn, 2024) and campus boundaries encroach and become starkly policed against pre-existing local communities (Haar, 2011; Baldwin, 2020).

Back at the boundary of the Glamorgan Building, the imposing steps I descend enrol rhythms (Lyon, 2019) of stalling, pausing, meeting, projecting. These practices variously contest the 'fast' temporalities of contemporary academia. The steps are the threshold where students and colleagues smoke and vape at the academic changeover period that hovers around the hour. During teaching times and at this scheduling pinch point, the steps resound with the rapid and sometimes violent thwack of the narrow wooden revolving door in the centre of the building: big enough for one person alone, spinning at a velocity determined and distributed by the energy and intensity of the queue pushing through it. Effort is required to enter. The periodic renewal of the 'student body' happens hourly, termly, annually. The 'student body' rings as though a permanent, mega-corporeal fixture, but is really a series of lives – complex, variously brave, lives – transitioning through spaces and positions over the course of semesters, years, degrees. Another mutable body stalls at the steps periodically, made of members keen to be seen as stable. Union members, their dogs, their children, spread out or cluster in groups midway down the steps during strike pickets. We stand in limbo, playing on the impulse – hope? – that, as per the chalk slogan scrawled across the pavement beneath the building during a recent dispute, 'la beauté est dans la rue'. We implement a stoppage in the academic work cycle and mark it corporeally: looking out and across to the rest of the university campus, but also out and across to the civic spaces nestled among educational ones. The placards leave at the end of the day, but union stickers occasionally stubbornly resist tidying, leaving traces of resistance beyond stoppages restarted.

Cathays Memorial Park: homing from work and renewing roots

> 3 July 2023
> Build myself up with grounding techniques before bimbles; experience sensory overload as the participant describes theirs. She dislikes how collaboration seems to only mean 'bums on seats' and 'everyone-in-on-Wednesdays'. I feel my brain scrape towards awkward overhearings, jokes falling flat, frazzled swan-kick smiles. With both interviewee and interviewer feeling rootless, replaceable, the go-alongs stop-alone. Afterwards, I swipe guiltily into my temporary 'principal investigator's office' – a privacy my participant has not been afforded – and sit on the floor with my back against empty cupboards, hands scratching up the carpet to my laptop; shrinking from glass, feeling fishbowled out to watchful space. (100)

At the bottom of the steps, down at road level, I move in the dog-legged direction of SPARK. Squeezed through the mess of cars, the beeping pay meters and their crouched, clenched users, I step into Cathays Memorial Park. I wonder again about the detour those with wheelchairs or pushchairs hoping to navigate this park must make, since drivers, with no force apparently to stop them, generally park against the dropped kerb at its entrance. Across tarmac and once within the square, order, symmetry and memory are inscribed on tarmac paths that intersect and surround lawns, flowerbeds and stone memorials to occasions as varied as war, organ donation and the victims of the thalidomide catastrophe. Cherry trees dominate the formal park's planting, and a short window in late spring sees the air thick with slow swirling pink and white petals. Now, the cherry tree petals are gone but the trees are verdant, planted in unnatural isolation, mowed grass in light crop circles around their bases.

This spell of very hot weather brings groups and individuals out from the benches that line the periphery and into its centre, on grass, leaning against trunks, bags, back-stretched arms, joints locked, fingers curled. Though awkwardly prescribed in this way through design, the park initiates a whirlpool for colleagues and strangers meeting. Staff members from the university buildings that line several of the sides of this park cross the park to get from A to B; others pace the periphery in walking meetings alone, in pairs, sometimes clutching china mugs brought in from home. Mobility here is for moving bodies and thoughts: people take their work pause for a walk. The stop-start rhythm of task-orientated work is, perhaps, smoothed through domesticity. The taking of mugs – or the not taking of throwaway ones – seems a nod to a permanency, a stability, a domestication of movement. The mugs are a reminder that we come here often; we have a base here. Perhaps we feel at home.

These appeals to stabilising objects come about within a present-tensed approach to planting. Among the longer-standing cherry trees there are the flowerbeds which are regularly renewed by council gardeners: the shallow roots of bedding plants and tulips are pulled up every few months and replaced. This shallow renewal feels similar to some of the processes cycling through academia. There is the move towards fixed-term employment. Here, we are fashioned to appear permanent to those who need to receive an affect of permanency at that time – students, funders – but are in fact rolled over, exchanged, stopped or extended: mutable when expedient. Fast fashion over long term. What might be called a 'renting mindset' infiltrates the fixed-term, funded project, open-to-renewal version of academia, and it affects how we position ourselves, and also how we are positioned by others. While in the 'fishbowl' *100* above, my own position of instability destabilised my reading of participants, at other times participants' reading of me felt instructive. Before starting one particular go-along interview a senior professor talks loudly, in open space, about the unlikeliness of my contract being extended. As Larrington-Spencer et al. (2024) have recently argued, these kinds of encounters illustrate the mutual accomplishment of care, and carelessness, between interviewer and interviewee during the go-along interview.

The city/campus divide: circulation, spread and deletion

16 June 2023
Sweet maple sap on the pavement so thick and mirrored it seems the trees have been recently watered. Landscaping, greyscale smooth tiling, electric car ports charging Teslas on this side of the road – the Innovation Campus side. Pockmarked tarmac, uncollected rubbish – bags, broken, scattered, plastic containers – and tall purple weeds on the opposite, where student housing intersperses homes owned by tenacious locals. I read the two sides as non-permeable, even oppositional: a distorted mirror image of glut meeting drought. But an empty interloping 35 cl vodka bottle sitting proudly on the university's walled periphery smiles resistance at the city/campus divide. (100)

I go left around the park's central war memorial in a vaguely diagonal line that takes me to the contact points of the university, Welsh government and the law courts. Despite the formality of the park and surrounding streets, and the visibility of local council motifs, ownership here is transient and ephemeral. Sliding between bright and shadowed dominance, between institutional might and everyday reclamation, the university, the state, capital and publics recompose dominance over days and nights, years and governments, White Papers and initiatives. It has materiality: Cardiff Council is permanently adorned on bins and periodically visible on the outdoor maintenance vans that roll into the park. The university has its own signposts in signature dark grey and red branding. Parking regulations are stipulated on signs with commercial insignia. Alongside material jostling for dominance – or generous desires for intelligibility to multiple publics – publics themselves overlap in subtler ways. The night-time and daytime publics meet in this square for an hour or so during the morning commute, homeless residents of the square squeezing final minutes of snatched sleep – begun while the square was theirs (mostly) alone – before bundling away carrying coverless duvets and making way for students, staff, tourists.

Beyond this meeting point, and after traversing busy crossroads, I pause at the Arts and Social Sciences Library that sits just to one side of the railway line, beleaguered and set back. The library, an ambivalent institution that facilitates 'learning and leisure' (Hayes and Morris, 2005), shelter and exclusion (Santamaria, 2020), order and chaos (Benjamin, 1999), has been steadily deleted in the public sphere (Corble, 2019), and is ever more tightly bound in the academic one (Quinn, 2024). I speak to college-going teenagers in the nearby Cardiff ward of Grangetown who ask – with justified irritation – why they can't use this university library as a space to study in the evening, since their local public library has had its opening hours cut down to the bone. Though Grangetown communities are a prominent focus of Cardiff University's civic mission, and the conversation I'm having has been facilitated through its funds, the idea of the public university seemingly cannot extend to buildings being made public. Public impact translates to purposive interventions rather than inoperative communities (Nancy, 1991). Out on the street, the railway line boundary signals an – incomplete – shift from teaching and learning (campus buildings with lecture theatres) to research and living (research institutes and student housing). That university estates grow in ways that sit in tension with local communities is well known. Baldwin (2020) has referred to this in the US as the coming of the 'UniverCity'. Locals move out, landlords move in. On the ground, Puwar details the ways in which higher education finances and rent extraction coincide on the littered streets of Coventry: 'Investors carve up housing for multiple occupation without turning an eye to how the properties will be maintained and rubbish collected … The old conflict between town and gown is exacerbated by the enterprising university without civic responsibility' (Puwar, 2019: n.p.). A similar story plays out in Cathays, with the transient student body villainised for the failures of government reform on the renting crisis.

Pernicious divisions don't only emerge between city and campus. There are also, perhaps increasingly, shifting bonds stretched among constituent parts of the university. I trace this route across the changing priorities of the university campus during a period not only of personal instability but also of sectoral fractiousness and industrial action. The fieldwork coincides with the highly stressful Marking and Assessment Boycott (MAB) of 2023. As a fixed-term lecturer, I can withdraw this labour, and I do. The confusion and bitterness of this period – bitterness in many nebulous directions – recalibrates how I position myself in the research project again, and, to some extent, how I am positioned by others. It sets a particularly stark context to my conversations with participants about their views on the future of the university, and SPARK-like propositions, and the politics of teaching, research, competition, funding. These politics play out materially across the walk. The following *100* responds to seeing a temporary plastic Cardiff University Open Day sign go up at this quasi-boundary between old and new, teaching and research, in and out. The sign, clumsily tethered to public infrastructure (a cycle path sign) at the threshold of the Innovation Campus that SPARK bookends, seemed to signal the clumsy splitting of the idea of the university as a public space, of research from teaching. SPARK – a building marked as non-teaching – was omitted from the sign. Since fee-paying students aren't taught there, they don't need to see it.

> 29 June 2023
> On MAB day sixty-five (who's-counting?), walking through early morning heavy air from Cathays to SPARK I see a middle-aged man in a security uniform bent kneeling on grinding tarmac, fixing struggling temporary Open Day signs for tomorrow's marketing push – tomorrow's local strike against MAB deductions. Hands clicking cable ties at base, a share-with-care sign, greyscale plastic corrugation temporarily folding over him. The sign gestures hopefully towards student spaces – arrowed acronyms float up Maindy Road (CUBRIC, Haydn Ellis). SPARK, the road's culmination, is an absence conspicuous to me. A non-teaching building warrants apparently no wayfinding but will be hard to miss. (100)

Materials for movement

> 3 April 2023
> The building was originally designed to resemble a disrupted bookshelf; three blocks of black metal and glass (the books) hold six floors of hot desks and collision opportunities. The budget couldn't stretch to wholly irregular angles, so 90° was as far as the disruption could go. Inside the building-block-book-1, first floor, there stands a 'policy library': fixed sign, empty shelves, excessive hindsight: 'Nobody reads

> books anymore'. Books become lagging objects – out-of-date, slow-to-consume, with marks too permanent? Their production might outlast the funded project, the research contract. The library becomes a leftover space for waiting visitors; space synchronised to shorter cycles. (100)

Approaching the entrance area to SPARK, past the chauffer-driven Bentley that sits in the drop-off-only parking bay beyond its stipulations, I see a smartly dressed woman sit down on a bench, take heeled shoes out of her handbag, and replace the trainers she wore to walk along the perimeter line of the campus. She stands as I pass, and we walk towards this mirrored building together. Unlike the individual thwack of the Glamorgan door, SPARK's revolutions are supersized, transparent, hushed. It is distanced, too, moving round and beyond in response to bodily proximity, not touch. We move through this boundary space in lagged togetherness, and I look out for my next participant to move through all this with.

I have cursed the fifteen-minute walk it takes to get from one site to another; clearly not long, but a journey longer than can be made without notice. The walk bore benefits, however; encouraging a transition from interior to exterior identity, necessitating slow observance of the university's polyrhythmic swells, physically moving ligaments tensed from typing. In walking from my office to that building I saw these internal themes also play out in the space of the campus overall: differential rhythms and layers of permanency and impermanence. In the end, the walk's time and presence encourages reflection on dynamics essential to the broader projects, personal and academic – that of the idea of the university, and that of the so-called 'academic journey' I have recently made steps within. With both, and with *100s*, I move among dynamics of temporariness and permanency, territory and transience, the fixed and the fleeting, the bounded and the permeable.

References

Back, Les, and Puwar, Nirmal (2012) A manifesto for live methods: Provocations and capacities. *Sociological Review*, 17 (S1), 6–17.

Baldwin, Davarian L. (2020) *In the Shadow of the Ivory Tower: How Universities are Plundering our Cities*. New York: Bold Type Books.

Benjamin, Walter (1999) Unpacking my library: A talk about book collecting. In Hannah Arendt (ed.), *Illuminations*, ed. and with an introduction by Hannah Arendt. London: Random House.

Berlant, Lauren and Stewart, Kathleen (2019) *The Hundreds*. Durham, NC: Duke University Press.

Corble, Alice (2019) The Death and Life of English Public Libraries: Infrastructural Practices and Value in a Time of Crisis. PhD thesis, Goldsmiths, University of London. Available at: http://research.gold.ac.uk/26145/ [accessed 4 October 2025].

Cruickshank, Justin (2016) Putting business at the heart of higher education: On neoliberal interventionism and audit culture in UK universities. *Open Library of Humanities*, 2 (1), 1–33.

Dakka, Fadia and Wade, Alex (2019) Writing time: A rhythmic analysis of contemporary academic writing. *Higher Education Research and Development*, 38 (1), 185–97.

Davies, William (2024) How the Tories pushed universities to the brink of disaster, *Guardian*, 2 July. Available at: www.theguardian.com/politics/ng-interactive/2024/jul/02/how-the-tories-pushed-universities-to-the-brink-of-disaster [accessed 22 February 2025].

Dolton, Peter (2020) *The Economics of the UK University System in the Time of COVID-19*. Policy paper 19. London: National Institute of Economic and Social Research. Available at: www.niesr.ac.uk/publications/economics-uk-university-system-time-covid-19 [accessed 21 July 2021].

Fred, Mats and Godenhjelm, Sebastian (2023) *Projectification of Organizations, Governance and Societies: Theoretical Perspectives and Empirical Implications*. Cham: Palgrave Macmillan.

Haar, Sharon (2011) *The City as Campus: Urbanism and Higher Education in Chicago*. Minneapolis, MN: University of Minnesota Press.

Hayes, Emma and Morris, Anne (2005) Leisure role of public libraries: A historical perspective. *Journal of Librarianship and Information Science*, 37 (2), 75–81.

Holmwood, John (2011) The idea of a public university. In John Holmwood (ed.) *A Manifesto for the Public University*. London: Bloomsbury.

Holmwood, John and Bhambra, Gurminder (2012) The attack on education as a social right. *South Atlantic Quarterly*, 111 (2), 392–401.

Larrington-Spencer, Harriet, Verlinghieri, Ersilia, Lawlor, Emma and Aldred, Rachel (2024) Troubling go-alongs through the lens of care. *Qualitative Research*, 25 (3), 690–710.

Lyon, Dawn (2019) *What is Rhythmanalysis?* London: Bloomsbury Academic.

McDonnell, Terence E. (2023) Cultural objects, material culture, and materiality. *Annual Review of Sociology*, 49 (20), 1–26.

McKnight, Lucinda (2020) Meet the phallic lecturer: Early career research in a neoliberal imaginary. *Gender and Education*, 32 (4), 505–17.

Nancy, Jean-Luc (1991) *The Inoperative Community*. Minneapolis, MN: University of Minnesota Press.

O'Neill, Maggie (2014) The slow university: Work, time and well-being. *Forum: Qualitative Social Research*, 15 (3), 1–20.

Puwar, Nirmal (2019) *Walking through Litter*. Life Writing Projects. Available at: https://reframe.sussex.ac.uk/lifewritingprojects/place/nirmal-puwar/ [accessed 22 February 2025].

Quinn, Katherine (2022) The university library as bellwether: Examining the public role of higher education through listening to the library. *Civic Sociology*, 3 (1), article 32635.

Quinn, Katherine (2024) The bookshelf's 'magic circle': An ethnographic study of classificatory encounters in library spaces. *Poetics*, 103, article 101888.

Quinn, Katherine, Cornish, Ben and Orlek, Jonathan (2025) Between co and solo writing: Experimenting with constraint, composition, and community through writing *100s. Culture and Organization*. https://doi.org/10.1080/14759551.2025.2449924

Quinn, Katherine and Lewis, Jamie (forthcoming) The lanyard. In Angela Woods and Des Fitzgerald (eds) *Constructing Sites: Surveying Scenes of Interdisciplinary Collaboration*. London: Bloomsbury.

Quinn, Katherine, Orlek, Jonathan and Cornish, Benjamin (2020) Writing alone together: Making sense of lockdown through hundreds, *Sociological Review Magazine*, 24 November.

Santamaria, Michele R. (2020) Concealing white supremacy through fantasies of the library: Economies of affect at work. *Library Trends*, 68 (3), 431–49.

16

Your feet may change size: murder mystery, motherhood and the anti-carceral imagination

Phil Crockett Thomas

Chapter one: lost in the woods

> In a wood, you go for a walk. If you're not forced to leave it in a hurry to get away from the wolf or the ogre, it is lovely to linger … . (Eco, 1994: 50)

An old man wakes up alone in the woods with a woman's name in his mouth but no recollection of his own. His first steps are stumbling, pained, his arms bleeding from fresh knife wounds. He looks at his arms in wonder – it is not only his name that he does not recognise. He thinks he sees through the trees a woman being harmed and wants to help her, but can't trust his unfamiliar eyes. He doesn't realise how close he is to Blackheath House, a stately home and a possible haven, until a mysterious benefactor slips a compass into his pocket.

A 'geriatric' mother is walking in wintery woods on a path that leads to Pollok House, a stately home in the Southside of Glasgow. There are rainforests in Scotland, and the moss and lichen dangles off the trees like designer knitwear. The frozen ground thaws to a jungly wetness under her feet. She looks like she is alone but there is a newborn nestled into her chest. They are wrapped together in an enormous puffer coat, like a big black duvet. The baby has colic and is 'unputdownable', so her parents take turns wearing or holding her. So young and she has already redefined their practice of love. As she slowly walks in loops the mother is reading an 'unputdownable' novel, a chunky murder mystery called *The seven deaths of Evelyn Hardcastle* (2018) by Stuart Turton. A man is lost inside the book.

He has been sentenced to walk in loops, compelled to relive the same day eight times, waking up in the body of eight different guests of Blackheath House to try and solve the murder of Evelyn, the daughter of its aristocratic owners, scheduled to take place that evening. He is a prisoner of the house until he achieves this. When the reader first encounters him, he is in the body of an old man in the woods, who, although he doesn't know it yet, has been failing in his task for thirty years, stuck in a time loop and unable to remember anything from his previous attempts.

It is during the COVID-19 pandemic and the mother has become accustomed to seeing other people out walking in Pollok Country Park, but not so today and its woods feel unknowable again. To her untrained eyes, the pace of change here feels slower than in the city's streets, and a lonely walk in the woods makes her feel like a time traveller, perhaps a trespasser in the time before the woods were gifted to Glasgow City Council. Just off the path the reddish bark of Scots pine stands out against the fade to black beyond. She reaches a point in the book where the protagonist has his throat slit by an adversary who appears from nowhere and calls him a 'brave rabbit'. She thinks about what she would do if she was attacked on this path; how she could fall in a way that protected her baby; whether running would cause the stitches from her C-section to come undone. The anaesthetist had said, 'it will feel like someone is rummaging in a handbag, but the handbag is your tummy'. They found a baby in her handbag, like in *The importance of being Earnest*.

Chapter two: murder mystery

> The corpse must shock not only because it is a corpse but also because, even for a corpse, it is shockingly out of place, as when a dog makes a mess on a drawing room carpet. (Auden, 1948)

Reader, when I first read *Seven deaths* I was that 'geriatric' mother, existing in a milky fog of waking and sleeping at odd hours. Watching Nigella Lawson on television cooking in her empty flat would move me to tears, and I was so sleep deprived that I started reading books twice, forgetting I had just read them. I felt like a stranger to myself, a bruised and swollen body with alien priorities. As Emma Jackson notes, walking with a baby changes the rhythm and pattern of your walking; you walk slowly – weighed down with things for the baby, or by a buggy – and often in circles. Walking in circles embeds you further into a place rather than taking you off to new destinations (Jackson, 2019). But as an exhausted new parent I didn't always want to be a good sociologist and be attentive to my surroundings. At times I needed fantasy with an urgency I had not experienced since childhood. Hitherto a speed-walker, I learned to move slowly enough to read at the same time. So, when I picked up *Seven deaths* I wasn't seeking unfamiliar woods, but a cozy parlour, a well-placed corpse and a puzzle to solve.

As exemplified by the novels of Agatha Christie, the clue-puzzle form of the 'golden age' of detective fiction (most of which was published between the two world wars) has a number of recognisable features – a primary focus on murder, an enclosed setting (often a country house) far removed from worldly events, multiple suspects with plausible motives, characters drawn from the upper or upper middle classes, a victim that no one really mourns, a criminal that knows the victim socially and rational detective work (Knight, 2003: 77–9).

The plot of *Seven deaths* is extremely complex and the presence of the familiar tropes of a murder mystery helps the reader focus on solving the puzzle. Like many murder mysteries the book contains a map and a list of characters in the first pages. Most of these characters are awful aristocratic types and others from their orbit – the idiotic playboy, the frosty dowager, the alcoholic earl, the nouveau riche thug with dirt on everybody, and numerous put upon servants. Like many other golden age mysteries, shame over the exposure of 'moral failings' such as addiction and illegitimate children have a part to play in the plot.

Contemporary adaptations and pastiches of golden age detective fiction such as *Seven deaths* use the trauma of the First World War to hint at plausible psychological explanations for some of the casual violence that fills the pages of the genre. But these remain hints rather than psychological studies, because otherwise the horror of war would distract from the pleasure of solving puzzles. It has been argued that the contemporary readers of golden age detective fiction turned to these books as 'a literature of convalescence', an escape from the memory of war (Light, 1991: 69; Knight, 2003: 90). Readers like myself continue to take refuge in the genre, and many scholars have conjectured that this is to do with the clue-puzzle form and the way that the reader is invited and challenged to solve the murder alongside the detective.

In *Seven deaths* the puzzle is explicitly laid out by a character our protagonist refers to as the Plague Doctor (due to his outfit), who acts as both jailer and helper, stating that if he can solve the murder and catch the killer, the protagonist will have won his freedom by rectifying this injustice. In a reversal of the stripping of a name and its replacement with a number that is iconic in cultural representations of prisons as a 'mortification of the self' (Goffman, 1961), the Plague Doctor tells the protagonist what his name was before he entered the prison: Aiden Bishop. It doesn't stir any memories, but Aiden holds on to his former name like a life raft as his hosts' appetites and attributes become more powerful. As he moves through his hosts' bodies he retains the new memories made in them, commenting that he is 'no longer a man, I'm a chorus' (Turton, 2018: 402).

Chapter three: bodies

I too feel like a chorus. My mother body feels too heavy for my bones and its appetites completely beyond my control. Instead, I focus on our daughter and try to make myself invisible. Her body is changing all the time in ways that are remarkable. As her long-distance vision improves and her neck becomes stronger, we turn her round in her sling so she can face the world. I experience strangers bursting into ecstatic smiles as I near them, their eyes transfixed on our baby. I feel guilty as an unintended witness to their private joy. My partner marvels that when he is out walking with our daughter, he can now smile at women without being seen as a creep. Older strangers put coins and sometimes banknotes in our pram, a Glasgow tradition. In a museum another stranger prises her from my arms and holds her tightly, tears rolling down her face. A younger woman hands her back saying, 'I'm so sorry, my mother is very ill.' I wonder if my daughter will ever have to do this for me. I hope not.

Aiden has strong feelings about the bodies and personalities that he gets to inhabit. He is disgusted by the heavy body of the banker but values his intelligence, he is ashamed to discover that the elderly doctor is really the guests' drug dealer, and he is so appalled by the rapist playboy that he volunteers to have his throat slit (echoing an existing hierarchy among prisoners where sex offenders are placed lowest on the social scale). The body that he enjoys inhabiting the most is that of a heroic and handsome young policeman, who can fight, has experience of detective work, high moral standards and useful friends. This character is able to piece together clues and drives the solving of the mystery, perhaps also by giving Aiden the experience of inhabiting a character who is universally loved and respected by the others.

Aiden only hops into the bodies of male characters, which implies a disappointing gender essentialism and denies the reader the pleasure of queered relationships that are a mainstay of body hopping narratives. In keeping with golden age detective fiction, the world of Blackheath is distinctly white, cis-gendered and heterosexual, and there is romance when Aiden teams up with another player known as Anna. This provides him with a way to externalise his detective work to the reader, and Anna also acts as an emotional anchor in a world of cold formality, violence and class prejudice. Unlike Aiden, Anna's punishment allows her to inhabit only one character, a maid who spends most of the novel trying to be as inconspicuous as possible, and writing down notes about everything that has happened, for their mutual benefit. As Aiden runs about getting into fights and solving the mystery, Anna hides in a gatehouse tending to two of his hosts, protecting them from their unscrupulous rivals. All the young female characters in *Seven deaths* are like the sidekicks invented by female writers of the 'golden era', like Dorothy L. Sayers' Harriet Vane. These characters are cute, bright, brave and breezy, but they leave the central task of solving the puzzle to male detectives and are happy just to help out. They would all have been nurses if they had been members of a social class that needed to work for a living. There is no Miss Marple at Blackheath House; the one elderly female character in *Seven deaths* could be played by Maggie Smith phoning it in.

Blackheath House itself is a character in a way that is closer to the horror genre than detective fiction. The house is dilapidated, usually abandoned, with parts of it shut off and others covered with rugs and throws to disguise the decay. The grounds of the house are most often described as caked in mud. I think of the mud as something that holds our protagonist together as he hops through different bodies. However, mud is also important for clues. Things are left on the ground, tucked into crevices in the brickwork of old wells, the mud gets bloody and mixed with broken glass. Mud also sticks to boots, providing incriminating footprints: gracious, these prints are from shoes far too small for a man to wear!

I keep to the path as it slowly curves; the frosty gravel crunches underfoot, obnoxiously loud in the still winter air. My feet grew during pregnancy, gaining half a size as the bones spread due to the effects of the hormone relaxin on my muscles. They are now in the process of shrinking back, making me glad I didn't throw out all my old shoes. Pollok House resembles a doll's house from a distance. It is set in a vast park that once belonged to the estate of the Maxwell family. Designated a country park on its opening to the public in the 1980s, it was intended to be wilder and more informal than a standard park. It has a radical history too, as in the 1990s the park became the home of the Pollok Free State, a tree-house protest camp organised against the building of the M77 motorway which would cut the park off from communities living in the post-war housing schemes on its north and west sides. The motorway was eventually built and my route to the park takes me through streets lined with enormous well-kept houses, whose continued access to the park was ensured. You need to pay to see the house apart from the warm cafe in the basement that was once the kitchen, which normally sells salty soup, and ice creams in the summer. The house is cared for, but closed up for now, like everything else. The Pollok House guidebook refers to the Maxwell family of three keeping fifty servants in the house's heyday. Now walkers take the opportunity to tramp all over the closed golf course. We are united by our need for new loops to walk!

Chapter four: prisons

> [M]ost prisoners walk into prison because they know they will be dragged or beaten into prison if they do not walk. (Cover, 1986: 1607)

Before my pregnancy I had been working on a project that involved going into prisons and making songs with the people who were incarcerated, and sometimes the people who worked there too. My attitude towards prisons was already that they should be abolished and efforts focused instead on developing responses to social harm that do not perpetuate it, but working in these carceral spaces reinforced my views. I saw that prisons made people sicker, poorer, more volatile and traumatised, and less connected to the world outside. As a result, the project I designed and undertook after my maternity leave involved supporting activists and scholars involved in the movement for prison abolition in the UK to write works of science fiction imagining futures that are more just. In other words, I hoped to foster a space for the expression of the anti-carceral imagination, and to support the development of alternatives to prisons and other carceral spaces (Crockett Thomas, 2022).

While reading *Seven deaths* I wondered whether it could be an anti-carceral text – intended to demonstrate the harms of detention – cunningly disguised as detective fiction? In Blackheath House the inmates remember nothing of their lives before imprisonment and are forced to relive the same day indefinitely unless they can win their liberation through their skill at solving mysteries. We are told nothing about the society that founded Blackheath House as a prison, but can infer that it takes a sadistic yet gamified approach to punishment, that it has mastered the technology of time travel and that it has a fondness for golden age detective stories. In terms of its penal philosophy and practices, time loops enable the society to have their punitive cake and eat it; the prisoners of Blackheath House are sentenced to indefinite imprisonment with no chance of parole (torture), but are also killed repeatedly (capital punishment), and are forced to labour intensively for no remuneration (slave labour) as characters in a murder mystery entertainment (public spectacle). So, does redemption and rehabilitation have a role to play in the world of *Seven deaths*?

In my work in prisons and with former prisoners, I saw how those who progressed within the system towards liberation were those who learned the 'redemptive script' (Maruna, 2001) and performed it well, convincing others and themselves that they had changed and were rehabilitated 'new men'. Aiden only becomes capable of escaping Blackheath when he no longer remembers the values and motivations of his former self. When people argue for the redemptive power of prisons in the real world, this tends to be tied to the idea that prisons enable those incarcerated to reflect on their harmful actions and take responsibility for them, but *Seven deaths* made me ponder – how much of rehabilitation is actually a process of forgetting? I don't remember concretely who I was at 18 or 24 years old, and that is a blessing. After she died, I read an interview with Anne Perry, the crime writer who murdered her friend's mother as a teenager, an act that was dramatised in Peter Jackson's 1994 film *Heavenly Creatures*. The interviewer expresses incredulity that Perry cannot remember committing the murder but chose to write about crime for the rest of her life through the prism of fiction (Darnton, 1995). To me, this makes perfect sense: the memory of trauma as a haunting, something that follows you around but that you can't quite make out, until something shocks it into view.

In *Seven deaths* the Plague Doctor is disturbed by Aiden's partnership with fellow prisoner Anna and reveals to him that prior to her imprisonment at Blackheath House she tortured and murdered his sister and others. He explains that Aiden then voluntarily entered the prison in order to torment and kill Anna in revenge. At the start of this section I quoted the legal scholar Robert Cover (1986) reflecting on the violence that underpins the speech act of judicial sentencing. Aiden's choice to enter the prison freely purely to cause harm is horrifying, as is the idea of a punishment regime that would enable this. However, when Aiden learns the truth about his own monstrous motivations he redoubles his efforts not only solve Evelyn's murder, but to try and prevent it from happening. This leads him to act in ways that alter the sequence of events significantly.

Part of the appeal of time loops as a narrative device is that they offer a chance to 'do things over' that is rarely afforded in real life. Wibke Schniedermann (2023) has written about 'involuntary time loops' and the ubiquity of their pairing with redemption narratives in popular culture. She comments, 'the hero redefines the successful outcome of his time loop story, which is to disregard the rules of the time loop. Destabilizing the loop becomes an assertion of individual agency' (Schniedermann, 2023: 297). The sketch of Aiden's walk loops in time, but is also divergent and increasingly agentic. He intersects with his previous routes and hosts, eventually targeting specific times to try and create or avoid encounters. He begins the book stumbling and ends up weaving pathways into a brilliant tapestry, guided by his nobler aims.

Chapter five: the end

> 'People are murdered every day', I say. 'Righting one wrong can't be the only reason for all of this.'
>
> 'An excellent point', he says, clapping his hands together in appreciation. 'But who's to say there aren't hundreds of others like yourself seeking justice for those souls?'
>
> 'Are there?'
>
> 'Doubtful, but it's a lovely thought isn't it?" (Turton, 2018: 217)

I had been hoping to think about prisons less during my maternity leave, but I kept looping back to them through reading *Seven deaths*. I was haunted by the people I had met there, however fleetingly, and by the ritual of my team walking away from the prison and going to the pub for an unofficial debrief, knowing that the people we had left behind couldn't come with us. During the pandemic many commentators and friends spoke about feeling like a prisoner in their own home, but we could still go for a walk in the woods. For actual prisoners during the pandemic it was business as usual, but with more isolation, more sickness and death (Morrison et al., 2023). Like Aiden, the shape of my walk is also a divergent loop as the mystery becomes clearer. I am never coming from or going anywhere other than home, but with each walk I am learning better how to take care of my baby. Together we trace paths as bees fly in spirals, building the courage and knowledge to fly further away from the hive each time. What are the things I need to remember to bring? I change her nappy on a park bench, telling myself that the freezing air hitting her skin can only make her hardier. I learn which bushes are good to pee in. One time I breastfeed her sitting on a tree stump and a deer rushes past us, flushed from the trees by a dog. I had heard that there were deer loose in the park but had never seen one. I see another one soon afterwards, a twisted corpse by the side of the path. Signs go up around the park threatening to prosecute the owners of out-of-control dogs.

Towards the end of the novel the Plague Doctor reveals that Blackheath House is one of thousands of similar puzzle prisons and, surprisingly, that the regime prides itself on being based on the principle of rehabilitation. He asks Aiden, 'do you know how you can tell if a monster's fit to walk the world again, Mr Bishop? ...

If they're truly redeemed and not just telling you what you want to hear? ... You give them a day without consequences, and you watch to see what they do with it' (Turton, 2018: 447–8). He continues to extoll the merits of the regime:

> instead of leaving our prisoners to rot in a cell, we give them a chance to prove themselves worthy of release every single day. Do you see the beauty of it? The murder of Evelyn Hardcastle was never solved, and probably never would have been. By locking prisoners inside the murder, we give them the chance to atone for their own crimes by solving somebody else's. It's as much a service as a punishment. (Turton, 2018: 448)

After thirty years of trying to solve the puzzle Aiden and Anna are judged to be rehabilitated, solving the historic murder as a community service by working together and being willing to sacrifice themselves to see justice served. In demonstrating the success of the prison regime, the novel cannot be said to be anti-carceral, although it implies that redemption and rehabilitation mean being prepared to forget. In terms of a progressive stance on crime it also models a (bizarre) form of 'restorative justice' in bringing together the offender and victim-survivor to work through their conflict.

Wearing other people's shoes, Aiden's walks often end in a grisly death, but his story ends with romance and walking into an unknown future with Anna. As well as an unknown future, Aiden and Anna choose not to remember their past lives before their incarceration – Anna no longer remembers her crimes and Aiden no longer remembers his pain or lust for revenge. Instead, they share their present love and the memory of their day at Blackheath in all its violence and uneasy allegiance. Fittingly, W. H. Auden (1948) argued that the pleasure of murder mysteries is that the detective's exposure of the murderer removes the reader's guilt about their own sins and restores them to 'a state of innocence, where he may know love as love and not as the law'.

References

Auden, Wystan Hugh (1948) The guilty vicarage. *Harper's Magazine*, May. Available at: https://harpers.org/archive/1948/05/the-guilty-vicarage/ [accessed 12 April 2024].

Cover, Robert (1986) Violence and the word. *Yale Law Journal*, 95 (8), 1601–29.

Crockett Thomas, Phil (ed.) (2022) *Abolition Science Fiction*. London: Independent Social Research Foundation.

Darnton, John (1995) Author faces up to a long, dark secret, *New York Times*, 14 February. Available at: www.nytimes.com/1995/02/14/arts/author-faces-up-to-a-long-dark-secret.html [accessed 27 November 2024].

Eco, Umberto (1994) *Six Walks in the Fictional Woods*. Cambridge, MA: Harvard University Press.

Goffman, Erving (1961) *Asylums: Essays on the Social Situation of Mental Patients and Other Inmates*. Garden City, NY: Anchor Books.

Jackson, Emma (2019) Walking in circles, *Sociological Review Magazine*, 4 October. Available at: https://thesociologicalreview.org/collections/thinking-on-the-move/walking-in-circles/ [accessed 2 October 2025].

Knight, Stephen (2003) The golden age. In Martin Priestman (ed.) *The Cambridge Companion to Crime Fiction*. Cambridge Companions to Literature. Cambridge: Cambridge University Press.

Light, Alison (1991) *Forever England: Femininity, Literature and Conservatism Between the Wars*. Abingdon and New York: Routledge.

Maruna, Shadd (2001) *Making Good: How Ex-Convicts Reform and Rebuild their Lives*. Washington, DC: American Psychological Association.

Morrison, Katrina, Anderson, Kirstin, Jardine, Emma, Maycock, Matt and Sparks, Richard (2023) *A Review of Interventions, Innovation, and the Impact of Covid-19 in the Scottish Prison System within a Comparative Analytical Framework*. Glasgow: Scottish Centre for Crime and Justice Research. Available at: www.sccjr.ac.uk/publication/impact-of-covid-19-scottish-prison-system-2023/ [accessed 21 February 2025].

Schniedermann, Wibke (2023) The narrative features of involuntary time loops. *Narrative*, 31 (3), 290–307.

Turton, Stuart (2018) *The Seven Deaths of Evelyn Hardcastle*. London: Raven Books.

17

Black dog, Brown disabled man, White world

Viji Kuppan

In this essay I invite the reader to walk with me and my canine companion as we move and interact with the people and spaces of my local neighbourhood. In these movements, I foreground sensing and sensation through human and non-human encounters and discuss the practice and embodiment of walking together as an interspecies relationship. These perambulations could be called phenomenological, because they are a way of noticing and making sense of what emerges in the walking experience. In my case, walking is not only about pleasurable time with my dog, or walking's health and fitness benefits. I am also interested in what is concealed, missed or evaded when walking, particularly in relation to matters of race and disability. The *body* is central to understanding these multilayered interactions because it not only connects us to our inner senses of self, but is the locus for mediating all our other relationships in the life world. As Merleau-Ponty (1969: 250) reminds us, 'flesh is at the heart of the world'. I am interested in our corporeal coexistence in the company of dogs as an intersubjective experience. Through the relationship with my dog, I aim to show the intimacy, sociality and misanthropy these rhythms and routines reveal between canids and humans in space and time leisure cultures (Holmberg, 2019).

I agree with Fletcher and Platt (2018: 214) when they argue that 'walking is a highly sensuous and complex activity'. Moreover, that dog walking is also a 'potentially important cultural space for making sense of human–animal relations' (Fletcher and Platt, 2018: 224). Where my argument differs from theirs is that, while most of the literature around dog walking is enfolded – unconsciously or otherwise – in Whiteness, I want to also expose the empirical moments, situations and processes where racism and disability surface, seemingly disappear, before re-emerging and reconfiguring anew. My contention is that, as an older, Brown disabled man, having a dog humanises my contact with the White world. It makes me less of a threat. Less potentially 'violent, fanatical … protean and unpredictable' (Valluvan, 2020: 5). More intelligible, perhaps, to White people. 'He must be alright; he has a dog!' The dog offers me provisional protection from the racialising gaze, but only to the extent that I conform to dominant ideas within the White imagination. As much as my dog helps me navigate the White world, this is not the case for all racially minoritised dog owners, as one of my interlocutors in this essay will shortly reveal.

I can offer these insights because I have lived in the same area for over thirty years (in a mixed-race relationship), walking, hobbling and even at times wheeling on these streets, with and without a canine companion. Below, I begin by sharing an everyday dog walk through urban space revealing the ways in which conversation, connection and community exist alongside silence, tension and hostility. My intention is to defamiliarise the dog walk as a benign quotidian activity, and instead, following Bennett (2016), highlight the affects, discourses and materialities of human, non-human and inhuman interactions in supposedly 'post-racial' and 'post-disabling' times. It is these paradoxical processes of convivial culture that are crucial to grasp if we are to envision new and more caring social relations.

Autumn in Carlton, an urban district located on the eastern edges of Nottingham – a culturally and economically significant city, widely known for its association with the legend of Robin Hood, as well as the former bicycle, lace and tobacco industries. It is situated in the central eastern part of England, known as the East Midlands. Carlton is a historically White but increasingly Black and Brown working-class suburb. Despite bright blue skies and late morning sunshine, it is decidedly chilly. I rub my hands together and blow into them in a desperate attempt to dislodge the biting cold from my gnarled arthritic fingers. While my impairment's effects are currently less painful and more effectively managed with medication, it should not mask the difficult lived realities for many disabled people; disability, far from being an individual problem, should instead be understood as a political and public issue (Oliver and Barnes, 2012) that touches the lives of many people.

Lax or Laxman, my black English Springer–Labrador cross, has no such impairment issues, and is up for it – he's always up for it! Straining at the leash, sniffing and scanning, intensely interested in the many nooks and crannies of built-up urban space – his olfactory senses cranked up to maximum. As Holmberg (2019: 31) observes in companionship with her dogs, it is as if 'every day is new, while it carries memories of yesterday'. Lax tugs me forward and I pull him back. We play this game for a while, both vying for control. I am the first to concede, as he doggedly leads me up a twitchell[1] that is often part of our daily walking practice. Fletcher and Platt (2018: 226) propose, 'rather than there being a one-way flow of power, the walk is where humans and dogs negotiate power within their relationship'. Sunlight bounces across bare branches of birch trees vivifying the copper-brown-coloured leaves which gather heavily on the path, making a satisfying 'crunch' when stepped upon. Lax buries his nose deep within its interiority, passionately inhaling, fully absorbed in this moment, his pleasure in curiosity palpable as he resurfaces from the leaf litter. This decomposing world is not dead to him but vibrant and alive. This canine sense of wonder is one of Laxman's lessons in which he teaches me the importance of opening up one's senses and being interested in the worldly sensibility of things. Put another way, it is an orientation towards touching and being touched by the world that he offers.

As we leave the wooded twitchell and emerge onto a main road, Lax is busily sniffing the wall for signs of other dogs. 'Ay up mi duck, how are ya? He's keen int eh … ahh he's lovely', a warm, friendly female voice, using the Nottingham vernacular, interjects. Lax sniffs her and then, turning to me, barks. 'Ay up duck. Sorry. He wants to get on. He's got ball on his mind – lovely to see you though', I hurriedly reply, as Lax yanks me towards the kerb. The older White woman, whom I recognise from walking the streets where we live, smiles and responds: 'Yes. I see you've got to go. Ta-ra duck.' I hear a car approaching and instruct Laxman to 'sit' and 'wait'. He immediately relaxes and obediently complies, recognising my authority in this moment. The vehicle passes and we cross in unison, whereupon he starts to pull again. I am familiar with this urging. He pulls me to a grassy area where he now carefully surveys the ground for signs of other dogs' scents, before determining his spot to defecate. Although unashamed in his toileting, there is a vulnerability in this open exposure that he communicates with the softness in his eyes. As Donna Haraway and Cary Wolf (2016: 94) suggest, 'we are training each other in acts of communication we barely understand. We are, constitutively, companion species. We make each other up in the flesh.' Bowel movement over and the poop scooped, Laxman's rhythm changes again, as he picks up another trail and insistently leads me on to investigate.

As we round the corner, we are pleasantly surprised by the presence of three dogs – a chestnut brown Pointer, a russet Dachshund and a grey-white Miniature Schnauzer. The dogs all bark from the excitement of this potential new assemblage, before becoming entangled and immersed in each other's bodies and odours. 'Hi Abigail', I say to the confident and composed Black woman who is responsible for these dogs. 'Not too many today then', I joke. 'I'm just on my way to pick another two up now', she wryly replies, grinning. Abigail is a local dog walker who we regularly meet when out walking. After disentangling the dogs, we cheerfully wave goodbye. Further along the road we meet a Brown woman with a young sable-coloured German Shepherd. She endearingly confides, 'He's cute, but not very bright, and if he gets off the lead I have to try and rugby tackle him.' I laugh out loud at the picture she has painted. Further along the road we say 'hello' to an East Asian woman with a silvery grey Shih Tzu. I mention these meetings with women of colour not because they are extraordinary, but, along with men of colour, these pedestrian interactions are part of our everyday encounters. There is a perception, both anecdotally and academically (through their omission), that racially minoritised people do not like dogs or are afraid of dogs. It could be argued that a generational trauma exists in the Black psyche because dogs were used to track down and capture enslaved people fleeing brutal plantation systems in the Americas (see Johnson, 2009). Yet such terror is assuaged by the comfort and companionship dogs have also historically offered Black people (see Phillips, 2007). I have noticed the increase in Black and Brown dog owners over the last ten years. Not only are people of colour dog owners, but they are increasingly professionally engaged as sitters, trainers and walkers.

As we approach the park, I can sense Laxman's eagerness growing, the lead becomes taut and his tail animated, wagging from side to side. In the park, he can barely contain his excitement. I remove his lead, and as I rummage inside the bag he sits scrutinising my every action. Waiting, his body now trembles in anticipation, as I finally find, and pluck, a luminous orange- and blue-striped ball from the bag's recesses. I kick it high and hard, and he hares off down the grassy bank and across the muddy field, fully focused, to retrieve it. Dayan evokes this presence when she writes:

> What would it mean to become more like a dog? How might we come up against life as a sensory but not sensible experience? We all experience our dogs' unprecedented and peculiar attentiveness. It comes across as an exuberance borne by a full heart ... What does it mean to think outside our selves with other beings? For dogs, thought is immersed in matter. Not sympathy or sentiment but something more acute and unsettling. (Dayan, 2015: 10)

I see Isaac enter the park and approach. 'Hey man! How's it going?' I enquire. 'Alright fella', he replies affably. His inquisitive, two-tone, lucid grey and white Old Tyme English Bulldog playfully pulls on his lead in an effort to greet Lax, who has just returned with his ball. 'No Collis', Isaac firmly interjects, while simultaneously pulling him back. 'He's alright. You know what Lax is like. He's just obsessed with that ball', I answer, nonchalantly stroking Collis' head in a compensatory action, to which he in turn responds by nuzzling my hand. 'I know he's only young', Isaac counters, 'but he's got to learn to respect boundaries. To be honest I'm just being careful. Some people have been on my case, asking me why I've got a Pit Bull'.[2] I retort, 'But he's not a Pit Bull', and besides, 'Collis is so affectionate, friendly and social; a bit boisterous at times, but wouldn't hurt anyone.' Isaac shrugs his shoulders. 'I know, but I'm a Black man.' Those words, 'but I'm a Black man', hang between us in the cold, bright midday air, illuminating the pervasive and insidious qualities of anti-Black racism. Whiteness is a process, and a technology of power, argued the sociologist Ruth Frankenberg (1997). It is also a complexly nested racial signifier; it forms the basis of 'socioeconomic, sociocultural and psychic interrelations' (Frankenberg, 1997: 1). But its signified multiple meanings often remain unexposed and uninterrogated in everyday forms of leisure activities such as dog walking.

This is not the first time that Isaac and I have spoken about race. The park provides a meeting place in urban multiculture for dog owners; it is a convivial culture, in which mundane conversations between differently positioned groups forge bonds of affinity between some, while also sowing seeds of suspicion and antipathy towards Others. As Gilroy (2004: p. xi) argues, conviviality does not describe the 'absence of racism or the triumph of tolerance'. In the interstices of this urban world, I want to suggest that there are also spaces to build solidarity, through forms of *communicative rationality* (Spracklen, 2013). That is, dog walking and the park provides opportunities to talk openly about complex forms of alienation and alterity. It is a topic of dialogue between racialised Others and their White allies that recognises how a White supremacist society continually reproduces the image of Black men as deviant and dangerous – in this instance, through the misrecognition by 'people' (who are White and plural) that Isaac is the owner of a 'dangerous' dog. The *fact* that he researched and carefully considered the type of dog appropriate for his lifestyle (which was not a Pit Bull), is casually and wilfully overlooked. The *fact of Blackness* is a racialising miasma, 'that does not permit us to understand the being of the [B]lack man', argued Fanon (2008: 82). The Black subject is given 'no chance' and is 'overdetermined from without' based upon his 'appearance' (Fanon, 2008: 87). I suggest that Isaac is taken to task because he is adjudged to be lacking the (White) moral standards that would allow him a *fair* hearing, let alone pass through the White world untroubled. What I find unsettling in this vignette is the way in which the complexity of Black life is stripped of its richness and diversity and rendered only as a vacuous stereotype. Race and gender become a toxic combination in the Black man, particularly when in the presumed possession of a proscribed breed of dog, meaning that Isaac is 'always already criminalised by virtue of the[se] social stigma[s]' (Bennett, 2016: 146). Racist expression appears in many forms; it does not have to be strident to be injurious, and indeed its subtle articulations can be just as psychically and socially harmful. Before we part company, I reassure Isaac that I will listen out for any criticism of him or his dog, and will try to engage with and correct any erroneous chatter I encounter.

Laxman is exploring in a corner of the park. I call over to him and he pretends not to hear. He knows that playtime is coming to an end, and we will shortly be leaving. I repeat my request for him to return, but he continues to ignore me. I call again. This time he looks up beseechingly at me, in a last-ditch attempt to stay a little longer. Realising the impossibility of that situation, he reluctantly sashays his way back to where I am standing. In a well-rehearsed script between the two of us, he sits. I tell him 'He's a good lad', and offer him a couple of treats, which he greedily snatches from my hand and wolfs down. We walk together for a few moments. Then, suddenly, Lax picks up a scent and, aroused, careers off into the undergrowth to investigate. I lose sight of him. 'Laxman. Come back!', I frustratedly shout. I spot him a few minutes later feasting on discarded take-away food. I know that he will pay no heed now until the vittles have been devoured. The observant reader will no doubt be aware of the numerous ways I have anthropomorphised Laxman thus far in this essay. I have an expectation that 'he' will be civilised and compliant in certain situations. In this particular situation Laxman demonstrates his own active agency: an instinctual, wild and wilful nature that has its own drives and desires. A refusal to remain tethered, tamed, domesticated and subservient. I cannot pretend that such moments of 'disobedience' are easy, and although I am sometimes angered by such expressions, I also feel a need to lean into these moments and fight against 'reductive forms of anthropomorphism' (Bennett, 2016: 125) to find a deeper relationship. In trying to loosen my desire for control and cultivate an awareness of interspecies sociality, I recognise that the dog is not 'my property'. I cannot possess an animal, but following Bennett (2016) and other Black writers in this vein – for example, Carl Phillips (2007), Jesmyn Ward (2011) and Zora Neale Hurston (1990) – imagine how we might practice kinship of 'being alongside' animals (Bennett, 2016: 125). Satiated, Laxman returns to me of his own volition, and we walk together again.

As we continue, I catch the white sails of Green's Windmill glinting in the distance as we descend into an adjoining urban area. Off the bustling thoroughfare, there are numerous narrow streets characterised by back-to-back terraced housing. Towards the top of one of these side streets I notice an older White woman with a white cane that she arcs from left to right, tapping the pavement in front of her. I recognise who she is. It's Lucy, my visually impaired friend. I can tell she's frustrated by the way she shoves one of the many wheelie bins that obstruct her route along her pathway. Laxman and I quickly walk up to meet her. 'Bloody hell!', she exclaims as she knocks a car's wing mirror and collides with one of the bins. 'Hi Lucy, it's Viji', I say. 'Oh Viji', she says, as she comes to a halt, her face brightening and relaxing. 'Bin day is it?' I utter ironically. 'No. It's so annoying – that was yesterday. I understand that people need to park partly on the pavement because the road is so narrow, and that they have to put their bins out. But can't they push their wing mirrors in and take their bins back inside once the refuse collectors have been?', she exclaims indignantly.

Lucy's anger is justified. As Bates (2018: 985) argues, 'the city is not, and has never been, equally accessible to all'. Moreover, Lucy has had conversations with her neighbours about these matters. While many are apologetic, and do initially try to be more considerate, even pointing out hazards and guiding her around obstacles, there continues to be a *forgetting*, in which, 'people are surprised that blind people come through' (Michalko and Titchkosky, 2018: n.p.). I contend that it is not that people 'do not care', but that the non-disabled imagination thinks that a car parked in a particular way, or a bin left on a pavement, will not prevent someone from doing something, or going somewhere, because they will navigate the object by *walking* around it. After all, this is 'common sense'. We live in a world dominated by visual culture, where vision has long been valued as the pre-eminent 'seat of sensation'. In his essay on 'The nobility of sight', the philosopher Hans Jonas (1966) undertakes a phenomenological discussion of the different senses, but sees no reason to strip sight of its superior status and concludes by exaggerating and exalting vision's capacity, thereby confirming the standpoint of the Greeks that 'sight is the most excellent of the senses' (Jonas, 1966: 135).

'I'm going into town. Can I take your arm to the bus stop at the bottom of the road, Viji?', Lucy asks. 'Of course', I respond. 'Is Laxman with you? I've not heard him?', she enquires. 'He's here. Don't worry. He found pizza and chips earlier in the park, which he ate with great relish. He doesn't feel the need to vocalise at the moment', I declare drolly. She laughs, 'I wondered why he was so quiet.' Lucy and I have been friends for many years and have had many discussions about the continuing politics of disablement (Oliver, 1990). She tells me that she has recently complained to the council about the hazards of poorly parked e-scooters, before segueing into the problems of 'shared space' in the city. 'It relies heavily on people noticing. You know, the ability to *catch someone's eye* as they negotiate the area together', she explains. 'But it doesn't take into account people not noticing, or disabled people who are visually impaired and can't see.'

Walking then, and walking fluidly, is the natural order of things, and therefore how we create and maintain disabling environments are processes that are not given enough attention, particularly in a world dominated by what the disabled post-punk artist Ian Dury acerbically described as the 'walkie talkies' (see Kuppan, 2017). Disability continues to be understood as a problem located in the individual, an aberration of body-mind corporeality, whose indeterminacy, like 'race' and gender, are phenomena that only seem to cause trouble (Butler, 1990). What a phenomenological perspective points out are the taken-for-granted frames in which bodies and culture are ruled by stealth, requiring 'critical cultural inquiry' to challenge the 'normative order that makes disability always-already a problem' (Titchkosky and Michalko, 2012: 140). Lucy, Laxman and I walk to the bottom of the road where we part company at the bus stop. My head is full, feeling into and thinking about disability, racism, embodied walking and connection with my local environment. I slowly return home with Laxman.

As my walk with Laxman has hopefully demonstrated, walking together is a socially engaged activity where we are offered the opportunity to learn about the world and ourselves in the company of humans and dogs. I have already begun recomposing, reimagining and reorientating myself. It feels like a long journey getting here. How did I get here? What is this new composition I am beginning to sketch? A newly discovered confidence with convivial culture. Understanding how racism sits unrulily alongside connection and community. My dog heart opening new possibilities to explore and new people to commune with. This recomposure, this different comportment, makes me feel more like myself, more at home in the world. An understanding of the long history of the Black and Brown presence in this land. Not a timeline that starts in 1940s Britain, but stretching back centuries. I belong here. This is my land too. This is our land. Histories of entanglement ameliorate the wounding of racism's touch, of the harms of hate – the pains of my body-mind. My dog heart has nurtured this renewal, this regrowth – a re-embodiment of the wildness within and without. Colonial conquest, dispossession, extraction, accumulation and racialisation are relatively recent events. This land is ancient. Connecting with this felt presence, allowing her to touch me deeply without withholding, is part of my journey to remembering and wholeness.

Notes

1 Twitchell is a regional word specific to Nottinghamshire that describes an alleyway or cut-through. It can also be referred to as a jitty or ginnel, although the latter term originates in Yorkshire.
2 In the United Kingdom, the Dangerous Dogs Act 1991 bans the ownership of Pit Bull Terrier breeds.

References

Bates, Charlotte (2018) Conviviality, disability and design in the city. *Sociological Review*, 66 (5), 984–99.

Bennett, Joshua (2016) Being Property Once Myself: In Pursuit of the Animal in 20th Century African American Literature. PhD thesis, Princeton University.

Butler, Judith (1990) *Gender Trouble: Feminism and the Subversion of Identity*. New York: Routledge.

Dayan, Colin (2015) *With Dogs at the Edge of Life*. New York: Columbia University Press.

Fanon, Frantz (1967/2008) *Black Skin, White Masks*. London: Pluto Press. First published 1967

Fletcher, Tom and Platt, Louise (2018) (Just) a walk with the dog? Animal geographies and negotiating walking spaces. *Social and Cultural Geography*, 19 (2), 211–29.

Frankenberg, Ruth (ed.) (1997) *Displacing Whiteness: Essays in Social and Cultural Criticism*. Durham, NC: Duke University Press.

Gilroy, Paul (2004) *After Empire: Melancholia or Convivial Culture?* Abingdon: Routledge.

Haraway, Donna and Wolf, Cary (2016) The companion species manifesto: Dogs, people and significant otherness. In Donna Haraway and Cary Wolf (eds) *Manifestly Haraway*. Minneapolis, MN: University of Minnesota Press.

Holmberg, Tora (2019) Walking, eating, sleeping. Rhythm analysis of human/dog intimacy. *Emotion, Space and Society*, 31 (2), 26–31.

Hurston, Zora Neale (1990) *Their Eyes were Watching God*. New York: Perennial Library.

Johnson, Sara (2009) 'You should give them blacks to eat' Waging inter-American wars of torture and terror. *American Quarterly*, 61 (1), 65–92.

Jonas, Hans (1966) The nobility of sight: A study in the phenomenology of the senses. In *The Phenomenon of Life: Towards a Philosophical Biology*. New York: Harper & Row.

Kuppan, Viji (2017) Spasticus Auticus: Thinking about disability, culture and leisure beyond the 'walkie talkies'. In Karl Spracklen, Brett Lashua, Erin Sharpe and Spencer Swain (eds) *The Palgrave Macmillan Handbook of Leisure Theory*. London: Palgrave Macmillan.

Merleau-Ponty, Maurice (1969) *The Visible and Invisible*. Evanston, IL: Northwestern University Press.

Michalko, Rod and Titchkosky, Tanya (2018) Travelling blind. *Disability Studies Quarterly*, 38 (3). https://doi.org/10.18061/dsq.v38i3.6481

Oliver, Mike (1990) *The Politics of Disablement*. Basingstoke: Palgrave Macmillan.

Oliver, Mike and Barnes, Colin (2012) *The New Politics of Disablement*. Basingstoke: Palgrave Macmillan.

Phillips, Carl (2007) *Quiver of Arrows: Selected Poems, 1986–2006*. New York: Farrar, Straus and Giroux.

Spracklen, Karl (2013) *Whiteness and Leisure*. London: Palgrave Macmillan.

Titchkosky, Tanya and Michalko, Rod (2012) The body as the problem of individuality: A phenomenological disability studies approach. In Dan Goodley, Bill Hughes and Lennard Davis (eds) *Disability and Social Theory: New Developments and Directions*. Basingstoke: Palgrave Macmillan.

Valluvan, Sivamohan (2020) *The Clamour of Nationalism: Race and Nation in Twenty-First-Century Britain*. Manchester: Manchester University Press.

Ward, Jesmyn (2011) *Salvage the Bones: A Novel*. New York: Bloomsbury Publishing.

18

Listening to urban change on the River Ravensbourne

Emma Jackson

It is always windy at Lewisham Gateway. I've been here multiple times through every season of the year and in all seasons. Today it's September. The sky is grey, but it is reasonably warm. We are standing in Confluence Park, a small patch of green between high-rise flats that are still under construction. This corner of south-east London where two rivers meet is undergoing major redevelopment. Lewisham is an intensely multicultural borough with a bustling town centre at its core, but the soundscape here feels far removed from the hustle and sonic richness of Lewisham market ('tomatoes, pound a bowl!') a stone's throw away. From where we are standing, the sounds of drilling and hammering overlay the keynote sounds of the Docklands Light Railway (DLR) and the trains passing through Lewisham station. The DLR serves as a direct transport connection to Docklands, London's financial district, and this new development echoes Docklands' high-rise formations, if not its strong business associations. This new architecture is highly unpopular locally (at present) and appears to be made in the image of the transient but affluent worker.

Moving towards the centre of the park, we face the river. Two rivers in fact, the River Quaggy coming in on the right from the direction of Lee, and the Ravensbourne from the direction of Catford. The rivers provide another set of connections. In one direction we can follow them to their sources just across London's border with Kent, a very different landscape to this one, suburban and leafy. And in the other direction to the Thames, and from there to the North Sea. This is the direction we will be walking in today. These rivers connect across administrative boundaries, across London's inner and outer boroughs, the suburban and urban, connecting places and people who might not have very much else in common in palpable ways – but what happens upstream impacts on what happens downstream. The route of our walk follows the River Ravensbourne as much as we can, as there are places on our route where the river cannot be accessed. This walk is an invitation to follow the river and its surroundings and to listen, to turn up the background (Back, 2007) rather than tune it out – even when the sounds seem unpleasant – to consider rhythms and types of urban change.

Originating in sound studies, the motivation for the development of the listening walk, or soundwalk, as a method was to get students to open up their ears to sounds they had never listened to before (Schafer, 1974). A whole host of listening and soundwalking techniques, to tune into the sounds of place and to interact playfully with them, have been honed and developed since (Arkette, 2004; Westerkamp, 2007; Drever, 2020). John Drever (2020) provides an excellent guide for anyone wanting to undertake their own soundwalk, covering different histories in sound studies alongside some practicalities and possible prompts for participants. But perhaps the sociologist might ask some additional questions to use listening to stimulate our sociological imaginations (Wright Mills, 1959)? For example, we might be attentive to how power works through soundscapes, or indeed in judgements made about which sounds belong and which are out of place (Martins, 2019; Summers, 2020).

On this walk together, I layer the soundscapes with the reflections of others that Louise Rondel and I have walked with along this stretch as part of our project Place-making and the Rivers of Lewisham. In listening to the river and its places we will attend to the layers that produce it, from top-down development interventions such as this one to the practices of those who care for the river or shape these watery spaces through their actions in other – sometimes unintentional – ways. Henri Lefebvre's (1991) work on the production of space has influenced how I distinguish between these different forms of spatial practices that shape place, as has Doreen Massey's (1994) insistence that places are processes rather than things frozen in time. We are thinking about urban change through sound as we walk – and in this slice of London, being attuned to urban development is key – but change happens at different speeds and not all change is linear, such as the rising and ebbing tide that shapes this watery landscape.

Every time I take this walk, I am accompanied by the voices of those I have walked it with previously. These include students, fieldwork participants and most of all Louise (see essay 4 by Louise Rondel) – who did the lion's share of walking interviews on this stretch of the river. We have walked this stretch repeatedly, together and alone. We have also been walking with the sounds of the river, even the inaudible ones rendered by sound recordist Konstantinos Damianakis. Konstantinos recorded soundscapes along this route that closely correspond to what we can hear as we walk, but also experimented with hydrophones and contact microphones to interact with what can't be heard. Thus, while I am the sole author of this essay, I am not the sole author of this walk. This is a piece of what my friend Agata and I term 'engaged walking' (Jackson and Lisiak, 2025), forged in dialogue with the ideas and voices of others. It is a product of these previous walks and the conversations and reflections that have been shared on this stretch – it is a recomposition. This written version of the walk also serves as a companion piece to the second episode of *Confluence*, the walking podcast we made, weaving together these conversations, observations and field recordings (Jackson and Rondel, 2024). I use 'we' in the walk to include everyone I have walked this stretch with so far, and now also you, as reader.

Back to Confluence Park: let's walk further into the middle of the grass. One visitor I brought here on a walk commented that it looks as if the new high-rise has been built around the river. But that is not the case. The two rivers were previously underground, culverted into concrete channels, and were 'naturalised' as part of the site's development. Whereas many of London's rivers are underground and many have been absorbed into the sewage system (Ackroyd, 2012), Lewisham's rivers have long stretches that are accessible, giving rise to a complex set of social relationships of care, maintenance and play (Jackson and Rondel, 2025). Nevertheless, the Ravensbourne is a highly engineered river – it has been moved at least twice. Along our walk it is mainly contained by smooth concrete walls used as canvases by local graffiti artists. At the confluence the rivers are about 5 m wide and are protected from the passers-by – or perhaps more accurately the passers-by are protected from them – by grey railings. Signs read 'Caution: deep water' and flotation devices are prominently displayed. The river here is to be looked at, and if you stand at the railings you can hear it, but you are not encouraged to touch it.

The place where we stand was long in the planning. A document from Lewisham Council's archive from the year 2000 gives a breathless account of what the place would be, conjuring a future of people drinking wine by the rivers. This was imagined as a place of consumption, even romance – the visualisation of place that accompanies this text shows a verdant landscape with young lovers embracing. We can imagine this past-future soundscape of laughing and tinkling glasses, with the river in the background. But so far at least, the reality is a little different. The only people in the space are on their way somewhere else. You can hear their fast footsteps as they power-walk to the station. One of the students I brought to this space described it as 'the sort of place you would bring a Greggs sausage roll to and then leave'. In English folk legend, confluences are considered places of spiritual power. Does this also count for rivers that have been moved, covered, uncovered and moved again?

Walking towards the viewing platform you might notice the rattle of a couple of discarded cans rolling across the wooden slats, and a vape lying on the ground. A sign that someone uses this space. Looking downstream you can see a heron. While the river groups that look after these rivers may be dissatisfied with this place, other animals are more forgiving and have made it their home. You can also see the white shape of one of the Lewisham stags as you look downstream. These feature across the local river network and are much loved by the river groups as art, rather than graffiti. The Lewisham stags feed into the ever-evolving mythology of the rivers. I recently saw an advert for a local Morris dance troupe, named 'Quaggy Morris' no less, that will be dancing at the location of the stag murals along the Ravensbourne. I wonder if their concertina music and ankle bells will cut through the overwhelming noises of construction.

It always feels a relief to leave Confluence Park. We turn right and go past the line of bus stops heading down to the main road. You can hear engines and the trains as they pass over the bridge above. The trains are a distinctive part of the south-east London soundscape, especially its river spaces. It is an area of London not served by the underground and, as is often the case, the overground train lines here were built along the natural valleys made by rivers. Here, we briefly part ways with the river as it weaves behind blocks of flats and a Tesco car park that awaits redevelopment. We must negotiate the edges of a strangely quiet retail park and more bus stops. We nip under a subway where a mural of a Kingfisher lets us know we are back on track towards the river, before coming to a flat walkway leading us towards Elverson Road Station.

The soundscape here changes, from the overwhelming sounds of transport to the domestic rhythms of this residential area and the passing cyclists. Today you can hear *Dire Straits* – sons of Deptford – coming out of a ground-level window ('Juliet, the dice was loaded from the start …'). And if you peer over the wall on the right, there is the river. Encased in graffiti. I wonder who Duncan aged 50 3/4 is – his ubiquitous tag along the rivers and elsewhere changing as he ages. When we started this project, he was just Duncan aged 50. Walking here with groups, this is always a place where people linger; perhaps it's the pleasure of being reunited with the river. Can you hear the river as we look down on it? One of our favourite river facts is that *Elver*son Road is named for the eels that move up and down the river, before returning to the Sargasso Sea.

From here we follow the path into Brookmill Park. This serves as another physical and sonic border. The wind rustles the trees and the birdsong intensifies. Almost immediately, as you enter the park, there is an opportunity (the first) to go down to the water's edge. Be careful on these steps, they are slippery. A whole cohort of Goldsmiths research architecture students' trainers were ruined here on such a walk, as they slid down the stairs and into the soft mud of the river. For about a year, a kitchen chair had been left by someone next to these steps. While Lewisham is a green borough of London, and is overall well served by parks, the north of the borough is less so. Perhaps bringing the chair was a way of carving out this place of relative quiet for themselves? The effect was certainly less fly tipping and more domestication of the park. We also often see tents in the park, here and elsewhere along the river, a reminder of the homelessness crisis engulfing London. The homelessness charity Shelter (2024) found that 1 in 47 people in London were homeless in 2024, compared to 1 in 160 in the whole of England. Often, we see people pitching up on the side of the river that is less accessible and where tents are less immediately visible, the river serving as protection like a moat.

This is a stretch of the river that is well loved and maintained by the Friends of Brookmill Park in monthly clean-up operations. They are one of a collection of groups that maintain these rivers and the parks around them. The regular volunteers express a close bond with the place. While researching Lewisham's rivers we have heard repeatedly from the volunteers who work on the rivers how they have become bonded to the river. In this park a volunteer tells us that the river has become 'her friend'. Talking to those who care for the rivers underlines how these stretches of the river don't just happen but are worked on over time, and that these acts of caring for the rivers act back on the volunteers and their sense of place (Jackson and Rondel, 2025). This is the most natural-looking stretch of the river on our walk. Did you see that flash of blue? A Kingfisher.

Birdsong features heavily in people's descriptions of these places. Listening back to the field recordings of the river spaces, it is a dominant sound. I lack the knowledge to properly read these recordings with my ears, but with my eyes I see Robins, Moorhens, Blackbirds, Goldfinches, Mallards, a nest of baby Herons – and Parakeets, which split the locals. I love the splash of green as they fly in flocks across the grey London skies. Flocks? The correct collective noun for Parakeets is 'pandemonium', no doubt due to the loud squawking that upsets some people, along with the idea that they will push out native species. I say they belong here.

This might all sound lovely – the birdsong, the sense of belonging of the volunteers, the sound of the water. And it is. But river spaces like this also have uncanny aspects. The river provides a place to hide and discard things. At the less alarming end we have found cut up credit cards, clothes and vapes – so many vapes. But knives and guns are regular finds on clean-up sessions. A colleague tells us of finding a bag of dead rats in the river here during a clean-up. A volunteer found a decapitated rabbit downstream at Deptford. These aspects of the river are more difficult to hear as we move along our walk. Although, cycling through this park one evening, as dusk turns to dark, I can feel it.

Konstantinos' experimentation with using contact mics on the concrete surfaces of these engineered rivers and the metal of the bridges that cross it render in sound some of the more liminal – even uncanny – aspects of the life of the river, that we can't access directly but are hinted at in stories of things being found that have been disposed of and concealed. These otherworldly clicks, whirrs and drones give us audio glimpses into the life beneath the river and provide another way of engaging with the materiality of these engineered watery spaces. The recordings sound industrial, with a strong drone. They are almost musical. The clicking sounds picked up by the hydrophone are not audible to us and speak of what lies beneath or what we imagine might lie beneath.

The geographer Maria Kaika (2005) describes how the separation of clean and controlled 'good water' and dirty non-processed 'bad water' was key to projects of urban modernity. London's small urban rivers can occupy both sides of this split. They are heavily engineered but uncovered. They look natural in places but worry abounds about pollution levels. The liminal and uncanny aspects of the river exist side by side with fluffy ducklings and, in the more accessible places on the river, splashing children. Working with the rendering of place through these recordings helps us to think about these paradoxes. It textures our understanding and conceptualisation of watery places (Rondel et al., 2025) and demonstrates how we might use sound in more sociologically imaginative ways when walking, through experimentation and collaboration.

Exiting Brookmill Park, we are briefly forced back onto a road, as we turn the corner across another metal and concrete bridge onto Broadway Fields. This was once Deptford Municipal Playing Fields and still serves as a place of play. There is a basketball court and a flat expanse of grass. On the left of the field as we look at it runs the Ravensbourne. The river feels quite cut off from the park as we are separated from it by grey fencing. The river is tidal here all the way up to Brookmill Park, rising and falling with the Thames. It is also much wider here than at the Lewisham confluence. The DLR passes overhead on a bridge that creates shelter and a temporary respite from the weather for a group of homeless people. The fields are quiet now. They feel flat and functional, but maybe if we came back later they would be animated with the sounds of basketball. They are surrounded with apartment blocks from this century. Grey is the dominant colour. We can hear the A2 road before we can see it. This is the old road to Dover and lorries still thunder along it, dominating the local soundscape, another route to the sea. Here we stick with the course of the river, passing Deptford Bridge station and crossing the busy road in front of us.

Join me in peering over the bridge on the other side. For months we could see a shopping trolley here. A repeated story from our project is about how previously three trolleys were pulled out of Deptford Creek by an enthusiastic volunteer. But the trolleys had become embedded, and their removal disturbed the wildlife of the creek. This tale is used as a reminder that deciding what belongs in the water isn't always self-evident. 'Is it rubbish? Or has it become habitat?' is a common refrain from one of the river leaders we have worked with. This can relate to both the sacred and the profane. On one river clean-up I took part in, the same silver tray was put in a bin bag and taken out again three times, as volunteers reacted differently to a religious offering being left in the river. One volunteer thought this should be respected and stay in the river; for another it was pollution; another reasoned that the tray could be a habitat and should stay in the river.

We now approach a different kind of riverscape, perhaps one more familiar, as we can start to feel the influence of the Thames. You can peek at the river here through the railings by the Birds Nest pub – you might also be able to pick up a patty from the vendor outside. Maybe you can hear and feel discarded oyster shells crunching under our feet? These are just remnants of a seafood van, but they add to the feeling of the Thames as a gateway to the sea. Deptford has a long maritime history as first the location for Henry XIII's boatyard and then the gateway for the so-called 'voyages of discovery'. The wharves and former warehouses we will walk past are intimately tied to histories of extraction and colonialism.

We take a right and walk along Creekside, a cobbled street lined by old warehouses that are now home to rehearsal rooms, bike workshops, art galleries and studios. Deptford has been shaped by every wave of regeneration in London since it received City Challenge money from central government in 1992 (Strasser, 2020), and this is a classic scene of post-industrial cultural regeneration/gentrification from the last century. You can hear the sounds of children shouting and playing from across the way in the twentieth-century blocks.

We turn down Creative Road – a decidedly uncreative choice of place name to signal the most recent wave in this redevelopment. Here we find a housing development, the *Faircharm Creative Quarter*, a mixture of six- and twelve-storey blocks and workshops. These developments raise the question of who these waterfront developments are for. Faircharm is a built-to-rent development that displaced artists who previously ran their workshops from the Faircharm estate, a low-rise business park (Trotter, 2013). A participant on one soundwalk we ran described the contrast between the 'hard sounds' of this new development, compared with the 'warmer sounds' from the older red-brick blocks of flats, which are also peppered with trees. This comment resonates with Konstantinos' experiments with contact microphones in drawing our attention to how changes in the built environment shape our acoustic environment. In the new development, the concrete and metal of the constructions shape the sonic environment as well as what we can see. This long-term Deptford resident had walked the stretch many times before but commented, 'I wouldn't have noticed that before. Because I wouldn't be listening.'

This environment isn't completely sterile, however. Wild plants have been allowed to grow along the river wall. In front of us is a raised ledge and a wire fence. If you climb onto the ledge, you can look out onto a muddy stretch if the tide is out, or a deep river if it is in. I recall seeing a one-woman performance, *Creekshow* (Witzel, 2023), about living on the creek. Yes, people also live on the river. For now, at least, you can see houseboats to your right. In *Creekshow*, performance artist Jenny Witzel described the strange feeling of living on a houseboat here, the tide going out and leaving your boat temporarily perched on the mud.

The guardians of this stretch are the staff and volunteers from the *Creekside Discovery Centre*. Maybe they will be visible today in their red waterproofs taking a group on a low tide walk, their eyes keeping a close watch on the time, as when the tide comes in, it comes in quickly. During the week they often take school groups, who are delighted to get into the mud. The centre, just to our left, and its grounds are an island in the middle of all the redevelopment. From the Discovery Centre there is a sloping entry point into the water. Nick, one of the staff members and fount of all knowledge about this habitat, explained to Louise and me its special ecology. Because of its position towards the upper end of the tidal limit of the North Sea, the creek is made up of a mixture of three waterbodies: the North Sea, the Thames and the River Ravensbourne. Despite being tidal, Nick tells us, it is mostly a freshwater ecosystem with a slight brackishness (meaning it is slightly saltier than freshwater, but less salty than seawater). A wide range of wild plants grow on the flood defence walls – the most diverse are the remaining Victorian walls. The worst walls for biodiversity in the creek are the modern steel sheet piling walls where not much apart from algae grows.

Maybe you will see or hear the Deptford Necker? I have never seen her, but as local folklore has it, she is a mermaid or serpent-like creature who lives in Deptford Creek, lurking in the mud. It's easy to see why such a legend might emerge from here and I can imagine her swimming with the eels that have made the journey from the Sargasso Sea. What song would she sing to lure us walkers into the mud?

She would have to sing it loudly as standing here the soundscape is intense and more industrial than you might expect, the noise from the industrial units in the neighbouring borough of Greenwich travelling across the river from the east. At least, this is how this place sounds at the time of writing. The city won't stand still for us to research and document.

Here, facing the wide and muddy creek, is where our walk ends – mirroring the boundaries of our research project. Together, we have walked from one new housing development to another, via a range of sonic scenes reflecting different layering of people's activities, wildlife and urban redevelopment. But the river keeps going and so could you, following the Ravensbourne down to where it meets the Thames and then along past the Thames Barrier towards the estuary and eventually to the North Sea. Or, like me, you could about-turn and stroll back up to Deptford Bridge, where the DLR allows you to make the return journey to Lewisham in just three minutes.

References

Ackroyd, Peter (2012) *London Under*. London: Vintage.

Arkette, Sophie (2004) Sounds like city. *Theory, Culture, Society*, 21 (1), 159–68.

Back, Les (2007) *The Art of Listening*. London: Berg.

Dire Straits (1980) 'Romeo and Juliet', track from the album *Making Movies*. Available at Spotify.

Drever, John (2020) Listening as methodological tool: Sounding soundwalking methods. In Michael Bull and Marcel Cobussen (eds) *The Bloomsbury Handbook of Sonic Methodologies*. London: Bloomsbury Academic.

Jackson, Emma and Lisiak, Agata (2025) You'll never walk alone: Theorizing engaged walking with Doreen Massey. *Sociological Review* [online first]. https://doi.org/10.1177/00380261241309715

Jackson, Emma and Rondel, Louise (2024) *Confluence: Episode 2* [audio podcast]. Available at: https://soundcloud.com/confluencepodcast/episode-2 [accessed 5 October 2025].

Jackson, Emma and Rondel, Louise (2025) The social production of small urban rivers: The (re)making of two riverside spaces in Lewisham. Paper presented at the British Sociological Association Annual Conference, Manchester, 24 April 2025.

Kaika, Maria (2005) *City of Flows: Modernity, Nature and the City*. London: Routledge.

Lefebvre, Henri (1991) *The Production of Space*, trans. D. Nicholson-Smith. Oxford: Basil Blackwell.

Martins, Allie (2019) *Hearing Change in the Chocolate City: Soundwalking as Black Feminist Method*. Sounding Out!, 5 August. Available at: https://soundstudiesblog.com/2019/08/05/hearing-change-in-the-chocolate-city-soundwalking-as-black-feminist-method/ [accessed 5 October 2025].

Massey, Doreen (1994) A global sense of place. In *Space, Place, and Gender*. Minneapolis, MN: University of Minnesota Press.

Rondel, Louise, Damianakis, Konstantinos and Jackson, Emma (2025) Listening to mermaids: The otherworldy life of Lewisham's rivers. *Seismograf*. Available at: https://seismograf.org/node/20849 [accessed 2 October 2025].

Schafer, R. Murray (1974) Listening. *Sound Heritage*, 3 (4), 10–17.

Shelter (2024) *At Least 354,000 People Homeless in England Today*. Available at: https://england.shelter.org.uk/media/press_release/at_least_354000_people_homeless_in_england_today_ [accessed 5 October 2025].

Strasser, Anita (2020) *Deptford is Changing* [ebook]. Available at: www.anitastrasser.com/deptfordischangingbook.htm [accessed 5 October 2025].

Summers, Brandi (2020) Reclaiming the chocolate city: Soundscapes of gentrification and resistance in Washington, DC. *Environment and Planning D: Society and Space*, 39 (1), 30–46.

Trotter, Sarah (2013) Deptford's Faircharm Estate development go-ahead is a 'nightmare' for artistic community, *News Shopper*, 3 May. Available at: www.newsshopper.co.uk/news/10399722.deptfords-faircharm-estate-development-go-ahead-is-a-nightmare-for-artistic-community/ [accessed 5 October 2025].

Westerkamp, Hildegarde (2007) Soundwalking. In Angus Carlyle (ed.) *Autumn Leaves: Sound and the Environment in Artistic Practice*. Paris: Double Entendre.

Witzel, Jenny (2023) *Creekshow*, directed by Lewin Davis, Actors East, London, 28 July.

Wright Mills, Charles (1959) *The Sociological Imagination*. Oxford: Oxford University Press.

19

Walking into the current

Charlotte Bates

Blue Lagoon, Pembrokeshire, Wales
11 January

I have driven over a hundred miles to reach the coast, arriving in the dark and waking the next morning on a windswept peninsula. The cliffs are covered in spiky bright yellow common gorse, a species that is synonymous with 'wild' landscapes. Although it can be found in many different habitats, I associate it most strongly with the coast. Inside my body, a gorse-weather-world prickles my skin. I am here to visit a group of swimmers who have welcomed me to join them for the weekend as part of a research project about swimming outdoors, community and well-being. It is January, when only the most committed swimmers continue to take the plunge. Swim locations and times have already been planned and shared, and I pack a towel, swimsuit and hot thermos flask into a bag and get ready to drive the short distance to meet the group. We are swimming at the Blue Lagoon, a former slate quarry on the west coast. The name alone is alluring. Flooded by the sea and bordered by beautiful beaches and craggy rocks, the lagoon is a popular spot for cliff diving and sea swimming.

I check my phone and receive a text: 'Due to the conditions we are changing location. We are going to a pond near Solva. I will send you directions now.' The storm that had blown through overnight meant that it would be too dangerous to attempt the steep descent down the cliff face, too difficult to lower our bodies safely into the water or to scramble back out onto the rocks again. Just a few steps prevent me from entering the sea. This essay rests here, in the movement between land and water, and explores how different terrains can shape our experiences in just a few steps, allowing or preventing entry and exit, requiring assistance and support, inducing discomfort or reassurance, and bringing swimmers together. Through these movements and moments, the essay explores the politics of trespass, nature and belonging, and offers an alternative to understandings of landscape, immersion and connection that are individualised and romanticised. My phone beeps again, and I receive the coordinates for a different location.

I search the map and find a small blue mark connected to the sea by a blue wiggly line. I drive a few miles south, the road following the coastline but the sea remaining just out of sight, and park in front of a five-bar wooden gate. On the map, I can see that the track beyond the gate ends five hundred metres before it would reach the cliffs that drop down to meet the sea. It is not long before other cars arrive too. Carrying bags and folding chairs, thirteen women walk together along the muddy track. This is private land, and I wonder if we are trespassing. Private landowners can be unwelcoming, and many rivers, reservoirs, lakes and ponds are fenced off with barbed wire and signs that read 'No Entry', 'Private Fishing', or 'No Recreational Swimming'. Water is reserved for others and can be difficult or impossible to reach. Even bodies of water that are designed to be swam in are often regulated and fenced off to control access (Bates and Moles, 2024). But today I am told that the owner has given the swimmers permission to access a small body of water on their land, a gift when the sea refuses entry.

In England and Wales access to land and water is disputed and protested, and the vast majority of the countryside is blocked from public access (Hayes, 2021). The right to roam movement has grown over the last century, from the first mass trespass of Kinder Scout in the Peak District on 24 April 1932, which saw around four hundred people walk together to protest for the right to access the countryside and helped lead to the creation of national parks in Britain, to recent campaigns to protect the right to wild camp on Dartmoor. These rights are understood to be vital for connection with nature and for health and well-being. The organisation Right to Roam is campaigning to change exclusionary laws of access and create a Right to Roam Act in England that would give everyone responsible access rights like those that already exist in Scotland

and Scandinavia. In 2021, the Outdoor Swimming Society took the protest to the water to fight for the right to swim in what became an annual protest at Kinder Reservoir, and in 2024 the Kinder Swim Trespass went nationwide, with swimmers meeting at lakes and reservoirs around England to protest for the right to swim. Filmmaker Hollie Harmsworth documents the atmosphere of the 2023 trespass, when more than five hundred swimmers gathered to duck under barbed wire, march past 'No Swimming' and 'Danger Keep Out' signs, and enter the reservoir together on a grey and chilly day. As poet and swimmer J. L. M. Morton writes in an essay on her relationship with the River Churn and the landscape of rural England, 'The feeling of a body being in landscape and of land being in the body has no boundary or limitation to pass over or across. To trespass' (Morton, 2024: n.p.).

There was no sign on the gate to make us feel unwelcome, but it is grey and chilly here too and there is a resolute feeling among the small group as we walk together. I am wearing a woolly hat, a warm winter coat and sturdy boots, but I am feeling cold, and I still have not seen the sea. There is some light-hearted banter about swimming today, and it is clear that I am not the only one having doubts in this moment. Someone is talking about eels, and I do not know if they are serious or not. We are not walking far, but these steps are important, bringing the swimmers together with humour and resolve.

Sea foam agitated by wind and waves floats through the cold grey air and lands on the rippling surface of the pond. The women gather at its edge, chatting and changing and leaving piles of clothes, tins of cake and hot thermos flasks on the soggy grass. Boots and thick socks are pulled off, and bare feet sink into the soft ground. The significance of footprints has been explored elsewhere, from the discovery of early hominin tracks, to the imprints left on the surface of the moon during the Apollo 11 spacewalk, and our ecological footprint (Subramaniam, 2022). As Radhika Subramaniam writes, the footprint is both a metaphor and a material imprint, signifying 'mobility and occupation, inquiry and imperialism, absence and presence, trace, and impact' (Subramaniam, 2022: 117). At the edge of the pond, feet register contact with ground that is part land and part water, and mud oozes between toes. The pond feels exposed and the wind chills the swimmers' bodies, raising goose bumps on their arms and legs. We all agree that on this blustery day the pond is uninviting, and a few women in the group decide to remain on land. I am here to swim, but I quickly choose to stay with them. Brightly coloured woolly hats and swimming caps are pulled on, and two women stand at the water's edge, offering their hands as a makeshift ladder.

Nobody wants to swim. But one by one the swimmers cross the threshold into the water, stepping into the brown silt with resolve and a polite 'thank you ladies', shortly followed by a series of loud expletives. Shrieking and swearing fills the pond as the cold water rises up the swimmers' bodies, enveloping all but their heads. Pond weed and imaginary eels swirl and twist around the swimmer's legs. I hold back, observing the scene from the other side of the threshold. Within a few minutes the swearing has turned to laughter, and the bobbing heads are lit up with bright eyes and smiles. Submerged in cold water, bodies, fears, pain and sadness dissolve like the organic matter that floats in giant bubbles on the pond's surface.

Gradually, the swimmers return to land. The hands of the makeshift ladder reach down, offering warmth, support and a way back up the slippery bank. Feet reconnect with soggy grass and wet swimsuits are peeled off, leaving pink skin momentarily exposed to the wind and the surprised gaze of passengers on a passing bus. The swimmers laugh and wave, too cold and too far from the road to care. Their bodies, young and old, scarred and saggy, defy social convention or consumption. Helping each other, and dressing as quickly as they can with numb fingers, the swimmers pour hot tea from thermos flasks and share homemade cakes and warm smiles.

As we walk back down the track together I reflect on the politics of swimming outdoors, and how swimming is not always desirable or possible. As Samantha Walton (2021: 29) writes in her critical exploration of the nature cure, 'The body, or the water, may resist.' There are many reasons for resistance. Rebecca Olive (2023) writes powerfully about not swimming in the crystal-clear waters of the tarn on the mountain kunanyi in Australia as a form of respect for place, while increasingly swimmers are choosing not to swim as an act of care for the polluted waters that they love. Sometimes getting to the water can feel impossible, whether the water is near or far away, and sometimes, like today, not everyone wants to swim.

But when the sea around us is too rough to enter, the pond offers a place of connection to water and to each other. The pond is uninviting and unappealing, but accessible and safe. It has none of the romanticism of the Blue Lagoon, but it does hold a certain magic of its own – hard to see at first, but knowable if you cross the threshold. In this moment even the most seasoned and stoic swimmers shriek and swear; it is both part of the fun and an audible expression of commitment. This stubborn attachment to water makes small and otherwise insignificant bodies of water like the pond remarkable, and reveals a commitment to immersion that goes beyond scenic or romantic notions of swimming outdoors.

Solva, Pembrokeshire, Wales
12 January

The idea of getting in the water yesterday seemed far-fetched. The cold grey pond told me to keep out, even though we were allowed in. But this morning the sky is light and bright, and I can feel a little warmth in the low winter sun as I walk along the edge of the harbour. Protected by green sloping hillsides, the water here is still and glistening. Small fishing boats gently bob on the surface, their anchors holding them in place so that when the tide goes out later, they are left behind, stranded in the silt until the sea returns and lifts them up again. A little further on I can see Green Scar, a small rock of an island rising out of the sea beyond the headland. Out there beyond the harbour the sea is dark and lively. White waves rise and crash against the black rocks.

Swimmers arrive from different directions and gather outside the boathouse, all ready to walk down the slip, a rough concrete slope used to launch boats into the water. Two gulls perch on the slip too, as if waiting to join the party. I find myself peeling off layers, exposing my body to the winter sun. Following the other women, I walk barefoot down the slip. The texture is uncomfortable, and the soles of my feet feel vulnerable. I am walking with a grandmother, an Ice Mile swimmer, a cancer survivor. We are all in 'skins', the vernacular used by swimmers for swimming in swimsuits, unprotected from the cold by neoprene wetsuits, gloves or booties, but also unconstricted, our senses not blunted. I am careful not to slip, to keep right so that I don't stumble off the ledge, to reach the sea and launch my body like a boat.

The women ahead shriek and chant and laugh and gasp and swear as they enter the water. I barely hear them, I'm so focused on making each step. The sea has a hypnotic pull, and the water is either not as cold as I expected, or so cold that it instantly numbs my feet, ankles, legs. As it reaches my waist I stop. At once out of my body and completely within it. I am on the edge.

I begin to question what I am doing, and whether I can do it. Voices urge me in. Instructing me into the water. 'Little bounces!' 'Keep breathing!' 'You're halfway there!' They tell me, supporting and guiding me on this rite of passage, my first winter swim. As I rise and fall the water gently moves up my body and the boundaries between me and it seem less solid. Without thinking, I am moving deeper. Accepting that I am past the point of no return, I take a breath and slide silently forwards, into the water. Released from the rough touch of the slip my feet seem to float away. I swim in small, rapid circles, breathing quickly but steadily. Out of my depth. 'Well done! Stay in for ninety seconds or you won't get the benefit!'

I slow down and look around at the scene I am swimming in. Swimmers bob between the boats, treading water and chatting in small groups. 'What temperature is it today?' 'It's not that cold. It doesn't feel cold.' No one has a thermometer, but the average sea temperature here in January is 9 degrees Celsius. My guides encourage me to swim further, to reach the next boat. I glide on, swimming breaststroke and keeping my head above water, passing swimmers and catching conversations. Shrieks and shouts of 'Seaweed on my leg!' and 'I'm having a wee before I get out!' Disgust, laughter and the shared warmth of bodily fluids intermingling in the sea.

The boat is closer than the land I left behind when I notice that my stroke is becoming less powerful, less effective at propelling my body forwards through the water. In the cold salty sea my limbs feel disconnected from my body, my boundaries undetectable. 'I'm feeling breathless' I murmur, and immediately my guides return me back to land. We swim together back to the slip. I wade out of the sea, my legs unexpectedly but firmly holding me upright on land. The slip had felt uncomfortable underfoot when I walked in, but now its hard solidity is reassuring.

Back at the bench my clothes are waiting, piled up in the order they will go back on my body. The winter sun is shining brightly as I peel off my swimsuit and layer on my clothes, without stopping to think about who might see. Other swimmers are back on land too, and I follow the wet footprints to the top of the boathouse to enter a cosy, wooden room where the swimmers are warming up together. My mind is still numb as I pour hot tea from my thermos and sit, surrounded by smiles, my fingers curled around my cup. Casual conversations unfold around me, about the temperature of the sea today, and where and when the next swim will be. Small talk about swimming and the weather mingling easily with intimate exchanges about illness, pain, loss and recovery. Other women tell me how swimming has helped them, and how the water and the community have become part of their lives, a way of reclaiming their bodies. Some swim together and alone, enjoying both the support of the group and the personal intimacy that comes with solitary swims. Someone asks if this was my first winter swim, and I am presented with a small pin badge – proof of my entry into the water and the community.

Together, the women and the water have dispelled my fears, and resolved the glaring problem of my entry into the 'current'. In *Ocean* (2020), Steve Mentz suggests that thinking and writing about water needs a less grounded vocabulary. Mentz offers the 'current' as a replacement for the 'fields' or academic disciplines in which we usually think. The field is also a key word in ethnography. Ethnographers enter the field to conduct fieldwork and write field notes. Entering the field means gaining access to a group or culture. It is an opening and an accomplishment. For ethnographers who study embodied practices, entering the field often becomes a performance of authenticity. To understand boxing or mountaineering, ethnographers train to become boxers and mountaineers. Apprenticeships in these fields involve broken noses and frostbitten fingers and toes, and call into question just how far we will go to understand and know a practice. The field, the boxing ring, and the mountain act back on our bodies in ways that change us both physically and mentally. As Emma Jackson (2024) notes, ethnographic heroism is a recurrent theme. But not all ethnographers become tournament winners or conquer the highest peaks. I am not entering a swimming race or attempting an Ice Mile. I have no confidence or authority as a swimmer, and my engagement is far from seamless. Still, I am immersed, and this swim is my rite of passage. All I had to do was leave land behind and enter the flowing current.

In *The living mountain*, writer and poet Nan Shepherd recounts her relationship with the Cairngorms. There, she writes, 'I discover most nearly what it is to be. I have walked out of the body and into the mountain' (Shepherd, 2014: 106). Here, in Solva harbour, I find that I have walked out of the body and into the sea. It comes as no surprise when I later look up the name of this body of water and find its Latin root: Solvere. To melt, loosen, or release. Swimming is all of these things. The cold water melts my bodily boundaries, loosens my thoughts, releases my pain. In Solva harbour I dissolve. This feeling of dissolving, a smudging of boundaries, makes me feel small, vulnerable, enlivened, powerful and connected all at once. There is water in mountains too, and I share this vital feeling of disintegration with Nan, 'This plunge into the cold water of a mountain pool seems for a brief moment to disintegrate the very self; it is not to be borne: one is lost: stricken: annihilated. Then life pours back' (Shepherd, 2014: 104). Astrida Neimanis (2017: 148) writes about water's power to dissolve our conceptual boundaries and ways of thinking, a loosening of the idea of human embodiment as a unity, through which 'we might drift, disperse, and dissolve in a new watery imaginary'. Reading and thinking about water is often metaphorical, but swimming in cold water makes this thought feel literal.

Waving goodbye to the swimmers, I leave the boathouse and walk back along the path and away from the sea. The bright coldness within my body is the vitality of the sea, a zinging feeling that slowly drifts away as warmth and land return. Writer and swimmer Roger Deakin (2000) called the heady rush of endorphins from a swim 'endolphins', and more recently scientists have begun researching the physiological effects of cold water in order to understand why swimming outdoors might be good for you. But on this swim, what strikes me most strongly is water's capacity to bring us together into community. Landscape, immersion and connection are often individualised and romanticised, but paying close attention to the steps between land and water that we make together introduces vulnerability and discomfort, and an understanding of well-being that is relational. These steps show how 'differently textured terrains' (Lorimer, 2012: 83) – the soft edges of the pond, the hard concrete of the slip – are felt, and how they shape our movements and emotions. For geographer and runner Hayden Lorimer, these sensory impressions are encountered over many miles, on surfaces and slopes that create a sense of belonging and attachment that is felt and remembered in the body.

These steps are shaped by the ground on which we walk, and they are shaped by the bodies that make them. As writer and poet Polly Atkin (2023: 209) writes in her memoir exploring place, belonging and chronic illness:

> Sometimes, I limp all the way to the lake. I saw 'all the way' and it makes the walk seem epic. To the abled it would seem a tiny distance, not worth thinking of as a walk, even. But when each placement of your foot on the ground triggers shooting pain in a foot or a hip, when carrying just a towel and a water bottle pulls too much on your shoulders and back, even a few metres becomes a marathon.

Many swimmers remark that they feel more comfortable in the water than on land. More comfortable in a different element, and more comfortable in their own bodies. In the water, bodies are supported and released to move with ease. The return of gravity and the pull of earth can be reassuring, but it can also make limbs and bodies feel heavy, weak and painful. As movements in and between land and water, swimming and walking recompose our bodies and boundaries, and our ways of being, belonging and becoming.

References

Atkin, Polly (2023) *Some of Us Just Fall: On Nature and Not Getting Better*. London: Sceptre.

Bates, Charlotte and Moles, Kate (2024) Bobbing in the park: Wild swimming, conviviality and belonging. *Leisure Studies*, 43 (6), 887–99.

Deakin, Roger (2000) *Waterlog: A Swimmer's Journey through Britain*. London: Vintage.

Harmsworth, Hollie (2023) *A Right to Swim* [film]. Available at: https://youtu.be/iyajtL49LFY [accessed 5 October 2025].

Hayes, Nick (2021) *The Book of Trespass: Crossing the Lines that Divide Us*. London: Bloomsbury.

Jackson, Emma (2024) How to do social research with … a bowling ball. In Rebecca Coleman, Kat Jungnickel and Nirmal Puwar (eds) *How to do Social Research With* …. London: Goldsmiths Press.

Lorimer, Hayden (2012) Surfaces and slopes. *Performance Research*, 1 (2), 83–6.

Mentz, Steve (2020) *Ocean*. London: Bloomsbury.

Morton, J. L. M. (2024) Over, across. *Elsewhere: A Journal of Place*. Available at: www.elsewhere-journal.com/trespass-posts/2024/11/22/over-across [accessed 2 October 2025].

Neimanis, Astrida (2017) *Bodies of Water: Posthuman Feminist Phenomenology*. London: Bloomsbury.

Olive, Rebecca (2023) How to swim without water: Swimming as an ecological sensibility. In Charlotte Bates and Kate Moles (eds) *Living with Water. Everyday Encounters and Liquid Connections*. Manchester: Manchester University Press.

Shepherd, Nan (2014) *The Living Mountain*. Edinburgh: Canongate. First published 1977.

Subramaniam, Radhika (2022) Footprint. An Itinerary. *Borderlands*, 22 (1), 117–37.

Walton, Samantha (2021) *Everybody Needs Beauty: In Search of the Nature Cure*. London: Bloomsbury.

20

Walking away and returning: letting go of ashes in Blackpool and Stratford-upon-Avon

Nirmal Puwar

Walking away and returning are intimately connected – whether one seeks to return but never does, never wants to return but is caught up with what the return will bring, or returns as recomposing matter. This essay moves between oceans, boats and a tower, forging a diasporic embodied approach to walking while returning to landscapes. Walking to let go of ashes to the river and the sea, of diasporic, globally connected lives, having forged a *silting settlement*, formulates the flow of this essay.

Sites of leisure, in Blackpool on the north-west coast of England and Stratford-upon-Avon in central England, double up, as sites for return. The releasing of ashes presents new compositions from decompositions, entangled with more-than-human life worlds, including animals. Matters of death enable new imprints and connections. Returning, across time, manifests an altered relationship of landscapes. There is a grounded and panoramic decolonial tracing here. Unsettling settlements of sea, sand, stone and countryside, this essay pushes towards wider and longer approaches to migration, boats and oceans. New embodied connections – from the sea, the British shires, to the materialities of colonialism – occur through walking. Mass observations of everyday life at the seaside and picnic outings are skewed and considered anew, just as planetary catastrophe rises and beckons.

The beach: roar of Blackpool

At 11am on 15 February 2020, at Blackpool, the sun shines alongside a bitter cold, as we finally let go of our mother to the left of the North Pier. The froth of the waves rocks her back and forth, taking more of her away, creating rippling bubbles between the pebbles. Her specs of light brown dust join with grains of grey sand connecting continents. Curling and enfolding her into the vastness of oceans, across the Atlantic to the Indian seas, where she was born, possibly returning in her own granular journey. We have our thick coats buttoned up, bent over, silent in our aloneness in the very act of letting her go. Together as a family of her children, those they married, who she also loved, and her sparkle of grandchildren.

Our shoes make marks in the sand, our legs keep moving – the point of coming here is letting go and to keep moving. Our backs are turning away from her, yet our heads are tilted towards the sea, looking for where she may now travel. We keep looking over our shoulders as we learn to walk away from her. Pondering on what she will become and intermingle with; may be decomposing and recomposing with our father at sea, who we left here, on a blustery, windy, rainy day in 2013. Bibi's mixing with the histories of elements, extraction and bodies at sea.

Imperial historiographies have underlined the entangled underbelly of the migrations of human and more-than-human lives. Reorienting towards the roaring underside of seafaring addressed by post-colonial, Black and ecological scholarship, histories of being thrown overboard, reconfigured in the wake of the ship, with multiple forms of more-than-human life, as articulated by Christina Sharpe (2016), comes to me in this very moment at Blackpool. As do the foggy scenes of *Caribs' Leap* (dir. Steve McQueen), of indigenous Caribs, in Grenada, who in 1651 leapt to their death rather than surrender to the invading French by jumping into the sea. Critical studies of oceans and society have led scholars to indigenous knowledge systems for governance of the sea (Hofmeyr, 2012; Burton et al., 2013; Dawson, 2018; DeLoughrey, 2020; Champion and Strand, 2025), away from extractive mining and political governance structures (Khalili, 2020). Could the marine mammal kindred be breathing, as articulated poetically by Alexis Pauline Gumbs (2021), with Bibi alongside them. Could she also be the sediment at the bottom of the ocean trying to process methane.

Bibi related to the elements of the sea as something spiritual, compelling her to pull up her salwar to dip her toes and ankles into the edges, away from the larger-than-life expansive unknown ocean. My parents and their wider kinship relations travelled at least three hours by road to Blackpool for the mixture of seaside delights, of fish and chips, slot machines, candy floss, sticky rock sticks, and slot machines where Bibi gathered handfuls of two pence pieces, again and again. Her jangling jackpot sounds ringing in our ears with a smile in our watery eyes. The waters of Blackpool were also part of small intimate ceremonial gestures, as we would park up en route to see relatives in Huddersfield. She would take out a small, folded envelope from her tightly zipped small inside pocket in her black platinum handbag. We would walk to the edges of the pier, leaning on the banister, to release a first cutting of my nephew's baby hair to the sea.

The sun shines a way forward without Bibi, as we head towards a fish and chips cafeteria, sharing a bite to repeat what our parents relished with us, on regular trips to see the Blackpool lights over the last fifty years or so, before their health prevented them from doing so. We never discussed Bibi's ashes with her; she was for life in a big way. Did she want them returned to India, where we had taken her eldest child's – Harbans – our eldest brother, more than twenty years ago. To the waters of Kiratpur Sahib Gurdwara, in Punjab. We had asked my father, who readily discussed death due to ill health in his nineties. Vying between Blackpool and the rivers of Stratford-upon-Avon, a local picnic and boat ride day trip location in Warwickshire, only twenty miles away from Coventry, a city the family made 'home', far away from 'home' in the post-war era. Being a pragmatic spirit to the core, he did not want us to have to trek to India with him. So, he opted for Blackpool, settling his peace with the thought that all the seas are joined.

Ten years earlier, the small roller-coaster of Pleasure Beach became a stream of chuckles as Bibi, my aunt, sister-in-law Kulwarn (Pabi) and I looked across to the sea. This was Bibi and Pabi's last of many coach and car trips from the Midlands to Blackpool. A few years later, Pabi's ashes were left in Kiratpur, in Punjab, where she had taken my brother's (her husband) twenty years earlier.

Walking was an integral part of the volunteers' role in the Mass Observation studies conducted in Blackpool between 1937 and 1940, led by Tom Harrison, Charles Madge and the photographer Humphrey Spender (1982) (see Cross, 1990). If we were to repeat the notes, sketches and photographs today, we would observe South Asian visitors walking with ashes among many activities, alongside bathing habits, dance halls, pubs, fish and chips, and parathas cooked in large batches at home, bagged for coach trips to see the lights and rides.

Mass observation gave extensive coverage to the trips and holidays of workers from Bolton to Blackpool (Spender, 1977, 1982; Cross, 1990). Had this study been conducted in the seventies and eighties, they would have found South Asian workers, from the foundries and factories in the Midlands, north of England and even London, as regular annual visitors to Blackpool. *Bhaji on the Beach* (dir. Gurinder Chadha) features a group from a women's project in Southall taking a minibus to see the lights. Domestic violence, fantasy and orientalism, risqué humour, eating chilly-sprinkled chips, a dip on the edge of the sea, with salwar and saris hitched up, take us through the pier and blown-up plastic paraphernalia that lines the beachfront under the lights. A Martin Parr eye, with a different inclination, would have snapped these, while walking the sea front with a camera. Though usually one might be too caught up in the revelry of being there to pick up the camera in time. The film *Aaj Kaal* (1990), a project led by Avtar Brah and Jasbir Panesar, features a trip from Milan Day Centre in Southall to the seaside (Puwar, 2012). No doubt there are family albums with photographs of trips to Blackpool.[1] I am drawing on what happens when we return to put these complicated and full lives to an open-ended pathway of endings.

COVID-19 accelerated slowly changing practices towards the act of returning ashes across diasporas and 'homelands', as families and kin sought out locations nearby, without the logistics and costs of migration and border crossings. These acts change how diasporic home-making is reconfigured, with a remapping of place-based emotions, as well as the right to a place. A willingness and even a desire to return ashes to the soil one migrated *to*, rather than the place of emigration, belies a connectedness to the here – a *silting settlement*. This relationship of course varies in accordance with differentiations in migration status and the right to residency. The right of refugees to be here is displaced by far-right activists who target temporary shelters, and by what Stuart Hall (1979) described as the 'Great Moving Right Show' in the present conjuncture. However, the Windrush Scandal shows how even long-term residency and lifetime working commitments to nationally defined British services, including the armed forces and the NHS, have not guaranteed the right to settle here permanently.

New death rites and businesses are part of sociotechnical life–death place-based relations with soil, waters, land and seas. After considerable debate within the family, half of Bibi's ashes were scattered in Blackpool and the other half in the River Avon on 17 August 2019. One might see the two locations as a class apart. Blackpool is ranked as the most deprived borough in the country. While some sections of Stratford-upon-Avon constitute the least deprived parts in the country, there are significant pockets of multiple deprivation. Within a twenty-mile radius of Stratford-upon-Avon lies the post-industrial city of Coventry, where an estimated 20 per cent of the population are living on the breadline according to the EU.[2]

The boat: decomposing recomposing

Dino, our dear old golden Staffy family dog, had his ashes scattered in the Avon, a year before Bibi, on 27 May 2018. He spent hours keeping a close eye on carers who touched Bibi, attentively watching, with lifted quizzical eyes and a tilted raised head, from his sleeping basket in the living room. More-than-human relationships with Dino took us to the boat, embarking as a family group of at least twenty, from the moorings next to the Crowne Plaza hotel. As we stepped inside the covered vessel, our ears focused in on Jagjit Singh's 'Satnam Shri Waheguru', frequently played in a crematorium for Sikh funerals. The boat was steered a few miles away from the city centre, before it was slowed down to scatter the ashes. Along the way we pass a bridge, stated to be, to our surprise, a site visited by one of the Sikh gurus in the fifteenth century. This mythology layers the site-specific process of letting go. We are served chai from teacups and biscuits on our return to the hotel after scattering Dino, bringing the comforting setting of welcoming guests into the vessel. We returned to do this with half of Bibi's ashes, take a walk in the city centre, before returning to the family home in Coventry to eat together. The motion of the water vessel, Jagjit's music, short prayers and the aroma of incense and chai, while adding Bibi to the sill of the soil, puts in place a changing set of relationships with the elements. A *silting settlement* not entirely without ambivalence, with respect to national belonging.

On recollection, the guide on the boat stated, as we moved towards the ecological zones demarcated for disembarking ashes, that the Avon rises near Rugby, joins the River Severn at Tewkesbury and then flows into the sea. Hearing of the connectivity to the sea and oceans, spoken out aloud, is important for our imaginary sending off the ashes of diasporic lives lived in Warwickshire, UK. They are released to a bigger, global and extensive planetary network, perhaps returning, in their elemental decompositions and recompositions, to somewhere close to where they migrated from. Letting them go materially transforms them as dead and living matter, intermingling with other life forms. The act also transforms us, those who let them go onwards in different elemental biochemical life forms.

In November 1961, Bibi and all my elder siblings had travelled from Punjab, where she had to leave her dog Pondu behind, to Bombay (Mumbai) on the Punjab Mail rail line, part of British private investments in the rail networks in India, built for commercial gain, as well as strategic administrative and military points in the country (Satya, 2008). From the Ballard Pier they boarded the cruise liner *TN Roma* to Genoa, one of the many 'immigrant ships' of the period. This was a luxury liner carrying eight hundred migrants between Australia, Aden, Port Said, Singapore, Bombay and Genoa. It had earlier lives and names, as a Seattle–Tacoma SB Corp ship (named *Glacier*) in 1942, before being commissioned and altered by the Royal Navy in 1943 (HMS *Atheling*) to escort aircraft carriers in the war. In 1946, the ship was returned to the US Navy and then sat rusting for several years in the Reserve Fleet at Jacksonville, Florida. It was refitted by Flotta Lauro as a two-class luxury liner, with first-class and what was referred to as 'immigrant's quarters' (*Cairns Post*, 1951), including bars, swimming pools, cinemas, libraries, a writing room and a well-equipped hospital. Testimonies from Cairns Wharf, in Australia, refer to the interior as a 'floating hotel' or a 'gigantic pleasure yacht'. In the post-war period there were different pathways to migration, with varying dynamics to arrival and settlement. A combination of rail and ferry through France to Dover brought Bibi and the wider kinship group they were travelling with to London, where they were picked up by my father and driven to Leamington Spa. He was one of several men who had arrived some years earlier, working the nightshift at a big Ford factory in the Royal Spa town. I would love to occupy the writing room to write the stories and facts I gather. Alas, the *TN Roma* was taken apart and disbanded in Italy in 1967.

Walking to the tower: local global panoramas

Today, while walking along the river, the scattering of ashes in the Avon continues to alter my affinity to the place, from what has been a destination for local outings to a reparative resting journeying along the water. There are many ways to walk the same paths. Numerous walking trails are advertised in Stratford-upon-Avon, of canal histories, Tudor buildings, farmlands and woods. Like many cities, ghoulish walks are charted too, focused on tales of plague, murder, ghosts, beatings, witches, sewage and grave-robbing. Not surprisingly, given its tourist destination, there is a preponderance of references to William Shakespeare. Relic hunting was popular in Shakespeare's day, and on his grave is an epitaph (curse) attributed to him:

> Good friend for Jesus' sake forbeare,
> To dig the dust enclosed here.
> Blessed be the man that spares these stones,
> And cursed be he that moves my bones.

There are many ways to walk a path, including with Shakespeare. The Dell presents an open-air moving theatre as well as a less austere engagement with the stage. Post-colonial engagements with the colonial context of Shakespeare's plays, along with critical analyses and adaptations from ex-colonial, gendered and queered perspectives, have sparked a flurry of debate and creativity – unsettling, in some ways, what has long been revered as universal and settled (Bhatia, 2002).

In Punjabi, the word 'raste' serves a dual purpose, referring both to journeys of navigation on a map and to the pathways of life. Passing the footpath on the opposite side of the Royal Shakespeare

Theatre, I contemplate the busy timetable of the boat, as rituals and music are adjusted with hybridising religious, secular and post-secular adaptations. While Hamlet grapples with his conscience, the ghost of his father, and soliloquies in the theatre, I cross Clopton Bridge, walking towards the thirty-two-metre-high Royal Shakespeare Company (RSC) viewing tower. Forgoing the 174 steps to the roof, it's a clear day for seeing the snowy fields with irregular patches across twenty miles. In today's panoramic view, the waters stand out distinctly.

My attempted 'god's eye view' from the tower spans the four counties of Warwickshire, Gloucestershire, Oxfordshire and Worcestershire. In this panorama, colonial entanglements are not easily accessible in the United Kingdom; nothing like they are in Éire, where imperialism, insurgency, and royal force remain first-hand points of reference for guides to historic sites such as Dublin Castle. The erasure and amnesia of empire, as termed by Stuart Hall, is so replete, we are unable to see it in the sugar we dissolve in our coffee (Hall, 1991, 1999). Or there is active resistance to seeing it. Nonetheless, at the same time, there is growing public engagement from academics, cultural practitioners and artists, attending to what is steeped in critical history books, national archives and household accounts. For example, Catherine Hall's (2012) research on the links between Britain and empire has considered how slave owners were compensated, as evidenced in The Legacies of British Slave-Ownership (LBS) database.[3] None of these initiatives escape being cornered as 'woke' and taking away British history, when they are opening it up for further viewing, beyond what Paul Gilroy, in *After empire* (2004), has referred to as a continuing post-colonial melancholia.

Walking is an effective methodological practice for place-based archival decolonial education, with increasing initiatives engaged in this enfolding (Ware, 2022). The RSC tower offers an observation point, presenting an opportunity from which to approach how we view the urban landscape and countryside below us differently. Not as a scientised, distant view from above that institutes mapping as a form of control, ownership and extraction – but rather as a diasporic cartography that connects the soil, stones and water below to walking on the ground with global histories. Looking across the four counties from the RSC tower, Uncomfortable Oxford Tours focus on the links of empire, while Leamington's imperial history is shared through free local walking tours. In Coventry there are site-specific talks on when the anti-slavery campaigner Frederick Douglass delivered a series of social justice lectures at St Mary's Guildhall in 1847.

A four-and-a-half-mile walk from the RSC tower will take me to Charlecote Park, one of a third of National Trust properties connected to multiple types of colonial activity, as charted in *Colonial Countryside* (2020), a collaborative project with the National Trust, led by Corinne Fowler. Specific objects in the house at Charlecote Park offered schoolchildren clues, which were taken further with researchers, to the involvement of slavery, colonial wars and looting. This included a painting of a Black page boy wearing a metal collar, a sword from the First War of Independence in India (1857) and five pearls stolen from Lucknow, a site of colonial struggle.

Criticisms of this unfolding situation resulted in a Charity Commission investigation into whether the National Trust had breached charity law with its research. Although the investigation found no breach, it left a lasting mark of hostility towards Fowler and the Trust, as well as a legacy of caution and threat. Her follow-up book, *Our island stories: Country walks through colonial Britain* (2024), is based on walks with ten companions who trace ancestral routes connected to the British Empire. Fowler has designed walks which connect the local landscapes and former colonies with distinctive place-based stories of empire. Cotswold villages visible from the RSC tower have strong historical connections to the East India Company. Twenty miles away from the RSC tower sits the lavish Sezincote House, influenced by Mughal architecture, owned by two Cockerell brothers who each took different routes through the East India Company: one military and one financial.

The tower allows one to repurpose the compass, the observatory and the aerial view, to look across and walk with less well-known facts, figures and stories. Bringing into light the material legacies of buildings and cuts in the landscape below our toes, enabling a conscious embodiment of those histories. Buildings, large infrastructures, as well as plants in the vicinity, are part and parcel of global connectedness (Bhambra, 2014) and longstanding extractive relations with human and more-than-human worlds (Gray and Sheikh, 2021).

An eight-mile walk from the RSC tower will take you to Compton Verney Gallery, one of my favourite local trips, located in 120 acres of parkland designed in the 1770s by Lancelot 'Capability' Brown (also connected to the East India Company). There are several walking trails on the grounds, with and without dogs. Centre stage, a Lebanon Cedar tree, a signature import of Capability Brown, with multiple trunks sits between the house and the lake, begging to be placed in the context of extractive botanical migration (Brown and Williamson, 2016; Lester, 2024).

Those who articulate the links between violent histories and Britishness, especially in relation to the countryside, and who draw out the faint lines of what has been pushed out of the frame, risk being hounded. Nevertheless, as stated by Fowler (2024: xvi): 'This new knowledge may be disturbing, shocking at times, but, rather than alienating us from the landscapes we love, it can deepen our relationship with them' – thus enabling us to return and walk anew.

An anti-woke affective response to a fuller understanding of local connections to global modes of extraction manifests as the loss of a myth—caught up in a revelry of what Paul Gilroy (2008) refers to as the melancholia of empire after empire. Walking with loss can also, as this essay states, transpire into a *silting settlement* – one that reveals the material connectivity behind the erasure of empire within fixed notions of Britishness (Hall, 1999). Returning, returning and returning again, to live, to lose and to reconnect as a responsibility of planetary repair with more-than-human beings. Calling for a *Decolonial ecology* – that is a world ecology, as proposed by Malcom Ferdinand (2022) and by Ferdinand and Shela Sheikh in *Pluriverse: A Journal of Decolonial Ecologies* (2024) in the Earth–World Observatory.[4]

Notes

1 See the Apna Heritage Archive: www.bcva.info/about-2
2 www.socialchallenges.eu/en-US/city/26/Challenges/22)
3 www.ucl.ac.uk/lbs//
4 https://terremonde.org

References

Bhambra, Gurminder K. (2014) *Connected Sociologies*. London: Bloomsbury Press.

Bhatia, Nandi (2002) Imperialistic representations and spectatorial reception in *Shakespeare Wallah. Modern Drama*, 45 (1), 61–75.

Brown, David and Williamson, Tom (2016) *Lancelot Brown and the Capability Men: Landscape Revolution in Eighteenth-Century England*. London: Reaktion Books.

Burton, Antoinette, Kale, Madhavi, Hofmeyr, Isabel, Anderson, Clare, Lee, Christopher J. and Green, Nile (2013) Sea tracks and trails: Indian ocean worlds as method. *History Compass*, 11 (7), 497–502.

Cairns Post (1951) Italian liner Roma is the largest passenger ship to have berthed at Cairns, *Cairns Post*, 20 October, 1. Available at: https://trove.nla.gov.au/newspaper/article/42723310# [accessed 6 January 2024].

Champion, Giulia and Strand, Mia (2025) Other(ed) ocean knowledges: Unlearning integration in ocean governance for recognitional justice. *Ocean and Society*, 2, article 8875.

Cross, Gary (ed.) (1990) *Worktowners at Blackpool: Mass-Observation and Popular Leisure in the 1930s*. London: Routledge.

Dawson, Kevin (2018) *Undercurrents of Power: Aquatic Culture in the African Diaspora*. Philadelphia, PA: University of Pennsylvania Press.

DeLoughrey, Elizabeth (2020) Shipscapes: Imagining an ocean of space (37th Annual West Indian Literature Conference). *Anthurium: A Caribbean Studies Journal*, 16 (2), article 1.

Ferdinand, Malcom (2022) *Decolonial Ecology: Thinking from the Caribbean World*. Cambridge: Polity Press.

Ferdinand, Malcom and Sheikh, Shela (2024) *Pluriverse: A Journal of Decolonial Ecologies* (first issue February).

Fowler, Corinne (2024) *Our Island Stories: Country Walks Through Colonial Britain*. London: Penguin.

Gilroy, Paul (2004) *After Empire: Melancholia or Convivial Culture?* Abingdon: Routledge.

Gray, Ros and Sheikh, Shela (2021) The botanical mind: The coloniality of planting [podcast]. Available at: www.botanicalmind.online/podcasts/the-coloniality-of-planting [accessed 5 October 2025].

Gumbs, Alexis Pauline (2021) Undrowned: Black feminist lessons from marine mammals. *Soundings*, 2021 (78), 20–37.

Hall, Catherine (2012) *Macaulay and Son: Architects of Imperial Britain*. New Haven, CT: Yale University Press.

Hall, Stuart (1979) The great moving right show. *Marxism Today*, 23 (1), 14–20.

Hall, Stuart (1991) Old and new identities, old and new ethnicities. In Anthony D. King (ed.) *Culture, Globalization and the World System*. London: Macmillan.

Hall, Stuart (1999) Whose heritage? Un-settling 'the heritage', re-imagining the post-nation. *Third Text*, 13 (49), 3–13.

Hofmeyr, Isabel (2012) The complicating sea: The Indian Ocean as method. *Comparative Studies of South Asia, Africa and the Middle East*, 32 (3), 584–90.

Khalili, Laleh (2020) *Sinews of War and Trade: Shipping and Capitalism in the Arabian Peninsula*. London: Verso Books.

Lester, Alan (2024) Capability Brown and the British Empire [blog post], 2 September. Available at: https://alanlester.co.uk/blog/capability-brown-and-the-british-empire/ [accessed 8 January 2025].

Puwar, Nirmal (2012) Meditations on making aaj kaal. *Feminist Review*, 100 (1), 124–41.

Satya, Laxman D. (2008) British imperial railways in nineteenth century South Asia. *Economic and Political Weekly*, 43 (47), 69–77.

Sharpe, Christina (2016) *In the Wake: On Blackness and Being*. Durham, NC: Duke University Press.

Spender, Humphrey (1977) *Worktown: Photographs of Bolton and Blackpool taken for Mass Observation 1937/38*. Falmer, Brighton: Gardner Art Gallery, University of Sussex.

Spender, Humphrey (1982) *Worktown People: Photographs from Northern England, 1937/38*. Bristol: Fall Wall Press.

Ware, Vron (2022) *Return of a Native: Learning from the Land*. London: Repeater Books.

Hidden track

Exercise 4: Sketch a map of your walk

What shape does your walk take?
Write a short description of the route you have mapped
Annotate or illustrate your map with your observations and notes

Index

access 4, 5, 8, 41–50, 81, 83, 96, 134, 144, 149, 151, 218, 243, 252
accessible 45, 49, 169, 193, 232, 239, 241, 243, 255, 268
activists 28, 60, 68–9, 71, 219, 265
attention 2–3, 49, 69, 140, 233, 245, 258
austerity 2, 9, 18, 25, 103, 108

Back, Les 2, 4–5, 57, 91, 99, 163, 168, 200, 238
barriers 30, 41, 96, 110
belonging 10, 11, 108, 242, 252, 259, 266
bench 46, 49, 193–4, 205, 221, 257
bins 20, 44, 60–1, 206, 231–2
birdsong 10, 58, 107–8, 174, 241–2
bodies 4, 8, 11, 48, 49–50, 53, 109, 134, 139, 140, 190, 193, 203, 214, 216–17, 225, 228, 233, 253–4, 256, 257, 258–9
bridge 91–2, 108–9, 120–1, 143, 146, 169, 243–4, 265

care 8, 35, 37, 41, 43–6, 48–50, 105, 111, 132, 139, 206, 221, 226, 238–9, 242, 254

class 4, 29, 32, 48, 79, 103, 111, 217, 265
climate 10, 71, 155
colonialism 6, 9, 92, 104, 111, 116, 118, 122, 127, 128, 145, 164, 179, 233, 244, 261, 268–9
community 11, 27–8, 30–1, 34, 36, 43–4, 49, 78–80, 82–3, 96, 108, 110, 178, 226, 233, 257–8
connection 11, 96, 111, 226, 233, 237, 252, 255, 258
conviviality 44, 226, 230, 233
cost-of-living 8, 9, 18, 103
crossings 58, 81

decolonial 29, 145, 261, 268, 270
derelict 48, 54–5
desire line 59
diasporic 11, 32, 261, 264, 266, 268
disability 11, 48, 225–6, 233
displacement 33, 77, 81–2
dogs 37, 53, 193, 204, 221, 225–9, 233

ecology 245, 270
economy 18, 30, 32–3, 78, 146, 149, 151–3, 164, 166
edgelands 5, 8, 55, 61

edges 2, 5, 54, 56–8, 60–1, 151, 197
eels 241, 246, 253–4
embodied 4–5, 42, 47, 53, 132, 233, 257, 261
empire 164, 183, 268–70
everyday life 8, 9, 23, 43–4, 49, 54, 72, 116, 161, 261

factory 9, 22–4, 84, 103–6, 111, 150–1, 169, 176, 178–9, 182–3, 267
fiction 10, 116, 215, 217, 219–20
field guide 3
flâneur 4, 165
flooding 107, 155
footprints 75, 137, 197, 218, 253, 257
Fowler, Corrine 116, 122, 269, 270
future 2, 9, 36, 87, 91, 93, 111, 148, 152, 154, 163, 196, 199, 208, 219, 222, 240

gender 4, 48, 99, 217, 230, 233
gentrification 8, 9, 29, 31, 33, 77–82, 192, 244
global 18, 22–3, 29, 56, 70, 106, 116, 145–6, 151–2, 165–6, 178, 194, 266, 268–70
global warming 155–6
graffiti 30, 35, 109, 167, 171, 239–41

habitat 181, 244–5
haunting 9, 84, 95, 121, 220
heritage 9, 92, 95, 98, 182–3
histories 4, 6–11, 32, 92, 99, 104–5, 127, 163, 233, 244, 262, 267–70
home 2, 10, 21, 28–9, 43, 46, 55, 60, 91, 104, 110–11, 162, 167, 171, 202, 205, 221, 233, 240, 263–4
homelessness 1–2, 4, 18, 21, 30, 37, 206, 241, 243
hope 36, 48, 50, 163, 185, 204
housing 9, 11, 21, 55, 77, 79, 81–2, 86–7, 97–8, 103–4, 107–8, 111, 162, 183, 201, 206–7, 218, 231, 244, 246

illness 41, 69, 105, 109, 257, 259
imperialism 166, 253, 268
indigenous 196, 262
industry 5, 8, 70, 77, 83–4, 86, 118, 150, 152, 164, 193
inequalities 4, 32, 41, 45
infrastructure 8, 34, 41–2, 45–9, 53, 61, 68, 122, 128, 143, 150, 153, 269

kindness 44, 46, 49

Lefebvre, Henri 5, 33, 193, 238
love 9, 93, 96, 98–9, 100, 111, 213, 222
library 109–10, 168, 207, 209
lighting 34, 149
liminal 5, 92, 189, 242–3
listening 1, 11, 93, 138, 151, 174, 182, 184, 193, 195, 238, 242, 245

mapping 53, 136, 201, 268
Massey, Doreen 5–6, 57, 116, 238
materiality 154, 200, 206, 243
migrants 27, 181–2, 191, 266
migration 11, 32, 48, 151, 184, 261–2, 264, 266, 270
mobility 56, 132, 205
monument 94, 107, 109, 145
more-than-human 5, 261–2, 265, 269–70
movement 8, 10, 58–9, 61, 98, 132–3, 139, 185, 187
mundane 2, 5, 43, 99, 192, 230
mural 9, 28, 93, 97, 99, 240–1
music 8, 31, 93, 99, 165, 168, 266, 268

neoliberalism 7, 9, 77–8, 87
night-time economy 30, 33
noticing 2–3, 42, 44, 191, 195, 225, 233

olfactory 60, 193, 227

pandemic 41–3, 45, 50, 214, 221
park 5, 10, 41, 48–9, 58, 109, 168, 173, 180–1, 183–4, 202, 204–6, 214, 218, 221, 228–30, 237, 239, 241–3, 269
past 7, 9, 87, 91–3, 99, 104, 111, 116–17, 122, 128, 154, 163, 169, 183, 203
pavement 34, 44, 56, 59, 204, 206, 231–2
phenomenological 225, 233
photographs 19–20, 68–9, 94, 194, 264
plant 1, 55, 117–18, 205, 246, 269
plastic 7–8, 18–21, 24, 31, 42, 47, 55, 59, 67–72, 206, 208, 264
police 27–9, 35–6, 47, 131–2, 149, 217
pollution 60, 68–71, 126, 148, 191, 243, 244
poverty 33, 79–80, 95, 103, 108, 111

race 4, 8, 28–9, 48, 79, 225, 229–30, 233
racism 11, 28, 33, 166, 226, 229, 233
railway 25, 32, 34, 55, 67, 72, 86, 103, 105–7, 110, 119–20, 125–6, 202, 207, 237
regeneration 8, 32–4, 57, 178, 244
resistance 9, 28, 78, 87, 165, 204, 206, 254, 268
rhythm 5, 15, 32, 41, 43–4, 48, 58, 71, 91, 134, 183, 184, 189, 193–6, 201, 203, 205, 209, 215, 225, 228, 238, 241
rioting 29, 95
routines 41, 43–4, 225
rubbish 55, 58, 61, 68, 75, 107, 117, 206–7, 244

scaffolding 83–5
senses 137, 185, 192, 227, 232, 256
smell 15, 19–20, 33, 37, 83–4, 117, 170, 176, 194
sociological imagination 6, 111, 194, 238
sonic 151, 237, 241, 245–6
sounds 5, 11, 43, 83, 99, 163, 174–6, 180–2, 192, 195, 237–9, 241, 243–6, 263
soundscape 56, 180, 237–41, 243, 246
soundtrack 20, 23, 97
soundwalk 163, 238, 245
statues 145, 169, 202
suburbs 9, 46, 54–5, 61, 106, 119, 149–50, 151–2, 155, 161, 237–8
surveillance 34, 49, 146

threshold 91, 203, 208, 254–5
time 1, 5, 7, 19, 41, 45–6, 48, 71, 105, 111, 134, 184–5, 195–6, 201, 214, 219–20, 225, 238, 242, 245, 261
tourist 9, 103, 146, 149, 165, 189, 206, 267
toxic 68–71, 84, 178, 193
tree 67, 122, 170, 173, 175, 181, 183, 204–5, 213, 227, 270
trespassing 68, 252–3
tunnel 25, 81, 149, 184

university campus 170, 199–200, 203–4, 207

volunteers 8, 108, 132, 242, 244–5, 264
vulnerability 29, 228, 258

wandering 10, 70, 137–8, 163, 165, 190, 194, 197

water 5, 7, 46–7, 49, 57, 84, 92, 117, 135, 137, 143, 148, 150, 154–5, 176, 189–92, 194–5, 197, 238–46, 251–9, 263, 265, 268
weather 48, 109, 155, 169, 189, 205, 243, 257
well-being 41, 251–2, 258
working–class 77, 79, 80, 95, 98, 161–2, 168, 175–6, 226
Wright Mills, C. 3, 91, 111, 238

EU authorised representative for GPSR:
Easy Access System Europe, Mustamäe tee 50,
10621 Tallinn, Estonia
gpsr.requests@easproject.com

www.ingramcontent.com/pod-product-compliance
Lightning Source LLC
Chambersburg PA
CBHW051954270326
41929CB00015B/2649

* 9 7 8 1 5 2 6 1 8 4 9 1 7 *